Trade and Jobs in Europe

Trade and Jobs in Europe

Much Ado about Nothing?

Edited by

MATHIAS DEWATRIPONT
ANDRÉ SAPIR
KHALID SEKKAT

UNIVERSITY PRESS

OXFORD

UNIVERSITY PRESS

Great Clarendon Street, Oxford OX2 6DP

Oxford University Press is a department of the University of Oxford.
It furthers the University's objective of excellence in research, scholarship,
and education by publishing worldwide in

Oxford New York

Athens Auckland Bangkok Bogota Buenos Aires Calcutta
Cape Town Chennai Dar es Salaam Delhi Florence Hong Kong Istanbul
Karachi Kuala Lumpur Madrid Melbourne Mexico City Mumbai
Nairobi Paris São Paulo Singapore Taipei Tokyo Toronto Warsaw

with associated companies in Berlin Ibadan

Oxford is a registered trade mark of Oxford University Press
in the UK and in certain other countries

© Oxford University Press 1999

Published in the United States
by Oxford University Press Inc., New York

The moral rights of the author have been asserted
Database right Oxford University Press (maker)

First published 1999

British Library Cataloguing in Publication Data

Data available

Library of Congress Cataloguing in Publication Data

Data available

ISBN 0-19- 829360-7

1 3 5 7 9 10 8 6 4 2

Typeset by Oxford Publishing Services
Printed in Great Britain by
Biddles, Guildford

Contents

Acknowledgements

This book concludes a research project that has started thanks to the financial support of the European Commission's Directorate General V, Social Affairs and Employment, awarded to ECARE, the European Centre for Advanced Research in Economics of the Institut d'Etudes Européennes of the Université Libre de Bruxelles (ULB). We thank Jean-François Lebrun and Armindo Silva from DGV, and Jeanne de Ligne, Nancy Demunck, Dominique Dembour and Romy Genin from ULB for their help with the administration of this grant.

Most papers included in this book were presented on September 25 and 26, 1995, at a conference and workshop entitled: 'International Trade and Employment: The European Experience', jointly organized by ECARE and CEPII (Centre d'Etudes Prospectives et d'Informations Internationales). We thank Jean Pisani-Ferry, Director of CEPII at the time, and his staff for co-organizing this conference.

We also thank the Brookings Institution for allowing this volume to benefit from the inclusion of a paper by Paul Krugman that reproduces parts of his publication entitled 'Growing World Trade: Causes and Consequences', 1995, Brookings Papers on Economic Activity, 1: 327–62.

Finally, we are grateful to the participants to the conference and the workshop for their useful comments and suggestions. We thank especially Pierre Buigues, Daniel Cohen, Jean-Philippe Cotis, Jaime de Melo, Riccardo Faini, Jean-Philippe Gaudernet, Jordi Gual, Eddy Lee, John Martin, John W. Morley, Jesus Seade and Adrian Wood.

MD
AS
KS

Introduction

MATHIAS DEWATRIPONT, ANDRÉ SAPIR AND KHALID SEKKAT

In the last 25 years, Europe has experienced a change of regime: growth has slowed down significantly in comparison with the postwar period, marking the apparent end of the 'catch-up process' with the USA; unemployment has grown tremendously in many European countries; today, the welfare state, symbol of the 'European model', is under threat due to the economic situation which reinforces the ageing problem. Simultaneously, Europe takes part in the worldwide trend of globalization, deregulation and privatization. Part of it results from global negotiations (under GATT and the WTO); part of it is engineered at the European level (Single Market Single Currency); and all these institutional changes partly originate from technological developments and cuts in transport costs that enhance increasing returns to scale.

These challenges to the 'European social model' can be discussed first in terms of the assessment of the problem, then in terms of policy responses:

What are the Facts?

The first issue concerns the relative importance of trade, technology, demographics and domestic policies in causing the European unemployment problem. These issues are hard to disentangle since several factors seem to contribute to raising unemployment, at least temporarily: labour force trends (rise in female participation, slowdown in the long-term decrease in the length of the workweek), the rise in the burden of tax-financed pensions, a technology that reduces the need for unskilled workers, even in services, deregulation policies that lead to employment reductions in the public sector and, finally, the emergence of a number of Third World competitors that gain market shares in the manufacturing sector. The main goal of this book is to try and assess the relative importance of this last factor in contributing to Europe's unemployment problem.

What should be the Policy Response?

To a number of observers, the above trends are unavoidable, and the only solution is to adapt the set of domestic policies that cause European unemployment:

inflexible labour and product markets and excessive tax burdens on the one hand; macroeconomic policies that aim at fighting inflation and result in strong currencies at the expense of exports on the other hand. The British example, with its lower unemployment rate than most countries of the 'Deutsche mark zone', fuels this view.

Whether such a policy line would allow Europe to retain the essence of its social model is subject to debate. Particularly interesting for the purpose of this book is the position that this policy line has to be contrasted with a protectionist stance, aiming at 'controlling the process of globalization'. According to proponents of this view, allowing globalization to proceed as is happening currently will lead to enormous problems for European countries. How can European workers ever compete with Third World workers who earn less than $1 a day? Given the enormous number of unskilled workers who enter the world economy due to market-oriented reforms in Asia, convergence can only take place at low wage rates. The problem is even worsened by 'social dumping' practices by a number of countries: for example, anti-trade-union laws and child labour. Therefore, there has been a call for 'social clauses' as part of international trade regulations, as a way to protect workers in both developed and developing countries.

This book's contribution to the policy debate can be summarized as follows: the evidence does *not* point to trade with LDCs as a major cause of European unemployment. Technological evolution and domestic policy choices are much more important factors behind Europe's labour market problems. Consequently, protectionist policies are not to be advised: their benefits would at best be very limited in terms of employment, and would have to be weighed against the potentially immense costs associated with the disruption of world growth that would follow from trade wars and a collapse of the global trading system, as the interwar history has taught us.

The value added of this book is to provide a first comprehensive set of estimates of the impact of trade with LDCs on the European labour market. So far, most studies have concerned the United States of America (standard references include Krugman 1995; Lawrence and Slaughter 1993; Revenga 1992; and Sachs and Shatz 1994). The chapters in this book detail them at length. Thus we only summarize the main findings over which there is a very broad consensus:[1]

1. Trade with LDCs does not cause aggregate welfare problems for the USA, since these countries are not in current-account surplus in the aggregate.[2] Trade imbalances are, however, significant in some manufacturing sectors.
2. On the labour market, one should not fear any downward pressure on the

---

[1] An outlier in the literature is the book by Wood (1994), who computes quite significant effects of trade with LDCs on OECD economies. See footnote 2 on his methodology.

[2] Labour content input–output computations point to a limited effect of LDC trade on employment unless, as in Wood (1994), one revises upwards the labour content of activities that have been displaced by LDC exports. Such computations are, however, subject to much debate.

average wage level, but only a rise in wage *inequality*, since the emergence of LDCs mainly means a rise in the world supply of unskilled labour.

3. In a standard (Heckscher–Ohlin) trade model, the emergence of LDCs should mean not only greater wage dispersion in developed countries but also *lower* relative prices of unskilled labour-intensive goods—and thus an improvement of the terms of trade of rich countries—and, *ceteris paribus*, a *decrease* in the skill content of production (since unskilled labour becomes cheaper). These two facts do not show up significantly in the data, leading one to think that it is unskilled-labour-saving technological change that is dominating labour market outcomes, and not trade with LDCs.

4. Finally, applied general equilibrium counterfactual simulations corroborate these econometric findings, showing that the impact of the emergence of LDCs in world trade on relative prices and wages has probably been very small.

This book supports the view that, for Europe too, trade with LDCs has had so far a limited impact on the labour market, and in fact a more limited impact than intra-OECD trade. More specifically, the following lessons emerge:

1. Trade with LDCs should be even less harmful for Europe than for the USA, since Europe has a current-account surplus in the aggregate. Moreover, Europe is less open than the USA to LDC trade.

2. The inequality problem to be worried about in Europe is not wage inequality, as in the USA, since this has not grown significantly in Europe in the last 25 years. Inequality is, however, present in terms of massive unemployment for unskilled workers.

3. As in the USA, such unemployment, which indeed originates in particular in some trade-affected sectors, seems to be overall more a result of technology than trade: once again, one fails to observe a decrease in the relative price of unskilled labour-intensive goods, and one observes an increase in the skill content of employment across manufacturing sectors. Finally, long-term unemployment also seems to be caused more by technology than by trade.

4. Finally, here again applied general equilibrium counterfactual simulations suggest that the emergence of LDCs in the global economy has only resulted in modest labour market effects in Europe.

5. While the overall effect of LDC trade on European unemployment has been small, the specific impact of exploitative labour practices (child labour and the like) has been extremely small. This is not at all to say that such practices should be allowed to proceed without check, but to insist that they do not belong in trade negotiations: the risk would be to penalize LDCs in sectors where such practices do not exist but where trade flows are significant, while the practices would then be allowed to continue in activities where trade is not important.

The book contains nine chapters. The first seven try and assess the impact of LDC trade on the European labour market: three cross-country econometric studies, with

Freeman and Revenga looking at the OECD, Dewatripont et al. and Neven and Wyplosz analysing European data; two applied general equilibrium studies, by Krugman and by Smith; and two country studies, Cortes et al. focusing on France and Haisken-Denew and Zimmermann looking at Germany. Finally, two chapters explicitly address the social clause problem: Sapir links the evidence presented in the literature and in the previous papers with the debate on unfair labour practices. And Bairoch presents the emergence of this debate in a historical perspective.

Freeman and Revenga investigate the trade–labour–market link in Europe, Japan and the USA. They distinguish LDC trade from intra-OECD trade. They estimate three sets of identical relations across these countries to see whether different wage setting systems affect the link between trade and labour markets: (i) measures of trade flows as a function of time, country and industry dummies; (ii) measures of skills as a function of the same dummies; and (iii) measures of trade flows as a function of country dummies, skills and the gender composition of sectoral employment. The study considers 28 to 49 industries from 18 OECD countries. The authors show that:

- trade flows present a clear industry-specific pattern across countries;
- there exist strong cross-country similarities in skill structure by industry; and
- positive net imports from LDCs occur more frequently in industries with a high percentage of female labour and, to a more limited extent, in industries with low skill content.

The authors present several pieces of evidence that point to a limited impact of LDC trade on the European labour market: (i) they show that employment and wages are less sensitive to imports in Europe than in the USA; (ii) they show that OECD employment is less sensitive to LDC imports than to intra-OECD imports; (iii) they argue that LDC trade has been concentrated in industries with a high percentage of female labour, while women have been doing relatively better than men on the labour market in most European countries since they have seen a rise in their employment rate and a reduction in their wage gap relative to men.

Neven and Wyplosz analyse the link between trade and labour markets in Europe, performing two exercises, one done by Lawrence and Slaughter and the other by Revenga, both for the USA. Specifically, they first relate output prices to the evolution of wages, employment and skill intensity by industry, in order to see whether one observes Heckscher–Ohlin type effects on the relation between output prices and the skill content of employment. They also estimate a two-equation model relating wages and employment by industry to domestic and import price levels, capital–labour ratios and aggregate demand.

They do find drastic restructuring of unskilled labour-intensive industries (downsizing), which are industries affected by trade, not only from LDCs. However, there is no systematic evidence of a fall in the relative price of unskilled labour-intensive goods in their study. As in the USA, it looks like the adjustment comes more from technological change than from trade.

Dewatripont et al. complement Neven and Wyplosz by looking at the effect of trade on long-term unemployment[3]—an important feature of European unemployment—on the wage skill premium and on the skill content of employment by industry.

They show that:

- long-term unemployment is driven mainly by individual characteristics, like the level of education and gender; imports from LDCs also represent a contributing factor, but only when industry dummies are omitted. Once again, this view is consistent with the idea that it is technology more than trade *per se* that matters, in this case to assess the causes of the long-term hardship of displaced workers.
- as far as differences between skilled and unskilled workers go, the chapter finds more evidence of an association between LDC trade and the wage skill premium than between LDC trade and the skill content of employment. This may seem surprising given the conventional wisdom of a rigid wage structure in Europe. But the lack of a significant impact on the skill content of employment is consistent with previous findings derived in the Heckscher–Ohlin framework.

The next two chapters are based on computable general equilibrium exercises. The advantage of such exercises is that they endogenize not only trade flows but also trade prices, leaving exogenous only preferences, technology and institutional structures like trade policies and labour-market practices. In this perspective, *Krugman* assesses the impact of low-wage exports on industrialized countries under two scenarios: a European, fix-wage scenario, where trade will affect employment, and an American, flexible wage scenario, where trade affects unskilled wages. The admittedly very simple model is first calibrated using parameter estimates from the factor-content and econometric literatures. Krugman finds limited effects of the emergence of LDC exports in both scenarios: some 1.4 per cent employment reduction in the first case, 1.7 per cent real unskilled wage reduction and 3 per cent rise in the skill premium in the second case, and this in comparison with zero overall exports from these Third World countries.

Smith performs a similar exercise in a more detailed computable general equilibrium model, including 12 countries and 64 sectors (differentiated à la Dixit–Stiglitz) and two types of labour (manual and non-manual). This exercise mainly confirms Krugman's result of a very limited impact of LDC trade on the European labour market.

The two country studies nicely complement the aggregate picture detailed above. *Cortes et al.* provide a detailed picture of the French labour market, documenting

---

[3] Building on survey data that detail the length of the unemployment spell and the industry where the individual had his or her last job; individual data are then aggregated to construct 'long-term unemployment rates by industry'.

the steady rise of unemployment, the relative importance of long-term unemployment and the low level of wage dispersion relative to the USA. They also show that LDC imports are less important in France than in the USA or even Germany and the UK. France has, moreover, a trade surplus with LDCs even though imports are growing. As with other industrialized countries, LDC trade is mainly inter-industry trade—with a trade deficit (surplus) in low (high) skill sectors—while intra-OECD trade is mainly intra-industry trade. As in previous chapters, the skill content of employment has been rising in France in all industries, pointing again to technology as the main factor behind the labour-market problems of unskilled workers.

Haisken-De New and Zimmermann present results from a rich household survey data set, adding a comparison between trade flows and migration flows as explanatory variables for labour market outcomes in West Germany. The magnitude of East–West population movements in the late 1980s has been such that this comparison can be quite insightful. Interestingly, the authors find that trade matters more than migration in explaining earnings (both its absolute level and measures of the skill premium) and labour mobility (within and across firms). In particular, the authors find that LDC imports depress wages and stimulate inter-firm mobility (but not occupational or intra-firm mobility).

The last two chapters explicitly discuss the issue of policy prescriptions, and in particular the case of 'social clauses'.

Bairoch provides a historical perspective on this topic, explaining the origin of the idea that differences in social conditions can influence trade. This idea dates at least from the late eighteenth century, even though the term 'social clause' was coined in the 1970s. In fact, the debate emerged more than 100 years after the rise in wage inequality between countries, with the sharp wage gains in industrialized countries. In the nineteenth century, trade unions and socialist parties were more in favour of free trade than of protectionism. The idea of a social clause can be linked to the efforts towards the creation of an international labour organization that predated the founding of the ILO in 1919. This event was part of a pattern by which, to establish the social peace necessary for the industrial war effort, governments had to promise social benefits once peace would have returned (one-man-one-vote, welfare systems). Social clauses are then seen as a way to protect social conquests in the face of the gradual return of freer trade after the Second World War, after the interwar burst of protectionism.

Sapir, however, argues that the fight for social clauses is misguided because: (i) the wave of globalization is desirable since present world income distribution is unsustainable and Third World countries should see their share rise; (ii) moreover, globalization has had a limited impact on wage inequality and unemployment; it is only one part of the challenge facing unskilled workers, next to technological evolution; this challenge should be addressed anyway by industrialized economies; and (iii) finally, there is virtually no evidence that the rapid increase of LDC manufacturing exports is due to low labour standards. For all these reasons, the solutions to European unemployment lie in domestic reforms, not in protectionist measures that would only worsen problems through mounting trade dispute with LDCs.

We have argued here that this book provides a set of estimates that broadly point to a limited impact of LDC trade on the European labour market, which has as a consequence that trade instruments are not appropriate to solve Europe's unemployment problems. Each chapter in this volume could of course be refined to provide further tests of the robustness of its conclusions. This important topic indeed deserves further research, if only because the importance of LDC trade is bound to grow in the coming years. It is our hope that the research contained in this book will provide a stimulus for continued research in this area.

References

Krugman, P. (1995), 'Growing World Trade: Causes and Consequences', *Brookings Papers on Economic Activity*, 1: 327–62.

Lawrence, R. and Slaughter, M. (1993), 'Trade and US Wages: Great Sucking Sound or Small Hiccup?', *Brookings Papers on Economic Activity*, Microeconomics, 2: 161–226.

Revenga, A. L. (1992), 'Exporting Jobs? The Impact of Import Competition on Employment and Wages in US Manufacturing', *Quarterly Journal of Economics*, 107(1): 225–84.

Sachs, J. D. and Shatz, H. J. (1994), 'Trade and Jobs in US Manufacturing', *Brookings Papers on Economic Activity*, 1: 1–69.

Wood, A. (1994), *North–South Trade, Employment and Inequality*, Clarendon Press, Oxford.

1. How Much Has LDC Trade Affected Western Job Markets?

RICHARD FREEMAN AND ANA REVENGA

Trade has long been seen as a key to European economic progress. Fifteen or so years ago, many believed that the Common Market was the cure to Europe's economic ills—a potential catalyst for growth that would create jobs and bring European countries to the frontier of modern technology. Economists studied trade flows among advanced countries, generating non-Heckscher–Ohlin theories to explain intra-industry flows among countries with comparable factor endowments. More trade presumably meant a better economic world.

Recent discussions of trade have taken a less rosy view. Trade with the less developed countries (LDCs) is, according to some, harming the economic prospects of low skill Western workers through high unemployment in Western Europe and through declining real wages in the USA. Prominent European figures, such as Sir James Goldsmith, have been sufficiently concerned with the potential adverse effects of LDC trade to favour a world in which EU countries would trade freely with other advanced countries but would establish barriers against trade with LDCs.

In the USA, concerns over the NAFTA treaty spawned considerable discussion and research on the effects of trade on the job market (see *Journal of Economic Perspectives* 1995, Fall). Some analysts employed 'factor content calculations' (essentially estimates of the labour displaced from imports) to assess the potential fall in demand for less skilled workers due to trade (Borjas, Freeman and Katz 1992; Cooper 1994; and Sachs and Shatz 1994). Others have examined the relation between price changes and the skill composition of employment by sector (Lawrence 1994; Sachs and Shatz 1994).

In Europe, empirical analysis of the links between trade and labour has been more sparse. Adrian Wood (1994) has made a case for trade having a huge effect on both European and American job markets. On the other hand, the OECD has argued that 'except in a few sectors like clothing and footwear, major job displacement from import competition cannot plausibly be linked to . . . developing countries' (OECD 1994a: 37). More recently, the World Bank restated this position by claiming that 'on net, the effects of trade with developing and transition economies do not seem large enough to account for the massive shifts in labour demand that have occurred within the OECD' (World Bank 1995b: 3). Academic debate over the effects of trade has been more muted in Europe than in the USA, in large part because analysts do not have readily available data sets relating labour outcomes to trade flows.

In this chapter we seek to fill part of the gap in our knowledge of how trade affects labour markets by using a newly developed data set linking trade flows by industry and country to labour market outcomes in a sample of OECD countries over the 1970 to 1992 period. This new cross-country trade and labour data file (LAT) amalgamates information from two OECD files on trade and labour and two United Nations data files on labour. One virtue of the amalgamated file is that it allows analysts to examine the differential effect on labour, if any, of trade with LDCs and trade with other OECD economies. It also allows for an investigation of the differential impact of trade on labour outcomes in Europe, North America, and Japan.

Our analytic approach is eclectic. Rather than arguing over whether it is better to examine trade effects on the labour market through factor content analyses of trade flows or through changes in the prices of goods more or less affected by trade, we explore both links. To see if institutions affect the trade–labour market link, we estimate identical relations for countries with different wage-setting systems and modes of employment determination.

1.1 Issues and Analysis

The big question is to what extent, if any, the difficulties that less-skilled Western workers faced during the 1980s and 1990s have resulted from increased imports of manufacturing goods from LDCs.

1.1.1 Some Theory

There are three ways to argue that trade will affect labour markets, each of which suggests a different empirical approach to the 'big question'.

The first adopts a Heckscher–Ohlin (H–O) perspective and argues that advanced countries are likely to import unskilled labour-intensive commodities from LDCs and export skilled labour-intensive commodities. In this framework, trade with LDCs will necessarily reduce the relative prices of unskilled-intensive goods in advanced countries, and put downward pressure on unskilled wages. Under specific conditions (identical constant returns technologies, homogeneous products, the appropriate numbers of goods and factors, and so forth), this pressure will equalize factor prices among trading nations. In this model, trade is the sole determinant of pay: the domestic labour market has *no* real effect on labour outcomes. Everything depends on the traded sector, and the world labour market. If wages do not respond flexibly in a particular country to world competition, workers end up unemployed. Moreover, the pressure for factor price equalization may be poorly measured by imports and exports, which are endogenously determined. It is even conceivable, though far-fetched, that factor prices will be equalized in an open economy with *virtually no* trade. What matters are the economic conditions under-lying trade: relative factor proportions, trade barriers and technology. Adherents to this model have sought the effects of trade through relative prices, searching for declines in the relative prices of unskilled labour-intensive goods and eschewing measures of trade flows. US studies have had only limited success in this venture (see, for example, Lawrence 1994; Sachs and Shatz 1994).

A second (labour market) approach focuses on observable trade flows, arguing that imports of labour-intensive commodities from LDCs displace workers in those sectors and thus reduce the demand for those workers in the economy. The result will be unemployment or wage cuts. In this analysis, the magnitude of imports and displacement matters greatly. Cost curves are upward sloping and products are heterogenous, even within detailed industrial classifications. Hence, cost factors and elasticities of demand mediate the displacement effect of imports in the traded goods sector, and mediate the effect of displacement in the non-traded goods sector. The effect of the traded goods sector on wages/employment depends on its share of total employment. Adherents to the domestic labour market model have sought to uncover the effects of trade on labour primarily through factor content calculations.

The third (Ricardian) approach takes a labour productivity/labour cost per-spective, focusing on cross-country differences in productivity/cost by industry. Cross-country differences in labour productivity are typically taken as exogenous, driven by differences in technology or (unmeasured) labour skills. A country produces commodities for which domestic unit labour costs are less than or equal to foreign unit labour costs. Unit labour costs, however, are endogenously deter-mined, as they depend on both productivity (given by technology) and relative wages. The equilibrium condition is that trade must be balanced. An exogeneous rise in LDC productivity leads to a loss in domestic comparative advantage. This implies a reduction in the range of commodities produced domestically and a trade deficit. To restore the trade balance, domestic wages must fall relative to those overseas. The extent of the fall depends on which industries are on the margin of the comparative advantage ladder, and the potential for wage-cut induced expansion of exports in industries higher in the country's comparative advantage 'ladder'.

These differing models all share the same qualitative prediction for Western workers in the 1980s and 1990s. With trade barriers declining, modern technology spreading to LDCs, and LDC workers becoming increasingly competitive with low skill Westerners, all three predict reduced demand for less-skilled labour. But each model tells a different story about the potential magnitude of trade effects and suggests different empirical tests to assess those effects. The H–O model, for example, predicts that the effects of trade are filtered through to the labour market via declines in the relative prices of unskilled labour-intensive goods (industries). Many factors beyond trade can, however, produce a negative correlation between changes in prices and the unskilled labour share of employment (namely a drop in the minimum wage that is passed to consumers in price cuts), so that a negative correlation between price changes and the skill composition of production is necessary but not sufficient to demonstrate an important trade effect. Even as a necessary condition, the price effect has been hard to detect across industries: sectors with highly skilled workers may have relative price declines due to technological advances related to skills, while changes in the composition of goods within a sector may make industry price measures inadequate measures of the import pressure.

The labour market model predicts that trade effects depend on the size of the traded goods sector and on demand/cost parameters. Employment in import-intensive sectors is lower than it would be in the absence of those imports. The implicit fall in the demand for the unskilled (or alternatively, the implicit increase in their supply) spills over to the rest of the economy, dependent on the size of the traded goods sector, and reduces wages and/or creates joblessness for unskilled workers, in the economy at large.

The Ricardian model directs attention to labour cost differentials by industry between LDCs and the industrialized countries, and focuses on how employment may respond to changes in those differentials. The magnitude of the reduction in wages in the advanced countries relative to those in LDCs depends on the size of the sectors on the margin; on the difference between labour productivity among them; and on the elasticity of product demand for output, all of which in turn depend critically on the mix and characteristics of industries. Because this model makes strong demands on data, empiricists have shied away from it, though it has considerable analytic appeal.[1]

1.1.2 Measures of Trade Pressure:Quantities and Prices

The movement of goods and services across borders has grown dramatically in recent years, from 23 per cent of world GDP in 1970 to about 40 per cent in 1990. Much of this increase has taken the form of trade between advanced countries and LDCs. Between 1991 and 1993 developing and transition economies accounted for almost 75 per cent of the increase in world exports. According to World Bank estimates (World Bank 1995b), by the year 2010 these economies will account for about 30 per cent of world imports and 22 per cent of world exports of manufactures.

Four 'exogenous' changes have fuelled the increased LDC role in world markets:

- Reductions in trade barriers in advanced countries. The average size of tariffs in the industrialized countries declined significantly in the past two decades, although there still remain substantial non-tariff measures, ranging from voluntary restraints under the MultiFiber Agreement, to antidumping and countervailing duty actions, to various licensing requirements.

---

[1] An exception is Feenstra and Hanson (1994), who use a Ricardian approach to examine patterns in wage inequality in Mexico and the USA.

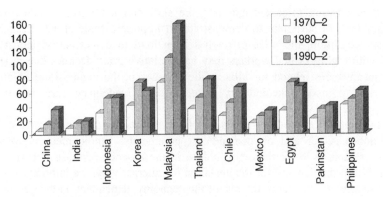

Source: OECD (1994a); Table 2.1.

Fig. 1.1. Magnitude of trade (M+X)/GDP from selected low wage countries

- Simultaneously, LDC development strategies have shifted from import-substitution to export-promotion, partly due to World Bank and IMF pressures (OECD 1994a: 5). China and India are entering the global market, and the former Soviet bloc countries are also moving from their previously isolated position. As a result, the trade share in GDP for many LDC countries has increased substantially (see Figure 1.1).
- The LDCs' share of the world work force expanded from 79 per cent in 1965 to 85 per cent in 1995 (World Bank 1995a: table 1.1). By itself, this shift in population should, *ceteris paribus*, lead to a greater role for LDC countries in the world economy. In fact, the LDC share of world manufacturing employment grew more rapidly than its share of the workforce (from 40 per cent in 1960 to 53 per cent in 1986).
- Mean years of schooling in LDCs has also increased substantially, giving more and more LDC workers the skills needed for industrial employment.

All of these factors have operated to increase LDC exports to the advanced countries (especially of manufactured goods), potentially to the detriment of low-skill workers producing import-competing goods in those countries.

There are two ways to measure the LDC trade pressure on workers in advanced countries. First, and most common, are measures of actual trade flows. Figure 1.2 shows imports of goods from advanced and LDCs, inclusive and exclusive of OPEC (oil) imports. Overall, there has been a rise in manufacturing imports from LDCs to the advanced countries. But it is easy to exaggerate the extent to which trade with non-OECD countries has increased, particularly in Europe. The increase in LDC imports to the USA has been much larger than to Europe. Indeed, inclusive of trade with OPEC countries, European imports of goods from LDCs have barely changed as a share of GDP. The West has 'gained' a windfall from the drop in oil

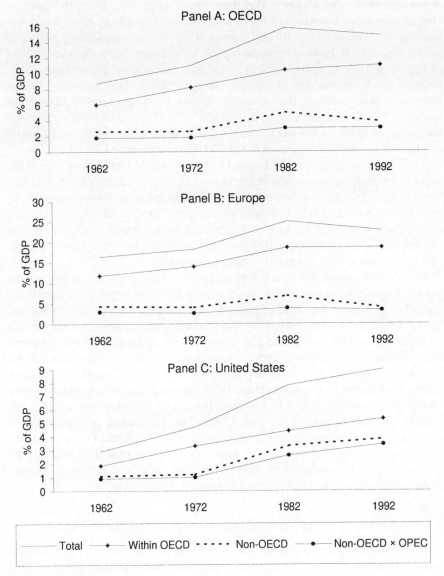

Fig. 1.2. Imports of goods/nominal GDP

prices that has been largely ignored in discussions of the effect of trade on the economy. Excluding OPEC trade, the ratio of imports of goods to GDP has been roughly constant in Europe while rising in the USA.

The ratios of imports to GDP in *current prices* in Figure 1.2 are, however, imperfect measures of the pressure of increased trade on job markets, particularly in manufactures. One reason is that these ratios reflect both price and quantity changes. Increased quantities of imports accompanied by falling prices could displace many workers in the affected sectors, while giving a misleading picture of falling import/GDP ratios. Given the relative price changes described next, ratios of imports to GDP in *constant prices* would presumably show greater increases in trade in goods on workers in Europe and in the USA. Still, assuming similar patterns of price changes, the message of Figure 1.2 would remain: Europe has increased its imports from LDCs less than the USA. If trade had similar effects on the European as on the US labour market, this would imply *a smaller reduction in demand for labour in Europe than in the USA* due to trade with LDCs.

While manufacturing imports from LDCs as a share of GDP has not risen, the share of employment in manufacturing in most advanced countries has fallen. The result is that LDC and other imports relative to manufacturing employment (or output) has increased. This potentially places great product market competitive pressure on firms and workers in the sectors facing import competition, and through spillovers could impact the economy more widely. Trade in services has also grown, though it is as yet only weakly documented.

As intimated above, the second way to measure trade pressures is through the prices of imported goods. Changes in the relative prices of imports and exports are normally reflected in the terms of trade. A decline in the price of imports relative to exports brings benefits to a country as a whole, but creates problems for workers in import-competing sectors and for those with the skills used in those sectors, more broadly. A potentially better indicator of the import trade pressure on domestic workers is the ratio of import to domestic prices. Feenstra and Hanson (1994) have shown that, throughout the 1980s, import prices have declined relative to domestic wholesale prices in the USA, Japan, and Germany. Presumably, this reflects the pressures of trade with LDCs. The magnitudes of these relative declines in import prices are, moreover, substantial: of the order of 0.5 per cent per annum in the USA, 1.5 per cent in Japan, and 0.8 per cent in Germany. The pressure from trade on labour markets is thus likely to be understated in analyses that focus strictly on the effect of changes in current price trade flows.

1.1.3 Deteriorating Labour Market Outcomes: Unemployment and Wages

The deterioration in the labour market for low-skilled workers in advanced countries has been amply documented. There are three important points to note about this major development:

- First, it has taken a different form in the USA than in Europe. In the USA relative earnings by skill group have risen, and the overall earnings distribution has become extraordinarily dispersed. Low decile workers make less relative to top decile workers than in the past, or than in any European country. In Europe, the problem shows up instead in increased joblessness of long duration. Groups with falling real wages in the USA—primarily less skilled young men—are long-term unemployed in Europe. But, despite falling real earnings for the less skilled in the USA, the employment rate for less skilled men has dropped, and 2 per cent of the potential male labour force is incarcerated.

- Second, among women, including those with few skills, the situation is very different. Women's earnings have risen relative to those of men in virtually every OECD country. The proportion of women who are employed has also risen. The ratio of female to male unemployment, however, varies across countries. In the UK, women are less likely to be jobless than men. In most European countries and in the USA, women are more likely to be jobless. Overall, however, the market outcomes for low-skilled women have not deteriorated as much as they have for men.
- Third, the measured growth of real earnings differs greatly among countries. In the USA, many earnings series show substantial declines. In Europe, real earnings have risen. The gap between the USA and Europe in average real earnings has thus been greatly reduced. The combination of a widening of the US earnings distribution and declining real wages has produced a striking difference in living standards between US and European low-paid workers. Fully employed Americans in the lowest decile, earn between one-half and two-thirds what Europeans in the lowest decile earn in Germany, Belgium or France.

In sum, workers in virtually all advanced economies experienced labour market problems during the 1980s and 1990s. These problems have taken a different form in different countries (which some analysts attribute to differences in labour market institutions), but are not markedly greater for the low-skilled in Europe than in the USA. They differ in magnitude between men and women. Both the cross-country and gender patterns are important in assessing the contribution of trade to the troubles facing workers in advanced countries.

1.2 The LAT Data Base

All of the approaches outlined above suggest that the potential impact of trade on the labour market should be analysed on the basis of industry-level data—whether these be industry prices, employment, wages, or net trade balances. This task, however, is often made difficult by the paucity of data collected on a consistent basis: trade information typically comes in the form of prices and quantities of goods, while labour and production data are gathered on an industry basis from establishments. The effort required to construct a consistent data base, one that links the information from trade and production sources, is substantial, particularly over periods when industry definitions change and new products are introduced. For the USA, Abowd and Freeman (1991) have put together such a data base—the NBER Trade and Labour data set combining trade, production, and employment information for some 450 four-digit manufacturing industries. To our knowledge, no comparable data set exists for Europe.

For this chapter, we have combined data from the OECD on bilateral trade among countries (the BTD file) and on trade, production, and the wage bill (STAN) with data from the United Nations on production, employment and earnings (UNIDO; UN) into a single cross-country labour and trade data base. This data base, described in Table 1.1, provides information on 28 to 49 industries (depending on detail and grouping) for 18 advanced OECD countries from 1970 to 1992. The trade data consist of two files: for the larger set of industries, the STAN file provides exports and imports; for the smaller set, the BTD provides exports and imports by country of origin/destination. The production data cover the variables contained on standard establishment surveys: value added, gross output, gross capital formation, employment and wage bill. The labour data provide also several measures of labour skill: a breakdown between production and non-production workers, the costs thereof (UN) and the number of women workers (UNIDO). By dividing the labour costs by employees, we can also generate an approximation of 'wages' in different industries and countries. We combine the files into two workable data sets: a BTD-based data set LAT1 (with 7,958 observations) and a STAN-based data set LAT2 (with 19,044 observations).

The data are far from perfect. The OECD gives explicit warning that its files are subject to problems and potential error. The UN data occasionally give inconsistent figures—more women employees than all employees, for instance. Indicative of these problems we have found that certain key variables, such as value added or employment, occasionally differ for the same sector/country in the same year between two different data sets. Still, there is a sufficiently high correlation between the figures in the different data sets to suggest that errors of misclassification will not seriously undermine our empirical analysis. The number of countries with data also varies depending on the source: the BTD has no information for Belgium, or Austria, nor usable data for Denmark. The UN data set has no information on production and non-production workers in France or Italy, and the data for Japan in that data set are suspect (Berman, Machin and Bound 1992). As a result, the number of observations in most of our analyses differs, and in some cases, the intersection of the data sets gives us only a few hundred observations. In particular, the UNIDO data for women workers is available for only 12 countries and ten years, and for just ten industries.[2]

Still, the potential for analysis offered by the LAT outweighs the data problems, serious though they are. Even with missing data and inconsistencies, the LAT1 has 7,956 observations, while LAT2 has approximately 19,000 observations. There is enough information by industry, country and years to allow us to control for variation in those dimensions when desired, and thus to test proposed linkages between trade and labour within industry–country–year cells.

---

[2] In principle, there is an additional year of data, but the diskette we received is missing 1988, for some reason. We are pursuing this and other data problems.

Table 1.1. The four building block data bases

OECD Stan Database: 18 advanced countries, 49 industries

Trade data	Imports, exports
Labour data	Employment, labour compensation
Production data	Value added, capital formation, gross output
Price data	Exchange rates, PPPs, implicit value added deflators

OECD Bilateral Trade: 16 countries, 27 industries

Trade data	Imports, exports by trading partner

UN General Industrial Statistics: 100+ countries, 48 industries

Labour data	Employment, wages and salaries of employees, supplements to wages and salaries, operatives employment, wages and salaries of operatives, hours and days worked
Production data	Valued added, capital formation, gross output, electricity consumed, gross fixed capital formation, machinery and equipment (some data in factor values and producers' prices), value of stocks, index numbers of production, number of establishments

UNIDO Database: 150 countries, 28 manufacturing industries

Labour data	Employment, wages and salaries, female employment
Production data	Value added, capital formation, gross output, number of establishments, index numbers ofo industrial production

---

Source: OECD (1994c); OECD (1994b); United Nations, *UN Statistical Division, General Industrial Statistics, volume 1 data base* describing data files sent to NBER, June 1994; UNIDO, Industrial Statistics Branch, United Nations Industrial Development Organization, *INDSTAT3*, User's guide to Database 1995 three-digit level of ISIC code on diskette.

1.3 Some Basic Relations

As a first step to investigating the trade and labour linkage using the LAT data base, we examined the industrial pattern of trade and labour across the full set of countries and time periods. All our analyses have industry–country–year cells as observations.

We focus on three questions that are critical to applying the section 1 models to the title question.

1. *Do advanced countries have comparable trade patterns by industry with less advanced countries?*

If, as seems reasonable, trade between advanced countries and LDCs is largely due to LDCs having a relatively greater endowment in less skilled labour, we would expect to see the advanced country's LDC trade 'problem' show up in the same sectors among advanced countries—those whose technology relies extensively on less skilled labour.

Whether trade *among* advanced countries should have a stronger or weaker industry dimension is less obvious. Non-H–O forces presumably underlie this trade, and there is much debate over how countries can gain and maintain competitive advantage in trade with countries with similar factor endowments—such as economies of scale and technological advantages. If trade among advanced countries does not depend on differences in unskilled labour endowments, this trade has no clear effect on demand for unskilled workers throughout the West, though non H–O advantages will affect the position of workers in particular countries.

Table 1.2 summarizes the results of an analysis designed to examine the industry dimension of trade. We regressed four measures of trade flows (TRADE) on vectors of dummy variables for year (T'), country (C'), and industry (I'):

$$\text{TRADE}_{ict} = T' + C' + I' \tag{1.1}$$

Our four measures are: the *net trade flow* (exports–imports per gross output or (X–M)/GO); the *direction* of the trade flow (M/(X+M)); the *magnitude* of the trade flow ((X+M)/GO); and a quantitative measure of *trade pressures* on domestic workers–imports per gross output (M/GO). The measures are related in relatively simple ways linking direction and magnitude:

$$\frac{M}{GO} = \frac{M}{X+M} \cdot \frac{X+M}{GO}, \quad \text{i.e. trade pressure = direction} \times \text{magnitude} \tag{1.2}$$

$$\frac{X-M}{GO} = \left(1 - 2\frac{M}{X+M}\right) \cdot \left(\frac{M+X}{GO}\right), \quad \begin{array}{l}\text{i.e. net trade = transformation of direction} \\ \times \text{magnitude}\end{array} \tag{1.3}$$

In these computations we have used gross output (GO) as the denominator for ease of presentation. It is common to assess imports relative to domestic consumption (GO-X+M) and exports relative to GO. Computations with domestic consumption as the base yield similar results to those reported here.

Table 1.2 reports the contribution of the industry vector to the pattern of flows in terms of the adjusted R^2 with and without the vector, and in terms of the F-test measuring the contribution of the industry vector to the sum of squares. The odd-numbered lines refer to trade flows with non-OECD countries. The even numbered lines refer to trade flows among OECD countries. The F-statistics show that the variation in net trade flows, trade pressures, and in the magnitude of trade is highly related to industry among non-OECD and OECD countries alike. The overall explanatory power of the calculations are stronger for OECD trade. One likely reason is the close relation and relatively small size and distances between many European countries in the European Union. The big difference between non-OECD trade and within OECD trade occurs in the direction of trade measure. The R-

Table 1.2. Contribution of industry, time and country dummy variables to OECD non-OECD trade, by individual OECD countries, 1960–92

	R^2 with all	R^2 without industry	F-test for industry	Number of observations
Measure of Trade				
Net trade flow $(X–M)/GO$				
1 Non-OECD	.14	.05	30.3	6124
2 OECD	.23	.14	28.6	6099
Import Pressure (M/GO)				
3 Non-OECD	.17	.08	26.9	6134
4 OECD	.29	.18	44.2	6110
Magnitude of Trade $(X+M)/GO$				
5 Non-OECD	.22	.15	24.9	6124
6 OECD	.35	.23	56.9	6099
Direction of Trade $(M/(X+M)$				
7 Non-OECD	.53	.18	248.0	7393
8 OECD	.28	.23	22.7	7354

Source: Tabulated from LAT1 database. Observations differ because of missing data points, or because data were inconsistent.

squares in lines 7 and 8 are much higher for non-OECD trade, and the F-statistic is huge.[3] *Conditional on the magnitude of trade, industries in OECD countries have similar trade patterns with the non-OECD world.*

Given the substantial industry pattern in trade flows, we turn to the second question:

2. *Is the skill structure (factor intensity) of production similar for sectors among the advanced countries?*

In part, this question can be viewed as a 'test' of whether the technology of production rules out substantial factor intensity reversals, due to different wage-setting or employment determination across countries. To answer it, we replicated the analysis of Table 1.2 with measures of labour and of other inputs or outputs to labour. We have five measures of labour:

---

[3] What contributes to this pattern is the basic fact that within OECD trade should, properly measured, balance out, so that for any given industry $M=X$, while non-OECD trade is open-ended in this respect. But with trade imbalances, particularly by sector (Japan or Germany exporting in particular areas with most OECD countries importing in those areas), this is not a major constraint on the regressions.

- Our first measure is the *proportion of employees who are operatives*. This measure has been used in many trade-labour studies because it is readily available. It is a crude measure of labour skill because many operatives are highly skilled. In our data, the earnings of operatives are some 20 per cent below those of non-operatives, supporting the notion that the proportion of workers who are operatives is a crude skill measure. But the ratio of earnings varies considerably across sectors, also.
- This motivates our use of a second measure, the *share of the wage bill going to operatives*. If higher operative wages relative to non-operatives wages imply greater skill for operatives, the wage bill measure will reflect this.
- Our third measure is the *proportion of employees who are women*. Abowd and Freeman (1991) found that in the USA women are highly concentrated in import-competing sectors, making them potentially the most vulnerable demographic group to trade pressures. If this is the case throughout the West, adherents to the 'trade has caused all problems' view must explain why women have fared better in the labour market than men in the past two decades.
- Our fourth measure is the *logarithm of wages* in a sector, calculated by dividing the wage bill by employment. All else the same, in an ideal competitive market, wages reflect skills. However, in many sectors there are economic rents, compensating differentials for adverse conditions, and so forth. In Europe, moreover, industry wages are more compressed than in the USA, while skills are not necessarily compressed.
- Our fifth measure is the *logarithm of operative wages*. This is calculated by dividing the wage bill for operatives by operatives' employment. It eliminates any difference in average industry wages due to differences in the proportion of operatives across sectors.

In addition, we have three measures of other inputs or outputs to labour.

- The *logarithm of the ratio of gross fixed capital formation to employment*, which can be taken as indicative of the capital/labour ratio. It is arguable whether capital should be viewed as part of a nation's endowments or as an internationally mobile factor. If capital and skilled labour are complementary, a measure of capital to labour provides some indication of skill.
- The *logarithm of the ratio of value added to employment*, which is a crude indicator of labour productivity. To turn this productivity measure into comparable units across countries, one can use the exchange rate, though it is important to recognize that a 20 per cent decline in value added/worker due to fluctuations in currency values is entirely different from a 20 per cent decline in value added/worker due to inefficient production.
- *Labour's share of value added*, obtained by dividing the wage bill by value added. Note that with internationally determined fixed prices, this measures unit labour costs. This measure can be transformed into unit labour costs on a common currency basis using the exchange rate.

Table 1.3 presents the results of regressions designed to determine the contribution of industry to the variation in the diverse labour measures just described, in terms of the R^2 with/without the addition of industry dummy variables, and the F statistics for addition of the industry vector. Because several measures of the same variable are available in the files, we often report the calculations with all measures. The lines labelled *a* use data from the STAN file. The lines labelled *b* are from the UN file. The table reports results for our largest data file (LAT2); results obtained from the smaller LAT1 file, which includes bilateral trade data, are similar.

Table 1.3. Contribution of industry to measures of labour skill by individual OECD countries, 1960–92

	R^2 with all	R^2 without industry	F-test for industry	No. of observations
Operatives' share of employment	.68	.24	216	6584
Female share of employment	.89	.03	576	2087
Operatives' share of wage bill	.71	.21	440	6609
Wages[a]	.95	.94	86	18784
Wages[b]	.96	.95	21	7222
Operatives' wages[a]	.96	.96	24	6597
Capital formation per employee[a]	.95	.87	514	14939
Capital formation per employee[b]	.97	.91	476	6610
Labour share of value added[a]	.54	.24	297	19248
Labour share of value added[b]	.78	.77	9	4045
Value added per employee[a]	.94	.91	191	18905
Value added per employee[b]	.80	.77	16	4024

Source: Tabulated from LAT2 database. [a]Based on STAN data. [b]Based on UN data. All regressions include year and country dummy variables. Results obtained with LAT1 are very similar.

The statistical analysis reveals powerful cross-country similarities in skill structures among industries. Taking our labour measures first, we note that the operatives' share of employment has a very strong industry dimension. But the most striking result is that the female share of employment is virtually exclusively related to industry. The R^2 is effectively zero absent industry dummies but rises to .89 inclusive of the industry vector. This reflects the industrial segregation of women workers, found in large numbers in some industries but not in others. The wage variables also show evidence of a significant industry dimension, even though the R^2 do not reflect it because wages are measured in national currency units, which show up in country dummy variables. But the industry vector is not as critical to explaining wage variation as it is in explaining the female or operatives' share of employment. This presumably reflects differences in wage-setting institutions among OECD countries: our data, like others, show substantial country differences in the variation of pay across industries, with the USA having a wider dispersion of pay by industry than most other countries.

The other variables—capital formation per employee, labour's share of value added and value added per employee—also show a substantial industry variation, though in the UN file both labour's share of value added and value added per employee have a weaker industry dimension than do those variables from the OECD, a result possibly due to problems of matching industries across the data sets.

The next issue to explore is the link between trade patterns and labour skill patterns across industries:

3. *Is the skill structure of an industry work-force related to measures of trade, with LDCs and with OECD countries?*

The *sine qua non* for LDC trade to contribute to the labour problems of less skilled workers in the West is that imports come largely in sectors that employ the less skilled. Table 1.4 examines the trade–labour link through regressions of the net trade flow, trade pressure, and the direction of trade on variables measuring the proportion of employees who are women (percentage female) and the proportion of employees who are operatives (percentage operatives). All the regressions include country and year dummy variables, but exclude industry dummies since the relations we are exploring are the industry correlates of the trade flows. The first line under each heading gives results for total trade (LAT2 data file). The second line presents the results for total trade obtained form the smaller LAT1 data set (included for comparison purposes with lines 3 and 4). The third and fourth lines use the LAT1 file to differentiate between trade with non-OECD countries and trade among the OECD. There are two main findings:

- There is a clear relation between the labour measures and trade flows overall, with the percentage female variable being particularly highly linked to imports. Industries with a higher percentage of women workers show more negative net trade flows, a higher import penetration ratio, and a larger import share in total trade. This is true for both the LAT2 and LAT1 data files. The results on percentage operatives are broadly similar, although smaller in magnitude and somewhat less powerful. The implication is that trade effects should be greater on women than on operatives.
- The labour measures are more strongly linked to non-OECD trade than to OECD trade. This can be seen most clearly in the net trade calculations ($(X-M)/GO$). Both the coefficients for the percentage *female* variable and for percentage *operatives* are negative and significant for non-OECD trade, but insignificant for OECD trade. With one exception—the coefficient on percentage *female* in the regression for $M/(X+M)$—this pattern holds throughout. The relation in total trade thus would appear to be driven by the patterns in trade with *non-OECD* countries.

Table 1.4. The effects of measures of labour skill on trade with non-OECD and OECD countries

Measure of trade	% female	% operatives	N	R^2
(X–M)/GO				
Total trade (LAT2)	−.48* (.07)	−.25* (.12)	1355	.07
Total trade (LAT1)	−.20 (.25)	−.36* (.14)	432	.32
Non-OECD	−.33* (.09)	−.16* (.07)	432	.10
OECD	−.01 (.13)	−.19 (.30)	432	.16
(M/GO)				
Total trade (LAT2)	.54* (.08)	.35* (.13)	1355	.08
Total trade (LAT1)	.67* (.32)	.06 (.21)	432	.24
Non-OECD	.35* (.12)	.14 (.08)	432	.24
OECD	.20 (.14)	.48 (.37)	432	.27
M/(X+M)				
Total trade (LAT2)	.20* (.03)	−.07 (.05)	1478	.15
Total trade (LAT1)	.33* (.07)	.18* (.07)	440	.28
Non-OECD	.32* (.08)	.20 (.16)	440	.22
OECD	17* (.07)	−.01 (.08)	440	.27

Source: Tabulated from LAT databases. All regressions include dummy variables for year and country. The first line of total trade figures correspond to those drawn from the LAT2 database. The second line of total trade figures, and the non-OECD and OECD figures are from the LAT1 database. Standard errors in parentheses. *denotes significance at the .05 level.

The fact that non-OECD trade has been concentrated in sectors with relatively many women workers—textiles, clothing—implies that, *the same women workers should have been most adversely affected by that trade*. But, this has not been the case. As noted, women's pay has tended to rise in most OECD countries relative to men's pay; and relative employment rates have also risen in most countries. The most likely explanation for this is that women have found jobs in the non-traded goods sector, and thus that developments in the sector affect labour market outcomes, contrary to the strong H–O model in which only the traded goods sector matters.

1.4 Trade Effects Through the Three Models

In this section we examine the evidence for trade effects on the labour market under the three models described in section 1.3. We have some results for the H–O and labour market models, but only glimmers of findings for the more complicated Ricardian model.

The *H–O model* directs attention at prices. The OECD–STAN dataset contains some information on prices in the form of current and 1985 constant price measures of value added for many industries. The ratio of the current value added to 1985 constant price value added yields an implicit price deflator for value added in the industry. It is not an ideal price measure, since it is not a measure of the final price of the relevant product but it does provide some clue to relative price changes.

In Table 1.5, Panel A, we examine whether the implicit value added deflator is related to imports and/or to the skill composition of the work force. We look first at price changes over a long period of time, specifically from 1978 (the first year for which data on most cells exist) to 1990 (the most recent year for which data for most cells exist). We have chosen to examine long period changes to finesse problems of timing. The dependent variable is the log change in the implicit deflator for each industry–country cell. Each of the regressions includes country and industry dummy variables, so that we are comparing changes within a country and industry with the relevant explanatory variables. Because relative price changes are presumably dominated by changes in relative productivity we also include the change in constant unit value added per worker as a key control variable in some of the calculations. Our analysis follows three steps:

- First, we relate price changes in an industry–country cell to changes in import shares, defined as the ratio of imports to gross output in the relevant cell in the end period (1990) minus the ratio in the initial year (1978). This is not the price relation that one would expect in a general equilibrium model, where the effects of import competition are 'splattered' throughout the economy. In such a model, the prices of all industries that use less skilled labour are driven down, not only the prices in the sectors facing import competition. We believe that looking for price effects in the industries most affected by import competition is reasonable, and indeed helpful to establishing the purported link from trade to prices. One reason is that, as noted earlier, other economic changes could underlie correlations between the share of unskilled labour in a sector and prices (*vide* minimum wages). We would feel more comfortable about interpreting the causality of that relation if we were given evidence that imports had a first-order effect on the prices in impacted sectors. A second reason is that in Europe, at least, institutional wage-setting could abort the general equilibrium effects, though there still might be first-order price effects.
- Second, we examine the relation between price changes and the less skilled labour share of employment in a sector in the base year, and the relation between price changes and the percentage of females in a sector in the base year. Because our data on female employment are available over a shorter time period than our data on operatives, we first report the results of this analysis for imports and the share of operatives in employment over the period 1978–92, and then report comparable results that include the share of women in employment for the period 1981–91.

- Finally, we examine prices conditional both on changes in import shares and the unskilled labour share of employment. This provides a crude decomposition of price effects between the first-order effects on impacted industries and potential splattering effects throughout the economy.

The results in Panel A of Table 1.5 suggest moderate effects of import competition on the implicit value added price deflators. The estimated coefficients on the change in import share are consistently negative and significant.[4] In a given country, industries with increasing shares of imports unambiguously experienced declines in prices relative to those with smaller increased shares of imports. The coefficient on the percentage of workers who are operatives in line 3 is also negative, consistent with the existence of price pressures due to trade or other factors on sectors intensive with operatives. Finally, lines 4 and 5 show that these two effects are sufficiently independent that the regressions yield negative coefficients on both the change in import share and percentage of operatives, when the two variables are jointly included in the equation. Because we control for industry and country, the implication is that relative prices among industries within a country have fallen more in those sectors where import shares have risen, and in those sectors that started off with a high percentage of operative employment.

Panel B of Table 1.5 gives calculations which also include the percentage of female workers for the period 1981–90 (this gave us the most observations on female employment for an extended period). The results on the change in import share are consistent with those obtained over the longer period: indeed, the coefficient on the import term tends to be larger and more significant. But the correlation between changes in prices and the per cent of operatives weakens significantly. In fact, there is effectively no correlation between either the per cent of operatives and the per cent of women in a cell and the changes in industry price over this period.

There are reasons to be wary of these price results: as noted, a value added deflator is not a final price measure; moreover, the three-digit/four-digit character of our industries implies that the prices are a mishmash aggregate of the prices of commodities; nor have we tried to estimate a full price model, as an industrial organization expert might do (neither has anyone else searching for price effects). Our suspicion is that the closer one gets to the real prices of real goods made in LDCs (namely Chinese toys), the greater will be the pressure of imports on prices, but this is simply suspicion. These weaknesses duly noted, the finding that sectors that have experienced increased import penetration have had relative price declines

---

[4] To see if this effect is more/less associated with the effect of non-OECD and OECD trade, we estimated the same equations in our LAT1 data file. In this case, the number of observations was smaller and the results correspondingly weaker: with a sample of 202 observations, we obtained a weak negative coefficient on OECD trade but a negligible negative on non-OECD trade (we do not report these results in the table, as we are still 'cleaning' this data file, and expect some modest changes as the data are improved).

Table 1.5. The effect of imports and initial labour skill on changes in prices, 1978–90 (Dep Var = long-period change in the value added price deflator)

	Panel A: Import shares and % operatives as explanatory variables, 1978–90					
	ΔImport share	Δln (VA/Emp)	%OPS$_{78}$	Ind/country dummies	R^2	No. observations
1	−.022 (.005)			Yes	.69	569
2	−.017 (.003)	−.759 (.029)		Yes	.87	562
3			−.426 (.268)	Yes	.68	307
4	−.019 (.005)		−.421 (.263)	Yes	.70	307
5	−.029 (.003)	−.799 (.043)	−.428 (.173)	Yes	.87	307

	Panel B: Import shares, % operatives and % female as explanatory variables, 1981–90					
	ΔImport share	Δln (VA/Emp)	%OPS$_{78}$	Ind/country dummies	R^2	No. observations
6	−.032 (.004)			Yes	.61	573
7	−.032 (.003)	−.734 (.033)		Yes	.80	569
8			.066 (.234)	Yes	.62	286
9				Yes	.71	186
10			.427 (.344)	Yes	.70	160
11	−.057 (.009)		.484 (.301)	Yes	.77	160
12	−.064 (.007)	−.641 (.071)	.492 (.234)	Yes	.86	160

Source: Calculated for the relevant periods using LAT2 database. Standard errors in parentheses.

would seem consistent with imports exerting pressure on those sectors. This should, in turn, affect employee wages and/or jobs.

This type of finding naturally leads us to consider the *labour market model*, which directs attention at workers displaced by trade. In the first stage, imports reduce potential output in a sector, and jobs are lost. Imports may also induce employees in the affected sector to take pay cuts to limit the potential loss of employment. Presumably, however, there is also a second-stage effect as displaced workers flow into other sectors, increasing labour supply there and reducing wages in those sectors as well. In Europe, where wages are set by labour market institutions, the wage responses are likely to be less than in the USA, with a resultant greater loss of employment in the first stage and fewer displaced workers obtaining jobs in the second stage. Similarly, within Europe we would expect to see some variance across countries in the relative magnitudes of the wage and employment effects, depending on the degree of wage flexibility that dominates wage-setting institutions.

Most analysts use the ratio of imports or net trade to gross output in a sector to measure the immediate trade effect on employment, under the assumption that absent trade domestic producers would fill the market demand, expanding output and employment. In factor content studies, output and employment are assumed to be proportionally related, so that a decrease in imports of 10 per cent would presumably raise employment by 10 per cent. Wood (1994) has suggested that proportionality understates the effects of LDC trade, because the more labour-intensive parts of an industry will be most affected. In other words, a 10 per cent reduction in LDC imports would raise employment by more than 10 per cent. One way to test this hypothesis is to examine whether an increase in LDC imports relative to gross output has a more/less negative effect than an increase in OECD imports relative to gross output or than a comparable change in output due to domestic market developments.

But there is an alternative possibility that should be addressed first. If imports were concentrated in growing industries, meeting demand that domestic producers could not meet, or if they differed so much from domestic products that there would be little domestic production of alternatives, the standard import share analysis might overstate the effects of imports on employment in that sector. One way to address this issue is to calculate the correlation between changes in imports and changes in employment by industry. Are sectors with growing imports gaining or losing jobs relative to other sectors? Within the manufacturing industries in our data set, the correlation between changes in log employment and changes in log imports (rather than the import share) is −.22 for the period 1978–90. This contrasts with the positive .44 correlation that Freeman and Katz (1991) report for the USA in the period 1958–84. In the 1960s and 1970s imports may have increased largely in industries with growing employment, but in the 1980s they have increased largely in industries with falling employment. Because of this, simply taking changes in imports rather than the standard change in import shares yields qualitatively similar results to those we report.

Table 1.6 presents our analysis of the effect of the ratio of imports to production on employment, with the import/gross output ratio, or change thereof, taken as exogenous, using our LAT2 data file. The dependent variable in line 1 is the change in log employment in an industry–country cell for the full period 1978–90. The independent variables are change in log output and change in the import share. The regression shows a significant negative correlation between increases in import shares and employment: industries that experienced the largest increases in import penetration also experienced the largest declines in employment. We also estimated the effect of imports on the operatives' or women's share of employment, but found no relation. Imports affect those workers because they are concentrated in import-intensive sectors, not by altering the operatives' or female share of employment within sectors.

The remaining lines of the table record the results of estimating similar regressions in first-differences (annual log changes) using the entire LAT2 data

Table 1.6. The effect of imports on employment in OECD countries

	Δ (import share)	Δ Log: (output) $_{t-1}$	R^2	N
Long-period changes (1978–90)				
Δlog (employment)	−.161 (.017)		.60	624
First differences				
Δlog (employment)	−.053 (.008)		.03	13328
Δlog (employment)	−.046 (.008)	.111 (.010)	.05	12777
Δlog (employment), US/Canada	−.112 (.048)	.147 (.021)	.06	1830
Δlog (employment), Europe	−.065 (.005)	.108 (.011)	.07	8310

Source: Line 1 calculated from LAT2 file, as long period changes, with dummy variables for country and industry. Lines 2–5 calculated from LAT2 file, as log-differences, with dummy variables for country and year. Results obtained with log levels and including industry dummies are similar.

file, with dummy variables for years and countries.[5] By estimating the regressions in first-differences, we eliminate the need to include industry dummies, as we are analysing year-to-year changes within industries (or more accurately, within industry–year–country cells). In effect, we are comparing year-to-year changes in employment within a cell to year-to-year changes in the import share within the same cell.

These regressions confirm the finding that increases in the import share depress employment in the relevant domestic sector. Line 3 adds the change in the logarithm of gross output to the regression, in part to test the robustness of import effect: the coefficient on the import share falls slightly but remains statistically highly significant. Since employment and output are jointly determined, we use lagged change in output as an imperfect 'instrument' for the contemporary change in output. We do not, however, want to give any particular causal interpretation to this equation, save to emphasize that the import share result, while modest in magnitude, is fairly robust. Lines 4 and 5 record results for the USA and Canada, which have 'flexible' labour markets, and for the European countries, where wages are largely institutionally determined. The coefficient on the import share is larger for the USA and Canada than for the European countries, which is consistent with trade having increased faster in the former. It also suggest *that North American*

---

[5] This is equivalent to estimating the regressions in log levels and including industry dummies. Using the levels approach we would estimate the deviation from the country–industry cell mean associated with changes in the import share. With the first-difference approach, we seek to explain what fraction of within-cell changes are related to changes in the import share. The first-difference specification, however, should reduce the potential problem of serial correlation in the errors that could result from the existence of one-period adjustment lags in employment. The first-difference specification should also eliminate any problems associated with the measurement of wages in different currencies.

labour markets are more sensitive to trade pressures than those in Europe. Put together with a body of literature that indicates fairly modest effects of trade on US employment (Cooper 1994; Revenga 1992; Sachs and Shatz 1994) this would suggest that import pressures cannot explain Europe's dismal employment performance over the last decade.

In addition to the calculations presented in Table 1.6, we also examined the differential effect, if any, of changes in import shares from non-OECD and OECD countries on employment, using the LAT1 data file. The preliminary results (not given in the table) show *greater employment effects within industries for OECD imports than for non-OECD imports.*[6] This raises the question of whether LDC imports into an industry may be more complementary with what an advanced economy produces in that sector than imports from another advanced economy. We need to do some further work testing the consistency of our data, however, before pursuing these results further.

Table 1.7 turns from the effects of imports on employment to their effects on wages. Line 1 examines changes in log wages over the 1978–90 time period. It shows that an increase in the import share, conditional on industry and country, reduced wages modestly. Line 2 mimics our employment analysis for the entire data set: the estimated elasticity of wages to the import share is again modest but still highly significant. The last two lines in the table compare the effect of imports on wages in the USA and Canada versus European countries. The results are again quite different for the two groups of countries. Import shares have a substantial negative effect on wages in the USA and Canada and a much smaller effect in Europe. Moreover, when the UK is dropped from the Europe group, the wage effect becomes negligible. This is not surprising given what we know about wage-setting institutions in continental Europe—what is surprising is that you might have expected employment effects in Europe to be larger than in North America, as a result. However, as discussed above, employment in Europe also appears to be less sensitive to trade flows than in the USA and Canada. Jointly, these two sets of results seriously weaken the argument that trade can explain rising unemployment in Europe.

The *Ricardian model* is the most complicated to analyse and we have not made much progress as yet in developing an empirical structure for exploiting its insights or testing its implications. It directs attention at three (or more) empirical patterns: the ordering of industries by net exports, which follows a 'comparative advantage ladder'; the characteristics of industries on the margin of comparative advantage in this ladder; and the potential for expanding trade or employment in industries with comparative advantages. To get a handle on the first two issues, we examined non-OECD net exports to the USA by industry for 1970, 1980 and 1990. There is a moderately similar ranking between 1970 and 1980 (a Spearman coefficient of

---

[6] In the levels equations, the coefficient on non-OECD imports is −.08, while that on OECD imports is −.22. In the first-difference equation, the coefficient on non-OECD imports is close to zero, while that on OECD imports is −.025.

.55), but the correlation weakens for 1990. The average wages in the 'marginal industry' are roughly unchanged from 1970 to 1980, but rise sharply thereafter. In addition, the range of goods that the USA exports has fallen. But with a trade deficit, this is likely even without any Ricardian model. To achieve balanced trade, exports in those sectors in which the USA has a comparative advantage should have skyrocketed, which they did not. The problem may lie in the relation between the wages paid to less skilled workers and those paid to more skilled workers, relative to US comparative advantage. Or it may lie in the industrial strategies of the NICs, or with competition with other advanced countries.

Table 1.7.   The effect of imports on wages in OECD countries

	Δ (import share)	Δ Log: (output) $_{t-1}$	R^2	N
Long-period changes (1978–90)				
Δlog (wage)	−.030 (.011)		.89	622
First differences				
Δlog (wage)	−.030 (.011)		.03	13328
Δlog (wage)	−.031 (.012)	.10 (.010)	.16	12664
Δlog (wage), US and Canada	−.085 (.023)	.078 (.012)	.07	1830
Δlog (wage), Europe	−.044 (.021)	.101 (.011)	.21	8209

Source: Line 1 calculated from LAT2 file, as long period changes, with dummy variables for country and industry. Lines 2–5 calculated from LAT2 file, as log-differences, with dummy variables for country and year. Results obtained with log levels and including industry dummies are similar.

There is another problem we encountered in trying to implement the Ricardian model. In most presentations of the model, the wage falls to restore the trade balance. But it is not transparent that domestic wage declines induced by trade will also restore full employment. The exchange rate, which is not treated seriously in the model, plays an important role in actual economic developments. The bottom line here is: lots of thinking and analysis is needed to implement this model in a useful way.

1.5 Conclusions

In this chapter we have used a new data file to examine the relation between trade and the labour market. While this new data set has some problems, it has illuminated several issues that merit attention in the debate over the effect of trade on the job market in Western countries.

To those who believe that the job market problems of European workers are due largely if not exclusively to LDC trade, our analysis highlights two major difficulties:

- Trade with LDCs has grown less in Europe than in the USA, and thus should have created smaller problems in European job markets. In addition, preliminary calculations show greater sensitivity of employment to OECD imports than non-OECD imports.
- Trade with LDCs has been concentrated in female-intensive sectors, but female workers have been doing relatively well in many European countries.

To those who believe that trade has no deleterious effects despite the clear prediction of factor price equalization, we find that this claim runs into two problems:

- Trade has fairly well-defined first order effects on employment and wages by industry and some effects on prices as well. The simple correlation between changes in imports and changes in employment for 1978–90 for all OECD countries in our data is -0.22, which contrasts with a .44 correlation in US data for 1958–84.
- Within industries, both employment and wages have been more affected by imports in the USA than in Europe.

The bottom line is that the evidence supports neither the extreme view that trade is the sole determinant of labour market problems nor the extreme view that it has no effect on Western workers. To paraphrase a famous statement about money, trade matters, but it is not all that matters.

References

Abowd, J. and Freeman, R. (1991), 'Internationalization of the US Labour Market', in J. Abowd and R. Freeman (eds), *Immigration, Trade and the Labour Market*, University of Chicago Press for NBER, Chicago.

Berman, E., Machin, S. and Bound, J. (1992), 'Implications of Skill-Biased Technological Change: International Evidence', July, manuscript.

Borjas, G., Freeman, R. and Katz, L. (1992), 'On the Labour Market Effects of Immigration and Trade', in G. Borjas and R. Freeman (eds.), *Immigration and the Work Force*, University of Chicago and NBER, Chicago, pp. 213–44.

Cooper, R. (1994), 'Foreign Trade, Wages and Unemployment', paper delivered at Egon Sohmen Conference, Salzburg, Austria, September.

Feenstra, R. and Hanson, G. (1994) 'Foreign Investment, Outsourcing and Relative Wages', October.

Freeman, R. B. and Katz, L F. (1991), 'Industrial Wage and Employment Determination in an Open Economy', in J. M. Abowd and R. B. Freeman (eds.), *Immigration, Trade, and the Labour Market*, University of Chicago Press, Chicago, pp. 235–60.

Lawrence, R. (1994), 'The Impact of Trade on OECD Labour Markets', Group of Thirty, *Occasional Paper 45*, Washington DC.

OECD (1994a), *Background Document for a study on Economic and Other Linkages with Major Developing Economies*, OECD, Paris, August.

—— (1994b), *Bilateral Trade Database Documentation*, OECD, Paris, May.

—— (1994c), *The OECD STAN Database for Industrial Analysis*, OECD, Paris, December.

Revenga, A. L. (1992), 'Exporting Jobs? The Impact of Import Competition on Employment and Wages in US Manufacturing', *Quarterly Journal of Economics*, 107(1): 225–84.

Sachs, J. D. and Shatz, H. J. (1994), 'Trade and Jobs in US Manufacturing', *Brookings Papers on Economic Activity*, 1: 1–69.

Wood, A. (1994), *North–South Trade, Employment and Inequality*, Clarendon Press, Oxford.

World Bank (1995a), 'Workers in an Integrating World', *World Development Report 1995*, World Bank, Washington.

World Bank (1995b), 'The Employment Crisis in Industrial Countries: Is International Integration to Blame', *Regional Perspectives on the WDR 1995*, World Bank, Washington.

2. Relative Prices, Trade and Restructuring in European Industry

DAMIEN NEVEN AND CHARLES WYPLOSZ

2.1 Introduction

In this chapter we explore the link between trade and European labour markets by using evidence on relative commodity prices and intra-sectoral skill levels. We document the evolution of relative (production and import) prices from developing countries since the early 1970s and relate the evolution of prices to wages, employment and the level of skills.

In terms of principles, the presumption that wages can fall in developed countries as a consequence of trade liberalization (relative to what would have happened in the absence of such liberalization) is associated with the Heckscher–Ohlin theory of trade and with the Stolper–Samuelson theorem. The simplest version of this theorem can be outlined as follows: consider two factors of production (skilled and unskilled labour) and two countries that differ according to their factor endowments. One country is relatively well endowed in skilled labour and the other is relatively well endowed in unskilled labour. There are two commodities and the production of these commodities requires different mixes of factors. One commodity requires a relatively high unskilled labour input, whereas the other one requires a relatively high skilled labour input. Production technology is well behaved (with decreasing returns to scale) and identical in both countries. In the absence of trade, relative prices of the commodities will differ across countries, with the unskilled (skilled) labour-intensive commodities being relatively expensive in the skilled (unskilled) labour rich country. In autarky, the relative price of skilled labour in the skill rich country will also be lower than in the unskilled labour rich country. As trade is liberalized, relative prices converge across countries, which leads to a reallocation of production within each country; the relative price of unskilled labour-intensive commodities falls in the skill rich country, which then specializes in the skill intensive commodity. At the same time, the relative price of the unskilled labour-intensive commodity increases in the unskilled labour rich country and its production increases. Trade liberalization has therefore led to a specialization in production. However, it has also provoked a shift in the demand for factors; there is an increase in demand for skill (unskilled labour) in the skill (unskilled labour) rich country, so that the relative price of skill (unskilled labour) increases. To the extent that the relative prices of commodities have converged, technology being the same across countries, the relative prices of factors will also converge. The real price of unskilled labour (in terms of either commodity) will actually fall and the real price of skilled labour will increase in the skill rich country.

If Europe can be seen as a skill rich area relative to developing countries, what should we observe if the parable is at work (recalling that the parable assumes full employment, a particularly unpalatable hypothesis for Europe)? First, the relative price of unskilled labour-intensive commodities should fall in Europe. Second, imports of unskilled labour-intensive commodities should increase in Europe whereas exports of skilled labour-intensive commodities should increase. Third, the price of standard (unskilled) labour should fall. Fourth, the skill labour ratio in the production of all commodities should *fall* in Europe (as relatively larger quantities of unskilled labour than skilled labour are reallocated from the production of unskilled labour-intensive commodities). Finally, *in any given industry*, the capital labour ratio will converge across countries.

Indeed, it is the fall in the relative wage of unskilled labour that has motivated much of the work undertaken in the USA. For instance, according to Freeman (1994) the wages for men with less than high school education have declined by 23 per cent between 1972 and 1990, at a time when the wages of workers with high school education stayed constant. This evidence can be corroborated with observed changes in the income distribution; according to Borjas (1995), workers at the thirty-third percentile of the wage distribution experienced a 14 per cent drop in real wage throughout the 1980s, whereas workers at the sixty-sixth percentile experienced only a 6 per cent drop and those at the upper tail of the distribution obtained a wage increase.

According to Wood (1994: 248), a similar rise in the relative earnings of college graduates can be observed in Northern EU countries. In particular, the relative wage of white-collar workers rose steadily in Germany and in the UK since the early 1970s. In other EU countries, the trend is, however, less clear (see Nickell and Bell 1995: table 3). More importantly, unemployment rates among less educated workers increased markedly relative to those of more educated ones; in the 1980s, the largest rise in unemployment is observed among the less educated workers (those with no more than basic secondary education), so that for instance in France the rate of unemployment among low education workers in 1990 is more than four times as high (10.6) as the rate observed among high education ones (2.6).

Various approaches have been followed in the empirical validation of the Heckscher–Ohlin and Stolper–Samuelson principles and each method has concentrated on a different aspect of the parable. The first method focuses on trade flows and computes the factor content of imports less that of exports to evaluate the net impact of trade on the demand for factors and in particular on the demand for skilled and unskilled labour (see Sachs and Shatz 1994; Wood 1991 and 1994). Others focus on the prediction that input mixes in production should change as trade is liberalized and accordingly use evidence on input mixes at the industry level (see Berman, Bound and Griliches 1994; Lawrence and Slaughter 1993; and Machin 1994). The third approach concentrates on prices and tracks down the evolution of relative commodity prices over time (see Lawrence 1994; Lawrence and Slaughter 1993; and Leamer 1994).

Each of these methods suffers from significant shortcomings (see Wood 1995, for a discussion). The main difficulty, which is common to all three methods, is to identify a reasonable counterfactual. Indeed, there are many factors other than trade that affect commodity and input prices. To name only a few, these include variations in factor supplies, including institutional changes that affect wage negotiations and labour costs; changes in demand related to evolving tastes or to trade integration; and most importantly, changes in both supply and demand prompted by technological progress. Separating out these factors is very difficult. In addition, there are some significant issues of simultaneity; for instance, changes in factor supplies (say human capital) can be themselves prompted by the antici-pation of changes in factor prices.

Many of the effects we want to look at can be related to technological progress as well as trade. For instance, the widely documented decline in low-skilled labour employment and relative (sometimes absolute real) wages may be the outcome of competition from developing countries; alternatively it may be related to techno-logical progress shifting jobs towards higher skills. Worse, trade and technological progress are interrelated: trade competition spurs the development and diffusion of new technologies, which, in turn, affect the pattern of trade. Whatever evidence will be gathered in this area will therefore be, at best, suggestive.

In this chapter, we first gather evidence on relative commodity prices. As indi-cated by Leamer (1994), the advantage of this approach is that changes in relative commodity prices are necessary to bring about sector reallocations and changes in factor prices. By contrast, trade flows are less informative as trade can remain unaffected despite changes in commodity prices (as the import competing industry is striving to adjust, possibly by cutting wages). Appropriate price data are, how-ever, difficult to gather. For most of the analysis, we have to resort to the use of unit values, which make no adjustment for change in quality over time. In this context, one cannot disentangle changes in relative (standardized) commodity price from changes in relative qualities. This may matter to the extent that commodities intensive in unskilled labour may have less scope for quality improvement than others. Accordingly, observed falls in relative unit values for unskilled labour-intensive commodities could very well exaggerate the fall in relative (standardized) commodity prices.

In Section 2.2 we provide evidence on the evolution of import and production prices by sector and check whether the relative price of unskilled labour-intensive commodities has indeed fallen since 1975. We find little support in favour of the hypothesis that import prices have fallen in unskilled labour-intensive sectors but we also find evidence of substantial specialization and restructuring in those sectors as witnessed by a large drop in (relative) employment and a significant (relative) increase in the skill intensity. Section 2.3 goes one step further and estimates a simple econometric model of wage and employment setting at the industry level, in which trade pressure is measured by import prices. Aggregate effects are found to be small or negligible but significant, and surprising adjustments can sometimes be found at the industry level. Some policy implications from the results are drawn in Section 2.4.

2.2 Relative Prices, Specialization and Skill Intensity: Some Hard Facts

As indicated above, trade liberalization with developing countries should lead to a reduction in the relative price of unskilled labour-intensive commodities in Europe, an increase in imports of unskilled labour-intensive commodities, a reduction in employment and output of those sectors and a decrease in skill intensity across all sectors. In what follows, we first document the changes in relative prices and subsequently turn to specialization and skill intensity.

2.2.1 Relative Import Prices

In order to gather evidence on relative prices, we compute unit values of imports for all three-digit NACE sectors,[1] for the period 1975–90 and for the four large EU countries (France, Germany, the UK and Italy). To isolate better the effects of competition with unskilled labour-intensive countries, we also compute separate indices for imports from developing countries and those from the developed world. The primary data are drawn from the COMEXT database. As import values and volumes are not available by NACE sectors for the period 1975–88, the primary data at the commodity level had to be aggregated into the NACE industry sectors (using a conversion table provided by EUROSTAT). Developed countries in the COMEXT database include the EFTA countries, the USA, Canada, South Africa, Japan, Australia, New Zealand, the former Yugoslavia, Turkey and minor European countries (Andorra, Malta). Note that EU countries are not included in this definition, so that changes in import price from this set of countries may be a rather poor measure of competition from the industrialized world as a whole. All other countries, except for the former COMECON countries are included in the category of developing countries. Our measure of competition from developing countries, which can be presumed to trigger Heckscher–Ohlin type effects, is thus rather comprehensive and well focused.

In addition to import prices, we also gather evidence on relative production prices from the OECD STAN database which provides data for a limited set of countries and SITC industries (unfortunately, the INDE database from EUROSTAT has no information on prices). As proxy for the level of skill in an industry, we use

---

[1] There are about 100 NACE three-digit sectors. We concentrate on about 80 sectors for which reliable data can be computed.

the proportion of white-collar workers. This variable, which is similar to that used in the US studies (production vs. non production workers) (see Lawrence and Slaughter 1993: footnote 32), is not ideal but it is the only proxy available at the industry level (from the INDE database).

In order to verify whether the price of unskilled labour-intensive commodities has fallen over time, several measures have been used in the literature. Lawrence and Slaughter compute a weighted index of prices changes at the industry level where the weights are given either by the share of all skilled workers or the share of all unskilled workers. If, indeed, the relative price of less skill-intensive commodities has fallen, one would expect the change in the former index to exceed that of the latter. In addition to this measure, Sachs and Shatz (1994), also regress (across industries) the changes in prices on the level of skill. We first concentrate on these two measures.

The first piece of evidence focuses on weighted prices indices. The evolution of import prices presented in Table 2.1 does not seem to depend very much on the weight factors. This suggests that the change in relative commodity prices may have little to do with the level of skills. This evidence confirms the findings of Lawrence and Slaughter (1993) for the USA and Germany. Similar conclusions can be reached from the second approach in which the change in import prices is regressed on the level of skills, proxied by the share of white-collar workers. We expect to see a negative coefficient of partial correlation. As indicated by Table 2.2, there is essentially no relation between these two variables: half of the times the sign is wrong and none of the estimated coefficient is significantly different from zero. This confirms the results of Sachs and Shatz (1994) for the USA.

The measures adopted so far could, however, be rather coarse if the pattern of changes in price is complex and this may occur if changes in relative prices result from various factors and not only from trade. For instance, a fall in the price of highly unskilled labour-intensive commodities may be occulted by a concomitant fall in the price of highly-skilled-intensive commodities so that on average no relation is observed between changes in price and levels of skills. This possibility was acknowledged by Sachs and Shatz (1994) who observe that import prices are significantly related to the level of skills if a dummy is introduced for the computer industry (in which presumably technological progress accounts for much of the fall in relative price). Accordingly, we shall also adopt a more disaggregrate approach in which we compute the change in price for various groups of industries that differ according to their factor intensity in production.[2]

In order to define a homogenous group of industries in terms of factor intensity, we use the clustering procedure presented in Neven (1994): it groups industries according to their proximity in the space of four variables chosen to proxy for factor intensity. As proxy variables, we use the share of wages in value added, the level of investments as a percentage of value added, the average (total) compen-

---

[2] Sachs and Shatz (1994) allocate industries by classes of skill intensity. The procedure adopted here is similar but controls for the level of capital.

Table 2.1. Change in import price (%, 75–90)

	Prices weighted by the share of white-collar workers	Prices weighted by the share of blue-collar workers
France		
Developing countries	104	108
Developed countries	121	133
Italy		
Developing countries	82	79
Developed countries	116	114
UK		
Developing countries	79	77
Developed countries	101	100
Germany		
Developing countries	80	76
Developed countries	97	87

Source: COMEXT, INDE, own calculations.

Table 2.2. Import prices and level of skills (dependent variable: percentage change in import price from developing countries, 76–90, OLS estimates)

	France	Germany	Italy	UK
constant	1.31	1.03	0.62	0.52
	(2.55)	(2.77)	(2.19)	(1.47)
Share of white collar (1977)	− 1.52	− 1.06	0.56	0.55
	(− 1.01)	(− 0.86)	(0.46)	(0.44)
R^2 (adjusted)	0.00	0.00	0.00	0.00
nbr observations	70	80	68	73

sation per worker and the share of blue-collar workers in the total number of employees. Since some of these variables are flows intended to proxy the corresponding stock, we use the average flow for the years 1985–90. A high level of investment as a percentage of value added is meant to represent a high capital intensity; a low average wage together with a high share of wages in value added is meant to pick up labour-intensive industries. By contrast, a high average wage, together with a high share of labour in value added is likely to be associated with

Table 2.3. Industry groups according to factor intensities (Germany)

	Share of white-collar workers	Average wage (million ecus per year)	Wage bill/ value added	Investment/ value added
1	0.48914	0.03177	0.77406	0.14573
2	0.35511	0.02581	0.79623	0.13388
3	0.22266	0.02269	0.85709	0.08042
4	0.24034	0.02281	0.75054	0.14676
5	0.37868	0.02808	0.64346	0.20981

Source: INDE, and own calculations

industries intensive in human capital. The share of white-collar workers is also a proxy for the intensity of skills (human capital).

We have applied the clustering procedure, which groups the industrial sectors in a predetermined number of homogenous classes, to the German data and subsequently checked whether clusters obtained for Germany would also provide an accurate description of the other three countries (see Neven 1994 for details). It turns out that industry clusters are remarkably stable across countries and easy to interpret.[3] Table 2.3 reports the average value taken by our proxies for factor intensities in Germany (averages over five years) when we allow for five clusters.

Group one is characterized by a high proportion of wages in value added, very high wages and a very high proportion of white-collar workers. These are high tech industries intensive in human capital, like office machinery and data processing, telecommunication equipment, pharmaceuticals and aerospace. Among the four remaining groups, we find two that are relatively intensive in unskilled labour and two that are relatively intensive in skilled labour (human capital); in each pair, there is one category that is relatively intensive in capital. The second cluster, which is intensive in human capital but uses little capital, is characterized by a relatively low level of investment relative to value added, high wages and a high level of wages in value added. Industries like machine tools, machinery, electrical engineering, domestic electrical appliances, photographic equipment and optical instruments belong to this cluster. The third group is intensive in unskilled labour and uses relatively little capital. These industries are characterized by low average wages, a high level of wages in value added and a low level of investment in value added. This cluster includes sectors like apparel, furniture, leather, footwear, shipbuilding and some metal products. The fourth cluster includes industries intensive in unskilled labour and capital (like carpets, heavy metal, steel, textiles, glass, rubber and plastics). They feature a high level of investment, relatively low

[3] The list of industries in each cluster is presented in Appendix 2.1.

40   *Neven and Wyplosz*

Table 2.4. Weighted change in import price by cluster (%, 1976–90)

Cluster	1	2	3	4	5	Average
Germany						
Developing countries	6	83	78	83	44	70
Developed countries	89	83	73	65	90	70
France						
Developing countries	52	66	109	123	101	103
Developed countries	57	174	170	105	116	128
UK						
Developing countries	30	131	69	56	85	77
Developed countries	145	131	78	92	84	100
Italy						
Developing countries	64	79	58	90	87	75
Developed countries	197	95	143	90	73	115

wages, a low proportion of white-collar workers and an intermediate proportion of wages in value added. The final cluster includes mostly food processing industries, which are intensive in both human capital and physical capital. They feature high wages, an intermediate proportion of wages in value added, a high level of investment and a high proportion of white-collar workers.

Table 2.4 presents the weighted (percentage) change (from 1976 to 1990) in import prices from developing and developed countries for each cluster, where the weight factor is the share of employment within the cluster (in 1976). The aggregate weighted change in import price is also given (in this case the weight factor is the share of employment in manufacturing, also in 1976).

The observation of this table reveals that import prices of unskilled labour-intensive commodities (cluster 3) have not decreased markedly relative to the average, at least in France, Germany and the UK. It is striking, however, that the relative import price of high tech commodities (cluster 1) has dramatically fallen over the period (in Germany nominal import prices have barely changed in 15 years). A closer look at the data reveals that this evolution is driven by the pattern of prices in electronics related sectors (like computers, office machinery and telecommunication equipment) from the newly industrialized countries of the Far East (Taiwan, Hong Kong, Korea). In turn, the observed fall in the relative price of these commodities could be associated with technological progress or with a misclassification of the industry. Such misclassification could arise from specialization in different activities within the industry in Europe and the Far East, to the extent for instance that EU countries have specialized in human capital intensive activities (like research and development), and that countries in the Far East have specialized in the more unskilled labour-intensive activities of mass production. If such a specialization within industry has occurred, the observed fall in the import price of electronics related industry should be more appropriately seen as a fall in unskilled labour-intensive commodities. However, on the basis of available data, it is hard to tell how much weight should be given to this interpretation (the observation that import prices from developed countries in those industries tend to increase faster than the average would, however, be consistent with the hypothesis of intra-industry specialization).

The evidence gathered so far still tends to support the view that the relative price of unskilled labour-intensive commodities has not fallen since 1975. Yet, much caution is required and some of the evidence could be interpreted otherwise. In order to enquire into the issue further, we have analysed whether the evolutions of domestic price, employment and skill intensity are consistent with the view that competition from developing countries had little effect on industry.

2.2.2 Domestic Prices and Specialization

As indicated above, data on domestic production prices at the industry level are not available in the EU industry database (INDE). Some indices are, however, available from the OECD, STAN–ANBERD database, in particular for France. This database uses the UN industry classification (SITC) at the three-digit level, so that the industry clusters defined above could not be used directly and we had to undertake a (somewhat imperfect) transposition. In what follows, the unskilled labour-intensive sectors are the textile (3,210), wearing apparel (3,220), leather product (3,230), footwear (3,240), wood products (3,310), furniture (3,320), ship-building (3,841) and railroad equipment (3,842) sectors. High tech products cover drugs and medicines (3,522), electrical machinery (3,830), aircraft and aeronautics (3,845), and professional goods (3,850).

Figure 2.1 reports the evolution of relative production prices[4] for high tech and unskilled labour-intensive commodities as well as services. The relative production price of high tech commodities falls, but by less than the relative import price observed above. This observation is consistent with the view that the fall in the import price could be due both to technological progress (which is reflected in the domestic production price) and intra-industry specialization across countries. For unskilled labour-intensive commodities, relative domestic production prices tend to fall rather more than import prices. Such discrepancy may suggest that domestic industries have felt the pressure from import competition and have adjusted more than what import prices indicate.

The extent to which adjustment has taken place can be observed in Table 2.5, which describes the changes in industry employment by cluster (from 1975 to

---

[4] The relative price in industry i is computed as the ratio of the price deflator (itself computed as the ratio of nominal to real output) in industry i relative to the price deflator of the economy as a whole.

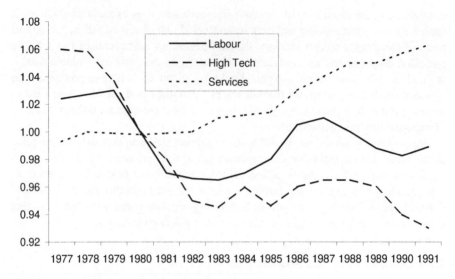

Fig. 2.1.   Relative production prices, France

Table 2.5.   Change in Employment by cluster (rate of change, 1975–90)

Cluster	1	2	3	4	5	Manufacturing
Germany	0.147	0.057	− 0.252	0.004	− 0.052	− 0.014
France	0.025	− 0.190	− 0.397	− 0.215	− 0.277	− 0.231
UK	− 0.106	− 0.413	− 0.442	− 0.368	− 0.377	− 0.383
Italy	− 0.221	− 0.056	− 0.179	− 0.186	− 0.107	− 0.157

1990). It is striking to observe that employment in unskilled labour-intensive industries has shrunk relative to other sectors by a wide margin (except in Italy). By contrast, employment in high tech industries has expanded in relative terms and in the case of France and Germany even in absolute numbers.

This evidence suggests that a significant specialization has taken place, and the extent of this restructuring is somewhat surprising given the changes in relative import prices observed above.

2.2.3 Skill Intensity

The mix of factors further helps detect signs of specialization. In the presence of full employment, if EU countries specialize in skilled labour-intensive

Table 2.6. Change in skill intensity (rate of change 1975–90) (weighted average by cluster)

Cluster	1	2	3	4	5	Manufacturing
Germany	0.145	0.068	0.134	0.053	0.032	0.082
France	0.070	0.066	0.027	0.080	−0.096	0.050

commodities, the ratio of skilled to unskilled labour should fall (see Wood 1995 for instance). The observed increase in the use of skilled labour in almost all industries in the USA is taken as strong evidence, for example by Lawrence and Slaughter (1994), that trade has not had a significant effect on wages and employment. In the USA, the ratio of non production to production workers increased by ten percentage points between 1975 and 1990. For Europe, the evidence is different. Table 2.6 shows that the share of skilled workers in total industrial employment has increased by about 5 per cent in France and 8 per cent in Germany. This is a modest increase relative to that observed in the USA (less than half as large).

Following Sachs and Shatz (1994), indirect evidence on the extent of restructuring in unskilled labour-intensive industries can be obtained by looking at the correlation between the change in skill intensity and the initial level of skill. If specialization is taking place, one can expect a negative correlation: sectors that have a high proportion of unskilled labour should experience a bigger rise in skill intensity as competition from developing countries forces unskilled labour-intensive activities to contract or to become more skill intensive by defensive innovation. In the USA, the correlation is slightly positive. For France and Germany, we find a strong negative correlation, respectively − 0.15 and − 0.29. This result is also apparent in Table 2.6, where we observe that the cluster including unskilled labour-intensive sectors experiences a relatively high increase in skill intensity (at least in Germany).

Overall, this overview of relative prices, employment and skill intensities provides a mixed picture. There is no strong evidence that the relative price of unskilled labour-intensive commodities fell significantly over the period. However, there is evidence of drastic restructuring in unskilled labour-intensive industries, in terms of downsizing and upgrading of skills. In this respect, the evidence for Europe is more favourable to the hypothesis that trade had an effect on industry structures than the evidence reported for the USA.

2.3 Direct Effects of Import Prices on Industrial Employment and Wages

In this section we look directly at the effect of trade on employment and wages. A number of studies (for example, OECD 1994) have already followed this approach, but rely on trade data to measure the pressure from imports. The problem is that trade volumes may fail to capture the effect of a decline of world demand for domestically produced traded goods on the derived demand for factors. If, for example, domestic producers respond to lower world demand by cutting prices, the volume of imports may remain roughly unchanged; observation of volumes will not detect the impact of foreign competition. Looking at prices, rather than at quantities, avoids this difficulty. The channel through which foreign competition makes itself felt must be through import prices, independently of the reaction of domestic producers.

According to the principles of the Heckscher–Ohlin model, a reduction in relative commodity prices is supposed to trigger a fall in employment of the industry concerned and a fall in the wage of unskilled labour throughout the economy, at least if the process of specialization induced by the change in price is significant at the aggregate level. Some deviations from this principle can still be expected if some of the hypotheses underlying the Heckscher–Ohlin model are not valid. Two such deviations seem particularly significant.

First, the Heckscher–Ohlin model assumes perfect mobility of factors of production across domestic industries so that there is an economy-wide level of wage for unskilled workers. We would expect, however, that because of imperfect mobility, wages will to some extent be industry specific. Accordingly, as competition from developing countries increases, a reduction in industry specific wages can be expected even if the industry considered is small relative to the aggregate.

Second, the Heckscher–Ohlin model does not consider strategic behaviour by firms. Once this possibility is introduced, the development of trade with low cost countries can elicit a wide array of reactions.[5] Facing competition from developing countries, firms in developed countries often react by developing niches for more sophisticated products. This may result in higher wages as firms hire more skilled workers. Competition may also trigger some technological developments which enable firms to increase their market shares world-wide. Thus, it is not even clear that unemployment must always decline.

Accordingly, in the presence of such strategic responses, a negative relation between import prices on the one hand and wages and employment on the other can be obtained. If such a negative relation is found, it will indicate that the restructuring taking place at the industry level involves upgrades and technological improvement rather than the traditional Heckscher–Ohlin specialization.

In what follows, we will also consider the effect of competition from developed countries. In principle, we have no prior knowledge regarding the effect of such com-

---

[5] For an analysis along this line, see Oliveira-Martins (1993).

petition on industry wages and employment. The specialization within industries triggered by competition from developed countries could involve either expansion or contraction of the industry, depending on a whole array of parameters including the type of competition taking place in industry (namely whether products are strategic substitutes or strategic complements).

2.3.1 The Model

To investigate these various aspects, we thus consider the joint behaviour of employment and wages, following the approach proposed by Grossman (1987) and also applied to the case of the USA by Revenga (1992). It is simple yet general and fairly robust, derived from a standard demand and supply model. We consider a country with N industries producing traded goods with well behaved production functions (namely, constant return to scale):

$$Y_i(t) = A_i(t) F_i(K_i(t), L_i(t)) = A_i(t) L_i(t) f_i(K_i(t)/L_i(t)) \tag{2.1}$$

where $A_i(t)$ measures exogenous technological progress in industry i. It is straightforward to derive the industry's demand for labour:

$$W_i/P_i = A_i(t) g_i(K_i(t)/L_i(t)), \quad \text{where } g(k) = f(k) - kf'(k) \tag{2.2}$$

The supply of labour can be modelled in a number of ways. From perfect competition subject to a reservation wage corresponding to welfare support (minimum wage, poverty alleviation schemes) to a monopolist trade union, a fairly general formulation is:

$$L_i(t) = G_i(W_i/P, ..W_j/P .., B_i(t)) \quad j=1, N, j \neq i \tag{2.3}$$

where P is the national aggregate price index and $B_i(t)$ is meant to catch a preference for leisure, trade union power, the reservation wage, and so forth.

Finally, good i is assumed to be an imperfect substitute for both other domestically produced goods and imported goods produced by the same industry abroad and selling domestically at the tariff-inclusive price P_i^*:

$$Y_i(t) = D_i(P_i^*/P_i, P/P_i, Y) \tag{2.4}$$

where Y is national income.

This system of $4N$ equations can be solved to yield reduced form equations for each sector:[6]

---

[6] See Grossman (1987) for a discussion of the signs to be expected for the partial derivatives. Our formulation differs slightly from Grossman's (allowing for a labour supply function and ignoring the cost of energy) but the estimating equations are identical.

$$L_i(t) = L_i(A_i(t), B_i(t), P(t), K(t)/L(t), L(t), P_i^*(t), Y(t)) \qquad (2.5)$$

$$W_i(t) = L_i(A_i(t), B_i(t), P(t), K(t)/L(t), L(t), P_i^*(t), Y(t)) \qquad (2.6)$$

These are the two equations estimated below. All the right-hand-side variables are considered exogenous and the terms $A_i(t)$ and $B_i(t)$ will be approximated by a time trend. The import price variable raises a difficulty as it could easily be modelled as endogenous, for example with imperfect competition and intra-industry trade. Revenga (1992) accordingly uses instruments to correct for this eventuality. This is one step that we intend to take in future work. On the other side, in contrast to Grossman (1987) and Revenga (1992), we take into account the fact that residuals in these two equations are likely to be correlated.

2.3.2 Data and Sample

We need to have data at the industry level on employment and wages as well as the prices of imported goods. For information regarding domestic industries, we use the INDE database from EUROSTAT presented above and focus on France, Germany, Italy, and the UK (which have reasonably complete series). Unit value indices of imports are the same as those discussed above. We focus on about 80 industries for which a reliable data set can be gathered (excluding, in particular, those industries for which unit value indices are very volatile, suggesting important changes in commodity composition over time).

The rest of the data are country-wide aggregates and therefore standard. The only difficulty concerns the capital–labour ratio. It is approximated by the ratio of machinery investment to industrial employment (source: OECD *Main Economic Indicators* on diskette). Aggregate output and the overall price level are measured either by the GDP and GDP deflator (source: *International Financial Statistics*, CD-ROM) or by the index of industrial production and the wholesale price index or the producer price and index (sources: *International Financial Statistics*, CD-ROM or OECD *Main Economic Indicators*) depending on availability. The period covered is 1976 to 1987, imposed by data availability.

2.3.3 Estimations With Constrained Import Elasticities

The equations to be estimated are a log-linearized transformation of (2.5) and (2.6):

$$\log L_i(t) = cst + \alpha_{i1}\, t + \beta_{i1}\, \log[K(t)/L(t)] + \gamma_{i1}\, \log L(t) + \lambda_{i1}\, \log P(t) \qquad (2.5')$$
$$+ \mu_{i1}\, \log Y(t) + \varphi_{i1}\, \log P_i^*(t) + \varepsilon_{i1}(t)$$

$$\log W_i(t) = cst + \alpha_{i2}\, t + \beta_{i2}\, \log[K(t)/L(t)] + \gamma_{i2}\, \log L(t) + \lambda_{i2}\, \log P(t) \qquad (2.6')$$
$$+ \mu_{i2}\, \log Y(t) + \varphi_{i2}\, \log P_i^*(t) + \varepsilon_{i2}(t)$$

Given that data are available only for 11 years, we performed pooled cross-section time-series estimations. To take into account the possibility that the innovations to employment and wages $\varepsilon_{i1}(t)$ and $\varepsilon_{i2}(t)$ are correlated, we resorted to the SUR (Zellner's seemingly unrelated regression) method.

A crucial question is how many constraints we impose across industries. Given the limited number of observations per industry, we had to be extremely parsimonious. We have assumed the same elasticity of industry-level employment and wages to all aggregate variables, that is:

$$\alpha_{ik} = \alpha_{jk}, \quad \beta_{ik} = \beta_{jk}, \quad \gamma_{ik} = \gamma_{jk}, \quad \lambda_{ik} = \lambda_{jk}, \quad \mu_{ik} = \mu_{jk}, \text{ for all } i, j \text{ and } k = 1, 2$$

In this section we report the results of regressions performed assuming also that the only industry-specificity is captured by a fixed effect captured by a constant dummy, in other words, we also impose the following restrictions:

$$\varphi_{ik} = \varphi_{jk} = \varphi_k, \quad k = 1, 2$$

Finally, the estimated equation must allow for dynamics. Again, for reason of parsimony we present below results obtained by using as a regressor the dependent variable lagged once. We have experimented with various other lag structures and are reassured that the substance of the results reported below is quite robust to this specification. For the same reason, we conduct our estimation for variables expressed in levels, as Grossman (1987), rather than first-differences as Revenga (1992).[7]

The coefficients of interest are the elasticities of employment and of wages to changes in import prices, φ_1 and φ_2. As noted above, in order to isolate better the effect of competition from developing countries, the import price variable $P_i^*(t)$ is decomposed into two different series: prices of imports from developed countries and prices of imports from developing countries.

The results are not very conclusive, much as is the case in other studies on the USA. A positive sign indicates that import competition pressure (a decline in import prices) pushes employment and wages down. Positive estimates are found most often in the case of import competition from the developed countries area. For imports from developing countries, some of the coefficients are either not significantly different from zero or negative, suggesting either no effect on the labour market or a favourable effect. The exception is Germany which seems to be sensitive in terms of wage. Interestingly, Germany seems also sensitive to import pressures from the industrialized world both in terms of wages and employment. The opposite is true for France whose labour markets appear to benefit from import competition.

---

[7] In addition, like Revenga (and unlike Grossman) we use prices and wages deflated by the GDP implicit price level.

Table 2.7. Effect of import prices on employment and wages (constrained estimates)

	Dependent variable: employment				Dependent variable: wage			
	France	Germany	Italy	UK	France	Germany	Italy	UK
Import prices developed countries	0.007	0.034**	0.005	0.008	−0.006*	0.003*	0.017*	0.001
	(1.01)	(2.72)	(0.36)	(0.98)	(−2.56)	(2.27)	(2.53)	(0.26)
Import prices developing countries	−0.011*	0.008	0.004	−0.011	−0.003*	0.003**	−0.011*	−0.004*
	(2.44)	(1.05)	(0.36)	(−1.47)	(−2.16)	(3.04)	(−2.50)	(−2.00)
Lagged dependent	0.86**	0.71**	0.77**	0.82**	0.0.63**	0.04**	0.21**	0.65**
	(59.87)	(33.68)	(40.97)	(63.66)	(28.42)	(6.50)	(7.25)	(31.25)

See text for sources and detailed explanations; **significant at the 1 per cent confidence level; *significant at the 5 per cent confidence level; 1976–87. Number of observations: France: 1,229; Germany: 1,155; Italy: 142; UK: 1,262.

2.3.4 Industry-Specific Responses

In this section we lift the restriction that the elasticities of employment and wages to import prices are identical across industries, that is we do not impose that $\varphi_{i1} = \varphi_{j1}$ in (5) and that $\varphi_{i2} = \varphi_{j2}$ in (6) for any pair of industries i and j. As we deal with more than 80 sectors we cannot report on all the detailed results in each of the four countries and we present instead a synthesis.[8] Table 2.8 presents the share of industries within each cluster and for the whole sample for which import prices are significant (at the 10 per cent level), by country, by dependent variable (employment and wages) and according to the sign of the coefficient. Focusing first on the results for the whole sample, we find that some 10 to 20 per cent (depending on the country and dependent variable) of the industries are affected by an import price. Importantly, it appears that the number of industries affected by competition from developing countries is similar to the number of industries affected by competition from the developed world. This indicates that, despite the relatively low share of imports from developing countries in total imports, their effect on industry in Europe is, *by this measure*, similar to the effect of competition from developed countries. This evidence confirms that trade flows may indeed be a misleading indicator of competitive pressure and gives an indication that competition from developing countries may be at least as significant as competition from developed countries.

[8] A summary of the results (in which all significant coefficients are reported) is presented in Appendix 2.2.

Table 2.8. Sensitive industries (%, by cluster)

		Employment				Wages			
		Developed		Developing		Developed		Developing	
		+	−	+	−	+	−	+	−
France	1	0	0	10	0	10	0	10	0
	2	11	5	0	11	0	0	0	0
	3	21	7	14	7	0	43	7	7
	4	8	4	4	8	8	21	4	0
	5	15	8	8	8	23	15	8	8
	Average	11	6	7	10	9	17	5	9
Germany	1	29	0	14	0	0	0	0	0
	2	5	10	0	5	0	5	5	0
	3	13	0	0	7	0	13	13	0
	4	0	0	0	3	3	17	17	3
	5	25	8	8	8	8	0	17	0
	Average	11	4	6	5	2	11	13	0
UK	1	0	11	0	0	33	0	0	11
	2	0	17	6	0	0	0	6	6
	3	0	7	14	0	14	0	0	14
	4	7	7	3	3	3	3	3	10
	5	42	0	8	17	8	25	8	8
	Average	7	8	6	4	9	5	4	11
Italy	1	11	0	0	11	22	0	0	22
	2	0	0	6	0	6	0	0	6
	3	0	6	6	0	6	6	0	6
	4	3	7	3	0	10	3	0	3
	5	11	0	0	11	11	0	11	11
	Average	4	5	5	4	11	2	1	10

As indicated above, if we have no prior information regarding the effect of competition from developed countries, we would expect competition from developing countries to reduce employment and wages. Simply counting the number of positive and negative signs associated with both import prices does, however, not reveal any clear pattern; there are 39 pluses and 43 minuses for developing countries, compared with 54 pluses and 48 minuses for developed countries.

As indicated above, the third cluster is *a priori* most sensitive to import competition from developing countries, being intensive in unskilled labour and requiring relatively little capital. Comparing the effect of competition in this cluster with the average is at first glance somewhat disappointing. It is only in France that sectors intensive in unskilled labour appear to be significantly more affected than the average (in particular in terms of employment). The pattern of sign is, however, more encouraging: in France, Italy and the UK, the response of employment is more in line (than the average) with the prior condition that import competition from developing countries should be associated with a contraction of the industry. In the case of Germany, the evidence supports the presumption that competition from developing countries should lead to lower wages.

Another way of assessing whether unskilled labour-intensive sectors are more or less affected than the average is to identify the sectors that are never (in any country) found to be affected. We find that whereas one third of unskilled labour-intensive sectors are never affected by competition from developing countries, as much of 42 per cent of the other sectors are never affected. Such differences give mild support to the view that Heckscher–Ohlin type effects are more significant in unskilled labour-intensive sectors.

Overall, it seems fair to conclude that this evidence fails to uncover an important effect of trade with developing countries along the lines of the Heckscher–Ohlin principles. It seems that if competition from developing countries may be of the same order of magnitude as competition from the developed world (when competition is measured by the number of industries being affected), the adjustments taking place at the industry level are not as simple as those predicted by Heckscher–Ohlin. The pattern of adjustment that we observe is certainly consistent with substantial defensive innovation.

Finally, the differences across the four countries of our sample are worth noticing. It is in Germany that industry is more clearly affected by competitive pressure, with a clear domination of an adverse impact of imports from developing countries on wages and on employment from imports from developed countries. In Italy and the UK, the effect on wages seem to be more frequently favourable for imports from developing countries, and adverse for imports from developed countries. France is in an intermediate position.

It is far from clear why countries that are part of the same free trade area with common protection exhibit such different outcomes. One possibility is that institutions matter, especially on the labour markets. This is a conclusion commonly reached in the labour economics literature, which is illustrated again in the present case. More detailed work is required to elucidate the forces at work here, ranging from trade union behaviour to minimum wage legislation and to state intervention.

2.4 Conclusion

We have tried to evaluate whether competition from developing countries has had an effect on wages in employment in Europe. Testing such a general proposition is bound to be fraught with difficulties, mainly serious identification and simultaneity problems, and conclusions can only be tentative.

We have assembled two pieces of evidence. The first is an overview of relative commodity prices, employment and skill intensities and it provides a mixed picture. There is no strong evidence that the relative price of unskilled labour-intensive commodities fell significantly over the period. However, there is evidence of drastic restructuring in unskilled labour-intensive industries, in terms of downsizing but also in terms of the upgrading of skills. Our second piece of evidence is a simple econometric exercise in which we estimate a reduced form for industry wages and employment. From this second exercise we conclude that competition from developing countries affects an important amount of industries, about as many as competition from the developed world, but that the adjustments taking place at the industry level are not as simple as those predicted by Heckscher–Ohlin.

These two pieces of evidence tend to reinforce one another; both uncover symptoms that can reasonably be traced to competition with developing countries and suggest that the effect of such competition is probably significant and almost certainly not overwhelming. Both also indicate rich patterns of restructuring at the industry level, which involve substantial defensive innovation. Such defensive innovation is reflected in the upgrading of skills, in the increase in production prices relative to import prices and in the positive wage and employment response.

Of course, it may be that the pattern of restructuring we observe has little to do with trade and it may be associated with purely exogenous technological shocks. At this point, it is hard to separate the two hypotheses. We suspect, in line with work on the USA, that both effects have been at work over the sample period. Ascribing responsibility to each of them is clearly an area for further research.

References

Berman, E., Bound, J. and Griliches, Z. (1994), 'Changes in the Demand for Skilled Labor within US Manufacturing: Evidence from the Annual Survey of Manufacturing', *Quarterly Journal of Economics*, 109: 367–97.

Borjas, G. (1995), 'The Internationalization of the US Labour Market and the Wage Structure, *Federal Reserve Bank of New York Economic Policy Review*.

Freeman, Richard B. (1994), 'Doing It Right? The US Labour Market Response to the 1980s/1990s,' unpublished paper, Harvard University, August.

Grossman, G. M. (1987), 'The Employment and Wage Effects of Import Competition in the United States,' *Journal of International Economic Integration*, 2, Spring, 1–23.

Lawrence, R. (1994), 'Trade, Multinationals and Labor', *NBER Working Paper*, No. 4836.

Lawrence, R. Z. and Slaughter, M. J. (1993), 'International Trade and American Wages in the 1980s: Giant Sucking Sound or Small Hiccup?' *Brookings Papers on Economic Activity*, 2: 161–226.

Leamer, E. (1994), 'Testing Trade Theory,' *NBER Working Paper*, No. 3957.

Machin, S. (1994), 'Changes in the Relative Demand for Skills in the UK Labour Market', *CEPR Discussion Paper Series*, 952.

Neven, D. (1994), 'Trade Liberalization with Eastern Nations: How Sensitive?', in R. Faini and R. Portes, *European Union Trade with Eastern Europe: Adjustment and Opportunities*, CEPR, London

Nickell, S. and Bell, B. (1995), 'The Collapse in Demand for the Unskilled and Unemployment across the OECD', *Oxford Review of Economic Policy*, 11(1): 40–62

OECD (1994), *Jobs Study, Evidence and Explanations*, OECD, Paris.

Oliveira-Martins, J. (1993), 'Market Structure, International Trade and Relative Wages', *OECD Working Paper*, 134.

Revenga, A. L. (1992), 'Exporting Jobs?: The Impact of Import Competition on Employment and Wages in US Manufacturing', *Quarterly Journal of Economics*, 107(1): 225–84.

Sachs, J. D. and Shatz, H. J. (1994), 'Trade and Jobs in US Manufacturing', *Brookings Papers on Economic Activity*, 1: 1–69.

Wood, A. (1991), 'The Factor Content of North–South Trade in Manufactures Reconsidered', *Weltwirtschaftliches Archiv*, Band 127:719–43.

—— (1994), *North South Trade, Employment and Inequality: Changing Fortunes in a Skill-Driven World*, Clarendon Press, Oxford.

—— (1995) 'How Trade Hurt Unskilled Workers', *Journal of Economic Perspectives*, 9(3): 57–80

Appendix 2.1 Industry Clusters

1	2500	chemical industry
1	2510	manufacture of basic industrial chemicals
1	2550	manufacture of paint, varnish and printig ink
1	2560	manufacture of other chemical products, mainly for industrial and agricultural purposes
1	2570	manufacture of pharmaceutical products
1	2580	manufacture of soap, synthetic detergents, perfume and toilet preparations
1	2590	manufacture of other chemical products, chiefly for household and office use
1	2601	chemical and man-made fibres
1	3300	manufacture of office machinery and data processing machinery
1	3440	manufacture of telecommunications equipment, electrical and electronic measuring and recording equipment and electro-medical equipment
1	3450	manufacture of radio and television receiving sets, sound reproducing and recording equipment and of electronic equipment and apparatus, manufacture of gramophone records and pre-recorded magnetic tapes
1	3640	aerospace equipment manufacturing and repairing
2	2430	manufacture of concrete, cement of plaster products for constructional purposes
2	2460	production of gridstones and other abrasive products
2	3200	mechanical engineering
2	3220	manufacture of machine-tools for working metal, and of other tools and equipment for use with machines
2	3230	manufacture of textile machinery and accessories; manufacture of sewing machines
2	3240	manufacture of machinery for the food, chemical and related industries
2	3250	manufacture of plant for mines, the iron and steel industry and foundries, civil engineering and the building trade; manufacture of mechanic handling equipment
2	3270	manufacture of other machinery and equipment for use in specific branches of industry
2	3280	manufacture of other machinery and equipment
2	3400	electrical engineering
2	3420	manufacture of electrical machinery
2	3460	manufacture of domestic type electrical appliances
2	3480	assembly and installation of electrical equipment
2	3600	manufacture of other means of transport
2	3700	instrument engineering
2	3710	manufacture of measuring, checking and precision instruments and apparatus
2	3720	manufacture of medical and surgical equipment and orthopaedic appliances
2	3730	manufacture of optical instruments and photographic equipment
2	4110	manufacture of vegetable and animals oils and fats
2	4150	processing and preserving of fish and other sea foods fit for human consumption
2	4170	manufacture of spaghetti, macaroni etc.
2	4190	manufacture of bread and flour confectionery
2	4290	manufacture of tobacco products
2	4380	manufacture of carpets, linoleum and other floor coverings, including leathercloth and similar supported synthetic sheeting
2	4930	photographic and cinematographic labouratories
3	2220	manufacture of steel tubes
3	2480	manufacture of ceramic goods
3	3110	foundries

3	3140	manufacture of structural metal products
3	3150	boilermaking, manufacture of reservoirs, tanks and other sheet-metal containers
3	3210	manufacture of agricultural machinery and tractors
3	3520	manufacture of bodies for motor vehicles and of motor-drawn trailers and caravan
3	3610	shipbuilding
3	3620	manufacture of standard and narrow-gauge railway and tramway rolling stock
3	3740	manufacture of clocks and watches and parts thereof
3	4350	jute industry
3	4360	knitting industry
3	4400	leather and leather goods industry
3	4420	manufacture of products from leather and leather substitutes
3	4500	footwear and clothing industry
3	4510	manufacture of mass-produced industry
3	4530	manufacture of ready-made clothing and accessories
3	4560	manufacture of furs and of fur goods
3	4630	manufacture of carpentry and of joinery components and of parquet flooring
3	4670	manufacture of wooden furniture
3	4920	manufacture of musical instruments
3	5000	building and civil engineering
3	5010	construction of flats, office blocks, hospitals and other buildings, both residential and non-residential
3	5020	civil engineering, construction of road, bridges, railway...
3	5030	installation
3	5040	building completion work
3	5100	building and civil engineering without specialization
4	2200	production and preliminary processing of metals
4	2210	iron and steel industry excluding integrated coke ovens
4	2230	drawing, cold rolling and cold folding of steel
4	2240	production and preliminary processing of non-ferrous metals
4	2400	manufacture of non-metallic mineral products
4	2410	manufacture of clay products for constructional purposes
4	2440	manufacture of articles of asbestos
4	2450	working of stone and of non-metallic mineral products
4	2470	manufacture of glass and glassware
4	3100	manufacture of metal articles (except for mechanical, electrical and instrument engineering and vehicles)
4	3120	forging, clossed-died forging, pressing and stamping
4	3130	secondary transformation, treatment and coating of metals
4	3160	manufacture of tools and finished metal goods, except electrical equipment
4	3190	other mechanical workshops not elsewhere specified
4	3260	manufacture of transmission equipment for motive power
4	3470	manufacture of electric lamps and other electric lightning equipment
4	3500	manufacture of motor vehicles and of motor vehicles parts and accessories
4	3510	manufacture and assembly of motor vehicles and of motor vehicle engines
4	3530	manufacture of parts and accessories for motor vehicles
4	3630	manufacture of cycles and motor-cycles and parts and accessories thereof
4	3650	manufacture of transport equipment not elsewhere specified
4	4120	slaughtering, preparing and preserving of meat
4	4210	manufacture of cocoa, chocolate and sugar confection
4	4300	textile industry
4	4320	cotton industry
4	4330	silk industry

4	4370	textile finishing
4	4390	miscellaneous textile industries
4	4410	tanning and dressing of leather
4	4550	manufacture of household textiles other make-up textile goods
4	4600	timber and wooden furniture industries
4	4610	sawing and processing of wood
4	4620	manufacture of semi-finished wood products
4	4640	manufacture of wooden containers
4	4650	other wood manufacture
4	4660	manufacture of articles of cork and articles of straw and other plainting materials, manufacture of brushes and brooms
4	4720	processing of paper and boars
4	4730	printing and allied industries
4	4800	processing of rubber and plastics
4	4810	manufacture of rubber products
4	4830	processing of plastics
4	4900	other manufacturing industries
4	4910	manufacture of articles of jewellry and goldsmiths' and silversmiths' wares
4	4940	manufacture of toys and sports goods
4	4950	miscellaneous manufacturing industries
5	2300	extraction of minerals other than metalliferous and energy-producing minerals; peat extraction
5	2420	manufacture of cement, lime and plaster
5	4100	food, drink and tobacco industry
5	4130	manufacture of dairy products
5	4140	processing and preserving of fruits and vegetables
5	4160	grain milling
5	4180	manufacture of starch and starch products
5	4200	sugar manufacturing and refining
5	4220	manufacture of animals and poultry food
5	4230	manufacture of other food products
5	4240	distilling of ethyl alcohol from fermented materials; spirit distilling and compounding
5	4250	manufacture of wine of fresh grapes and of beverages based thereon
5	4270	brewing and malting
5	4280	manufacture of soft drinks, including the bottling of natural spa water
5	4700	manufacture of paper and paper products; printing and publishing
5	4710	manufacture of pulp, paper and board

Appendix 2.2 Significant Industry Responses

France

Nace Code	Industry	Employment		Wages	
		Developed	Developing	Developed	Developing
221	Steel	+		+	
222	Steel tubes			−	
223	Steel rolling			−	
224	First transformation of metals			+	−
231	Extraction for construction	−		+	
232	Potassium and phosphorous	+	−	+	−
242	Cement			−	
243	Construction equipment		+		−
244	Asbestos	+	−		
245	Stone works		−		−
256	Chemicals for agriculture		+		+
260	Synthetic fibres				
311	Iron works			−	+
312	Casting			−	
314	Metallic construction		+	−	
315	Boilers and reservoirs	+		−	
352	Automotive bodies	+		−	
361	Ship building	−	+	−	
363	Cycles and motorcycles	−	+		
371	Measure/control equipment	+	−		
411	Fats (animal and vegetal)	−			
414	Fruit and vegetable canning			+	−
417	Pastas				
418		+	−	−	+
420	Sugar			−	
425	Wine			+	
427	Beer			+	
438	Carpets and rugs	+	−		
439	Other textiles			−	
456	Leather and furs	+	−		−
482	Tyres		−	−	−
495	Other manufacturing			−	+
Total:		9 +; 5 −	6 +; 8 −	8 +; 14 −	4 +; 7 −

Germany

Nace		Employment		Wages	
Code	Industry	Developed	Developing	Developed	Developing
221	Steel	+	−		
222	Steel tubes		+		
243	Construction equipment		+		
258	Detergents				
259	Other chemicals for home use		+		
344	Telecom/measur. equipment	+			
361	Ship building	+			
363	Cycles and motorcycles			−	+
422	Food for animals		+		
365	Other transport equipment		−	−	+
371	Measure/control equipment			−	+
372	Medical equipment	−	+		
411	Fats (animal and vegetal)	+			
415	Fish canning			−	+
416	Seeds		+		
417	Pastas	−			
418	Starch	+	−		
422	Food for animals			+	+
425	Wine	−			
427	Beer	+			
439	Other textiles			−	+
453	Clothing			−	+
456	Leather and furs	+	−		
462	Wood unfinished products			+	−
467	Wooden furniture			−	+
471	Paper and pulp	+			+
481	Rubber			−	+
495	Other manufacturing			−	+
Total:		9 +; 3 −	5 +; 4 −	2 +; 9 −	11 +; 1 −

Italy

Nace Code	Industry	Employment Developed	Employment Developing	Wages Developed	Wages Developing
212	Mineral extraction	+	−		
242	Cement			+	
243	Construction equipment			+	−
245	Stone works			+	−
326	Transmissions			+	−
330	Office equipment	+	−	+	−
344	Telecom/measur. equipment			+	−
351	Automobiles			+	−
361	Ship building			+	−
412	Livestock		+		
420	Sugar	+	−		+
421	Confectionary	−	+		
424	Alcohol beverages			+	−
453	Clothing			−	
455	Other textiles			−	
456	Leather and furs	−	+		
482	Tyres	−			
494	Toys and sport equipment	−	+		
Total:		3 +; 4 −	4 +; 3 −	9 +; 2 −	1 +; 8 −

United Kingdom

Nace		Employment		Wages	
Code	Industry	Developed	Developing	Developed	Developing
222	Steel tubes			−	
241	Materials for construction			−	
242	Cement	+		−	
244	Asbestos	−			
245	Stone works	−			
246	abrasives	−			
255	Paints and inks			+	
256	Chemicals for Agriculture				−
257	Pharmaceuticals			+	
260	Synthetic fibres	−		+	
314	Metallic construction			+	
315	Boilers and reservoirs		+		
323	Equip. for textile industry	−			
361	Ship building			+	
363	Cycles and motorcycles				−
365	Aircraft	+	−		
412	Livestock	+			
413	Milk	+	−		
414	Fruit and vegetable canning	+		+	
415	Fish canning	−	+		+
419	Bakery				−
423	Various food	+	+		
425	Wine				
426	Hosiery				−
427	Beer			−	+
463	Wooden framing and floors	−	+		
464	Wood packaging	+			
465	Other wooden products				+
471	Paper and pulp				−
Total:		6 +; 7 −	5 +; 3 −	7 +; 4 −	3 +; 9 −

3. Labour Market Effects of Trade with LDCs in Europe

MATHIAS DEWATRIPONT, ANDRÉ SAPIR AND
KHALID SEKKAT

3.1 Introduction

Trade with LDCs is a controversial issue. In the USA it is often blamed for widening wage dispersion. In Europe, it is instead often blamed for job losses and resulting unemployment.

What is the empirical evidence? The problem has been mostly studied in the US, both by labour economists and by trade economists. Estimates (detailed in section 3.2) vary from no effect to a significant effect on wages and employment, which is, however, small relative to the magnitude of the wage dispersion problem, for which technology is typically blamed. In Europe, the few studies that have been performed (stressed in section 3.3) point to similar conclusions.

In section 3.4 of this chapter, we provide an additional look at this issue. After a brief description of aggregate data, we try to assess the consequences of LDC trade on long-term unemployment, wage dispersion and the skill content of employment of northern European countries. We first rely on individual data on long-term unemployment that identify the sector of activity where the person lost his or her job. We aggregate these data by sector to end up with sectoral 'long-term unemployment rates'. We try and explain these rates by individual characteristics (education, sex), technology (industry dummies) and trade variables. Imports from LDCs are shown to increase our unemployment rates *only* when industry dummies are omitted, which we interpret as evidence that it is technology that matters, and not trade *per se*. To our knowledge, ours is the first study that tries to investigate whether trade with LDCs can be a source of long-term hardship on the labour market.

We then turn to unskilled-to-skilled wage and employment ratios by sector, again with trade indicators and industry dummies as explanatory variables. Somewhat surprisingly for supposedly rigid European labour markets, we find more evidence of an association between LDC trade and wage dispersion, than with respect to the skill content of employment. Moreover, the main effect we find concerns exports and not imports, and it suggests that sectors that export more to

With the assistance of Giovanni Guazzarotti and Andrea Lamorgese.

LDCs (in percentage terms) tend to offer better opportunities to unskilled workers. Concluding remarks are presented in section 3.5.

3.2 The Literature

This section provides a very brief overview of the methods of analysis and of recent findings obtained in the area. A first set of studies concentrates on the *factor content of trade*, in order to end up with a total net number of job creations (or destructions) due to exports and imports. Particularly spectacular is the study by Wood (1994), that comes up with a very significant level of net destructions: 5 per cent of total employment in the North just from manufacturing sectors. Key to this argument, however, is the idea that imports from the South are 'noncompeting goods' that have roughly disappeared in the North. Consequently, Wood argues that the labour–output ratio to use in order to compute employment destructions is that of Southern countries, which is much higher than that of Northern countries. This assumption is crucial for Wood's result, and has been the subject of debate.

Another study in this vein is by Sachs and Shatz (1994), who compute the job losses due to increasing import shares between 1978 and 1990. They argue that rising import penetration has resulted in job losses totalling 7 per cent among US manufacturing production workers and 2 per cent among US manufacturing non-production workers. However, this computation ignores the flip-side of inter-nationalization, that is, US export growth.

A second set of studies econometrically test the impact of imports on employ-ment and wages. The most careful one has been performed by Revenga (1992), both in terms of (instrumental-variable) estimation and in terms of data. One should indeed keep in mind that data problems can be very severe for export and import prices. Revenga finds significant import competition effects. In particular, she concludes that the severe US dollar appreciation between 1980 and 1985 has had a negative impact on wages and employment of trade-impacted industries, of 2 per cent and 4.5–7.5 per cent respectively. This relatively small impact on wages indicates a relative ease of relocation for workers in these industries. Moreover, while significant, this impact suggests that trade only modestly contributes to the wage dispersion problem in the USA.

Despite the limited magnitude of trade flows in the USA, trade economists have investigated, in a number of studies, the general equilibrium consequences of trade with developing countries. In a two sector Heckscher–Ohlin–Samuelson world with two factors of production (skilled and unskilled workers), opening trade with another country that is relatively richer in unskilled labour will lead to: (1) a rise in the skill premium in the skill-rich country; (2) a rise in the relative price of the skill-intensive good in the skill-rich country; (3) a fall in the skill-intensity of labour in each industry in the skill-rich country. While (1) has been widely noticed in the USA, the study by Lawrence and Slaughter (1993) fails to find evidence of (2). Instead, Sachs and Shatz (1994) do find some evidence of (2), but of admittedly small magnitude. Finally, (3) has *not* been observed, since skill-intensity is on the rise for all US industries, due to technological change. Lawrence and Slaughter conclude that this change is the chief cause of increasing wage inequality, after finding a strong correlation between total factor productivity growth and the intensity of use of non-production labour at the industry level.

This evidence of limited relative price effects is corroborated by Krugman's (1995) computable general equilibrium illustration. Although admittedly very simplified, his set of assumptions point to the ability of a 1–2 per cent change in terms of trade to accommodate a move from autarky to the existing level of trade for the USA. As Krugman stresses, this is well within measurement error for trade prices.

3.3 The Case of Europe

Most econometric studies concern the USA. One exception is the study by Neven and Wyplosz (1994). This study replicates in particular the approach taken by Revenga. Neven and Wyplosz's results are somewhat mixed: they find no significant aggregate effects; at the industry level, some evolutions are significant, but not all of them are consistent with a trade-only interpretation. As in a number of other studies, the authors point to the difficulty of disentangling trade and technology, but also to the limited impact of trade on labour market outcomes.

Krugman (1995) is the first to try and address European features in a general equilibrium analysis of this problem. Specifically, he runs his computable general equilibrium example under the assumption of rigid wages (for both skilled and unskilled workers) and thus rigid terms of trade. He comes up with a 1.4 per cent fall in unskilled employment when the economy moves from autarky to current trade flows. Once again, while non-trivial, the effect is small compared with the huge rise in unemployment in Europe, which is somehow the counterpart of the wage dispersion problem in the USA.

3.4 The Empirical Analysis

The purpose of this section is to test for potential effects of foreign trade on the European labour market. The objective is to investigate whether competition between European and non-European producers on the product markets spill over to the European labour market, hence increasing unemployment, reducing wages and so forth. The analysis will, therefore, concern the impact of foreign trade on both employed and unemployed persons. It is based on labour market survey data and foreign trade data collected and made available by EUROSTAT, the statistical institute of the European Union.

We rely on two survey data bases: the labour force survey and the labour cost survey. The first one gives information collected through annual surveys at the individual household level from 1983 to 1991. The surveys are national and divide population into three groups: unemployed (without work but currently seeking work), employed (self employed or in paid employment) and out of the labour force. For each group, information is available with respect to various characteristics, such as sex, level of education, and present and past economic activity. The second survey data bank gives information from a four-year survey at individual firm level (all employees in establishments of more than ten employees) concerning industry, commerce, banking and insurance. Available data concern years 1966 to 1988 and are broken down by country. In addition to the sectoral breakdown, a distinction is made between manual and non-manual workers.

Data for foreign trade are drawn from two data bases: VISA and VOLIMEX. In the first one, data are provided on 28 variables (like output, turnover, productivity), drawn from national surveys at the level of industrial firms. The sample covers the period 1980 to 1990. The second one, VOLIMEX, gives bilateral and sectoral foreign trade data. For both imports and exports, unit value indices, volume indices and values are provided from 1979 to 1988. Well-known reliability problems for unit values, together with the fact that wage rigidity can prevent terms of trade changes as argued by Krugman, have led us to focus on trade flows instead of unit values.

3.4.1 Descriptive Statistics

The next set of figures present the evolution of trade flows with LDCs for our European countries, as well as labour market evolutions. A couple of facts emerge: (1) an increase in European imports from LDCs relative to apparent consumption, but still of a very limited magnitude; (2) no upward trend in European exports towards LDCs as a percentage of European GDP. This is due in large part to the erosion of the oil price in real (and even nominal) terms; (3) the long-term unemployment rate follows the business cycle, and peaked just before the counter-oil shock of 1986; (4) as in the USA, the skill content of employment is on a steady rise; (5) in contrast with the USA, the skill premium is clearly *not* on the rise.

3.4.2 Foreign Trade and Unemployment

The focus, here, is on the long-term unemployed. The analysis is conducted on relatively disaggregated data. Using the labour force survey data we are able to compute for a given year and a given country the ratio of long-term unemployment to total employment by sex, level of education and sector of activity in which the person last worked. This will constitute the dependent variable. Indicators of the intensity of trade with LDCs by sector of activity are computed for given years and countries by combining information from VOLIMEX (bilateral trade variables) and VISA (output variables). These will constitute a part of the explanatory variables. The remaining explanatory variables consist of sets of dummy variables for sectors of activity, sex, education levels, countries and years. Given that reliable and homogeneous data are available only for at most four years and four countries, estimation is performed on pooled cross-section time-series data.

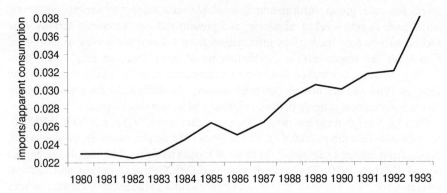

Fig. 3.1   Import penetration rate from LDCs

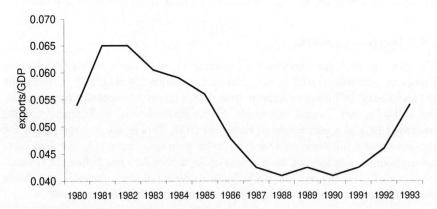

Fig. 3.2   Export toward LDCs over GDP

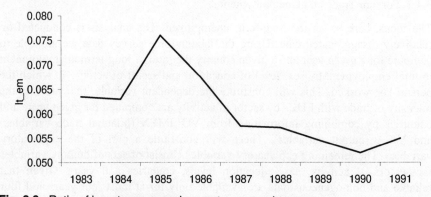

Fig. 3.3   Ratio of long-term unemployment over employment

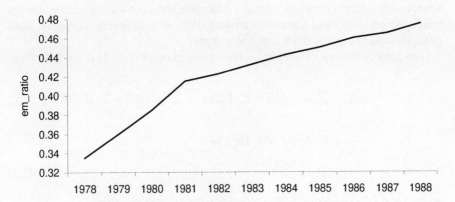

Fig. 3.4   Skilled over unskilled employment ratio

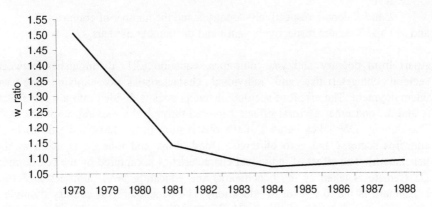

Fig. 3.5   Skilled over unskilled wage ratio

The most important features of the data are the following. The long-term unemployment variable, U, is defined as the number of unemployed persons who, at the time of the survey, had lost their (last) job in a given sector more than one year ago. The employment variable, E, is the number of persons who, at the time of the survey, were in paid employment in that sector. Two trade variables were considered for each sector: penetration of LDC imports, M, defined as the country's import from LDCs over its apparent consumption, and export to LDCs, X, defined as the ratio between the country's export to LDCs and output.

The sample covers 16 industrial sectors (two digit NACE classification; see Appendix 3.1), three education levels (low, medium and high), four years (1988, 1989, 1990, 1991) and four countries (Germany, France, The Netherlands and the Belgium-Luxemburg Economic Union, BLEU). As far as education levels are concerned, the following classification was adopted. Low education concerns no formal or first level education. Medium education concerns second level education leading to university and vocational training. High level concerns university, post-graduate studies and any other equivalent degree.

Disregarding indices for simplicity, the estimated equation (3.1) is the following:

$$\frac{U}{E} = \beta_0 + \beta_1^1 M + \beta_1^2 X + \sum_{i=1}^{I-1} \beta_2^i DN^i + \sum_{k=1}^{K-1} \beta_3^k DC^k + \sum_{t=1}^{T-1} \beta_4^t DY^t$$

$$+ \sum_{j=1}^{J-1} \beta_5^j DE^j + \beta_6 DE + m$$

$$(3.1)$$

where i and I denote respectively sector i and the number of sectors

  j and J denote respectively education level j and the number of educational levels

  k and K denote respectively country k and the number of countries

and t and T denote respectively year t and the number of years.

Apart from country and year dummies, equation (3.1) distinguishes between sectoral characteristics and individual characteristics to explain long-term unemployment. The effect of sectoral characteristics is divided into a trade effect, X and M, and other sectoral effects captured through the sectoral dummies DN^i. The dummy DN^i takes value 1 if the observation in the left hand side of (3.1) concerns sector i and zero otherwise (food, drink and tobacco is taken as the benchmark). The effect of individual characteristics is captured by the sex dummy DS (female is taken as the benchmark) and education level dummies DE^j (the benchmark is the low level of education). The benchmark for country dummies, DC^k, and year dummies, DY^t, are BLEU and 1988 respectively. The definition of all the dummies is analogous to the definition of DN^i. The method of estimation is OLS.

As far as the sign of the coefficients is concerned we anticipate the following: $\beta_5^j < 0$, since a higher educational endownment should reduce the risk of long-term unemployment; $\beta_6 < 0$ if women have a harder time on the labour market than men; and $\beta_1^1 > 0$ if LDC imports create hardship for workers who lose jobs and have a hard time relocating into other activities. Finally, β_1^2 could be negative if being oriented towards fast growing economies like East Asia reduces the risk of long-term unemployment.

Estimation results are reported in Table 3.1. To save on space, estimated coefficients of dummies for sectors, years and countries are omitted in the main text and presented in the appendix. Except for trade variables, the coefficients are to be interpreted as deviations from the benchmark case.

Table 3.1 reports the results for two specifications. Both specifications include year, country, sex and education dummies. The sectoral dummies are included in the second specification only. The overall quality of fit is good for both specifications. The F-statistics are always highly significant.

Table 3.1. Long-term unemployment

	Specification 1	Specification 2
Intercept	0.11*	0.13*
	(11.14)	(10.42)
M	0.14*	−0.19
	(2.82)	(−1.25)
X	−0.12	−0.23
	(−1.18)	(−1.06)
Male	−0.02*	−0.02*
	(−3.90)	(−5.24)
Medium education level	−0.05*	−0.05*
	(−8.36)	(−9.58)
High education level	−0.05*	−0.05*
	(−7.27)	(−7.86)
Sectoral dummies included	No	Yes
Number of observations	411	411
Adjusted R^2	0.22	0.35
Significance of the whole regression	0.0001	0.0001

Notes: Figures in brackets are *t*-statistics; specifications 1 and 2 are the same except for sectoral dummies: included in specification 2 but not in 1. All specifications include year dummies and country dummies. * indicates that the coefficient is significant at the 5 per cent level. The significance of the whole regression gives the probability level of the calculated *F*-statistic, i.e. the probability that all the coefficients in the regression are equal to zero.

The estimated coefficients of individual characteristic variables (sex and education levels) are always negative and highly significant. The values of these coefficients are also stable across specifications: the coefficient of the sex dummy is equal to − 0.02 and those of education level dummies are both equal to − 0.05. The sign of the coefficients are in accordance with our anticipations: males are less subject to long-term unemployment than females and medium and highly educated workers are also less subject to long-term unemployment than workers with less education. Note also that the impact of education on long-term unemployment does not differ between medium and high levels: the two groups of workers are equally subject to long-term unemployment. This may be due to the fact that medium education level also includes vocational training, which may compensate for the lack of high education. To sum up, workers' individual characteristics seem to be major determinants of long-term unemployment.

The coefficients of the sectoral characteristic variables are divided into two groups: trade coefficients and sectoral dummies coefficients. The sectoral dummies coefficients (reported in the appendix) exhibit reasonable behaviour: there is much more long-term unemployment in extraction and processing of metals industries, for instance, than in food, drink and tobacco industry. The significance of the trade variable coefficients depends on which specification is considered. In specification 2 neither the import coefficient nor the export coefficient are significant. In specification 1 the import coefficient is significant and positive but the export coefficient is not significant.

We take the lessons of these results to be as follows. In specification 1, we have evidence that sectors with higher LDC import penetration are also, *ceteris paribus*, sectors with more separations that lead to long-term unemployment. This can thus be consistent with the idea that LDC imports create real 'hardship' on the European labour market. Of course, this hardship may be there only because of an inadequate set of labour market institutions, so that policy conclusions are not obvious.

Another issue is whether it is really import penetration that is associated with long-term unemployment, or simply technology. Specification 2 sheds some light on this issue, by adding sectoral dummies. Interestingly enough, import penetration ceases to be significant. This means that, for any given industry, we fail to observe a positive correlation (across years and countries) between import penetration and the long-term unemployment rate. We interpret this evidence as saying that it is really technology and *not* LDC imports that seem to be a source of long-term unemployment.

Tables 3.2 and 3.3 provide robustness checks concerning the results of Table 3.1.[1] Specifically, Table 3.2 replicates the regressions of Table 3.1 after having excluded energy producing sectors from the sample. Indeed, these sectors have very different employment contents than manufacturing sectors and could bias our results. However, Table 3.2 shows that results are unaffected by the presence or absence of energy producing sectors. In a similar vein, Table 3.3 adds to the sectors of Table 3.2 non manufacturing sectors (setting their trade flows to zero). Here, not only does trade have no significant impact on unemployment once sectoral dummies are included, moreover their addition preserves its insignificance.

Note, finally, that Table 3.1 only concerns 'Northern' Europe, namely those countries where the debate on trade with LDCs and employment is the most active. Table 3.4 replicates the regressions of Table 3.1 for 'Southern' Europe and finds very similar results. We take these results as further evidence that it is really technology that matters and not trade, since the first can be thought to affect all European countries in a more similar way than the second.

---

[1] We also performed the regression of Table 3.1 while introducing the dependent variable and the trade variables in percentage changes instead of levels. This did not change our qualitative results.

Table 3.2. Long-term unemployment (without energy producing sectors)

	Specification 1	Specification 2
Intercept	0.11* (11.35)	0.13* (10.55)
M	0.10* (2.12)	−0.18 (−1.21)
X	−0.05 (−0.47)	−0.24 (−1.13)
Male	−0.02* (−4.22)	−0.03* (−5.27)
Medium education level	−0.05* (−8.66)	−0.05* (−9.61)
High education level	−0.06* (−7.85)	−0.06* (−8.36)
Sectoral dummies included	No	Yes
Number of observations	402	402
Adjusted R-squared	0.24	0.36
Significance of the whole regression	0.0001	0.0001

Notes: Figures in brackets are *t*-statistics. Specifications 1 and 2 are the same except for sectoral dummies: included in specification 2 but not in 1. All specifications include year dummies and country dummies. * indicates that the coefficient is significant at the 5 per cent level. The significance of the whole regression gives the probability level of the calculated *F*-statistic, namely the probability that all the coefficients in the regression are equal to zero.

3.4.3. Foreign Trade, Employment and Wages

We now turn to the impact of foreign trade on the conditions of employment. The discussion in the previous sections implies that such an impact may operate through either employment or wages. It was also argued that this impact is probably different for skilled and unskilled workers. We therefore investigate the effect of foreign trade on the ratio between the numbers of unskilled and skilled workers (E_u and E_S respectively) as well as on the ratio between wages of unskilled and skilled workers (W_u and W_S respectively). To compute these ratios we use the Labour Cost Survey data bank.

From the Labour Cost Survey data we compute for a given year and a given country the ratios of wages, W_u/W_S and of employment, E_u/E_S, by sector of activity. Wages are defined as direct pay for days worked and not worked (holidays) before deduction of taxes and social security charges (employee and employer contributions). They include other bonuses paid by the employer. The distinction between skilled and unskilled workers turns out to be about manual and non-manual workers as reported by the firms in the survey.

Explanatory variables consist of the same set of trade variables (drawn from the VOLIMEX and VISA data bases) as before, and sets of dummy variables for countries, years and sectors.

Combining information from the three data bases and focusing on reliable and homogeneous data, leave us with a sample coverage of 14 industrial sectors (two digit NACE classification; see Appendix 3.2), three years (1981, 1984, 1988) and four countries (Germany, the United Kingdom, Denmark and BLEU). For the same

Table 3.3. Long-term unemployment (without energy producing sectors, with non-manufacturing sectors)

	Specification 1	Specification 2
Intercept	0.09* (20.74)	0.11* (12.84)
M	0.07 (1.50)	−0.24 (−1.82)
X	0.13 (1.79)	0.14 (0.84)
Male	−0.02* (−6.77)	−0.02* (−9.13)
Medium education level	−0.05* (−15.77)	−0.05* (−17.43)
High education level	−0.06* (−16.29)	−0.05* (−15.63)
Sectoral dummies included	No	Yes
Number of observations	1361	1361
Adjusted R-squared	0.24	0.36
Significance of the whole regression	0.0001	0.0001

Notes: All non-manufacturing sectors included assuming zero trade flows. Countries in the regression: Germany, France, The Netherlands, BLEU. Reference: 1988, BLEU, DN41–42, female, low education. Figures in brackets are *t*-statistics. Specifications 1 and 2 are the same except for sectoral dummies: included in specification 2 but not in 1. All specifications include year dummies and country dummies. *Indicates that the coefficient is significant at the 5 per cent level. The significance of the whole regression gives the probability level of the calculated *F*-statistic, namely the probability that all the coefficients in the regression are equal to zero.

reason as before, estimation is performed on pooled cross-section time-series data. To take into account the potential link between wages and employment ratios, simultaneous equation estimation is performed.

The equations to be estimated are:

$$\frac{Eu}{Es} = \alpha_0 + \alpha_1^1 M + \alpha_1^2 X + \sum_{i=1}^{I-1} \alpha_2^i DN^i + \sum_{k=1}^{K-1} \alpha_3^k DC^k + \sum_{t=1}^{T-1} \alpha_4^t DY^t$$

$$+ \alpha_5 VX + \alpha_6 \frac{W_u}{W_s} + \varepsilon_E$$

$$(3.2)$$

$$\frac{Wu}{Ws} = \gamma_0 + \gamma_1^1 M + \gamma_1^2 X + \sum_{i=1}^{I-1} \gamma_2^i DN^i + \sum_{k=1}^{K-1} \gamma_3^k DC^k + \sum_{t=1}^{T-1} \gamma_4^t DY^t$$

$$+ \gamma_5 VY + \gamma_6 \frac{E_u}{E_s} + \varepsilon_W$$

$$(3.3)$$

where the definition of indices is the same as for equation (3.1) and the construction of dummies follows the same principles as before. The additional terms with VX and VY stand for other exogenous variables. Note, however, that the benchmark case is defined here with respect to BLEU 1981 and mechanical engineering.

Table 3.4. Long-term unemployment (Mediterranean countries, without energy producing sectors)

	Specification 1	Specification 2
Intercept	0.09* (10.19)	0.13* (12.37)
M	0.39* (2.76)	0.26 (1.01)
X	−0.01 (−0.09)	−0.01 (−0.11)
Male	−0.05* (−10.76)	−0.06* (−11.72)
Medium education level	−0.03* (−5.43)	−0.03* (−5.86)
High education level	−0.03* (−3.17)	−0.03* (−3.40)
Sectoral dummies included	No	Yes
Number of observations	357	357
Adjusted *R*-squared	0.34	0.44
Significance of the whole regression	0.0001	0.0001

Notes: Countries in the regression: Greece, Portugal and Spain. (Italy has data at one-digit level in the Labour Force Survey.) Reference: 1988, Greece, DN41–42, female, low education. Figures in brackets are *t*-statistics. Specifications 1 and 2 are the same except for sectoral dummies: included in specification 2 but not in 1. All specifications include year dummies and country dummies. *Indicates that the coefficient is significant at the 5 per cent level. The significance of the whole regression gives the probability level of the calculated *F*-statistic, namely the probability that all the coefficients in the regression are equal to zero.

Estimation results are reported in Tables 3.5a and 3.5b. Each table gives the results of two different specifications. Both specifications include country and year dummies. To insure that the system is identifiable, sales and labour productivity are introduced as explanatory variables in the equation of employment and wage ratios respectively. For the same reason as before we report only trade coefficients.

The two specifications are defined as in Table 3.1. The overall quality of fit of both specifications is good for both equations (employment and wages). The *F*-statistics are always above the 5 per cent critical level. Moreover the sectoral dummies seem to play an important role in explaining both employment and wage ratios. Their introduction into the equations significantly improves the quality of fit as shown by the adjusted R^2 which increases from 0.39 to 0.90 in the employment ratio equation and from 0.48 to 0.85 in the wage ratio equation.

Table 3.5a. Ratio of unskilled to skilled employment

Two stages least squares estimation	Specification 1	Specification 2
Intercept	11.40** (1.97)	1.99 (0.94)
M	0.28 (0.21)	−0.19 (−0.33)
X	0.06 (0.10)	0.62** (1.92)
Sectoral dummies included	No	Yes
Number of observations	96	96
Adjusted R^2	0.39	0.90
Significance of the whole regression	0.0001	0.0001

Table 3.5b. Ratio of unskilled to skilled wages

Two stages least squares estimation	Specification 1	Specification 2
Intercept	0.51* (3.79)	1.17* (4.81)
M	−0.16* (−2.04)	−0.08** (−1.97)
X	0.04 (1.05)	0.13* (2.44)
Sectoral dummies included	No	Yes
Number of observations	96	96
Adjusted R^2	0.48	0.85
Significance of the whole regression	0.0001	0.0001

Notes for Tables 3.5a and 3.5b: Figures in brackets are *t*-statistics. Specification 1 and 2 are the same except for sectoral dummies: included in specification 2 but not in 1. All specifications include year dummies and country dummies. * (**) indicates that the coefficients is significant at the 5 per cent (10 per cent) level. The significance of the whole regression gives the probability level of the calculated *F*-statistic, namely the probability that all the coefficients in the regression are equal to zero.

The estimated coefficients of sectoral dummies (not reported) exhibit a reasonable behaviour. In the employment ratio equation they are either positive and significant or non-significant. A positive and significant coefficient of a sectoral dummy, implies that the corresponding sector uses relatively more unskilled workers than the benchmark sector. Given that the benchmark sector is mechanical engineering, the result is not surprising. In the wage ratio equation the coefficients are in general either negative and significant or non significant. The intuition for this result is similar to the employment ratio equation.

The estimated coefficients of trade variables are never significant in the employment equation at the 5 per cent level. At the 10 per cent level, however, the coefficient of exports to LDCs is significantly positive in specification 2.

Table 3.6a. Ratio of unskilled to skilled employment (without energy producing sectors)

Two stages least squares estimation	Specification 1	Specification 2
Intercept	0.65 (0.15)	19.60* (2.32)
M	4.22* (2.93)	− 1.10 (− 1.50)
X	− 1.56* (− 2.21)	0.95* (2.59)
Sectoral dummies included	No	Yes
Number of observations	91	91
Adjusted *R*-squared	0.44	0.90
Significance of the whole regression	0.0001	0.0001

Table 3.6b. Ratio of unskilled to skilled wages (without energy producing sectors)

Two stages least squares estimation	Specification 1	Specification 2
Intercept	0.57* (4.60)	1.06* (5.77)
M	− 0.20 (− 1.53)	− 0.06 (− 1.49)
X	0.06 (0.97)	0.08* (2.45)
Sectoral dummies included	No	Yes
Number of observations	91	91
Adjusted *R*-squared	0.49	0.85
Significance of the whole regression	0.0001	0.0001

Notes: Figures in brackets are *t*-statistics. Specification 1 and 2 are the same except for sectoral dummies: included in specification 2 but not in 1. All specifications include year dummies and country dummies. *(**) indicates that the coefficients is significant at the 5 per cent (10 per cent) level. The significance of the whole regression gives the probability level of the calculated *F*-statistic, namely the probability that all the coefficients in the regression are equal to zero.

In the wage ratio equation the significance of coefficients depends on the specification. When no sectoral dummies are present, the coefficient of import penetration is significantly negative at the 5 per cent level and the coefficient of exports is non significant. When sectoral dummies are incorporated into the specification the coefficient of import penetration is significantly negative at the 10 per cent level and the coefficient of exports is significantly positive at the 5 per cent level.

The above results do not lend support to the view that trade with LDCs has a negative impact on the ratio of unskilled to skilled employment. This conclusion is interesting, since we saw earlier that aggregate data showed both increasing LDC import penetration and decreasing relative employment of unskilled workers. Here, with or without sectoral dummies, one cannot find an association between import penetration and the skill content of employment.

Somewhat surprisingly, there is more action on the wage front, where we saw that the European picture does not reproduce the increasing skill premium that is so spectacular in the USA. However, we obtain (somewhat weak) evidence associating a higher import penetration (in any given sector) with a higher skill premium. On the other hand, being in a sector with higher exports to LDCs is associated with a lower skill premium.

We also performed the same robustness checks as for the unemployment equation and they confirm the results of Table 3.5. For example, Table 3.6 reports the same regressions as in Table 3.5 after having excluded energy producing sectors. Once again, when sectoral dummies are present, the significant effect is on the export side, and positively affects the unskilled. In this set of regressions, import penetration even ceases to have a significant impact at the 10 per cent confidence level.

3.5 Concluding Remarks

Our study is the first, to our knowledge, to investigate the relation between trade with LDCs and long-term unemployment. Overall, our results fail to display any significant long-term hardship from LDC import penetration in terms of unemployment. Put together with our analysis of the skill premium and skill content of employment across sectors, the overall conclusion we draw is that trade has at most a second-order effect on European labour markets, and that this effect is dominated by that of technological factors. This conclusion is thus similar to that of the many studies performed on the US economy and the more limited evidence available for Europe. Let us end by qualifying our results a bit, which suffer from a couple of limitations: First, we had to work with a broad industry classification, at the two-digit instead of the three- or four-digit level, where more 'action' might be seen. Another limitation comes from the problematic quality of trade price data, which we thus chose not to use at all. Finally, one could argue that our approach is not 'structural' enough in its modelling of the impact of trade on labour markets. We hope to address some of these challenges in future research.

References

Krugman, P. (1995), 'Growing World Trade: Causes and Consequences', *Brookings Papers on Economic Activity*, 1: 327–62.

Lawrence, R. Z. and Slaughter, M. J. (1993), 'International Trade and American Wages in the 1980s: Giant Sucking Sound or Small Hiccup?', *Brookings Papers on Economic Activity*, Microeconomics, 2: 161–226.

Neven D. and Wyplosz, C. (1994), 'Trade and European Labor Market', mimeo, University of Lausanne and INSEAD.

Revenga, A. L. (1992), 'Exporting Jobs?: The Impact of Import Competition on Employment and Wages in US Manufacturing', *Quarterly Journal of Economics*, 107(1): 225–84.

Sachs, J. D. and Shatz, H. J. (1994), 'Trade and Jobs in US Manufacturing', *Brookings Papers on Economic Activity*, 1: 1–69.

Wood, A. (1994), *North–South Trade, Employment and Inequality: Changing Fortunes in a Skill-Driven World*, Clarendon Press, Oxford.

Appendix 3.1: Definition of the variables in equation (3.1)

Sectoral Dummies

DN1	Extraction of petroleum and natural gas
	Mineral oil refining
DN2	Production and distribution of electricity, gas, steam and hot water
	Water supply: collection, purification and distribution of water
DN3	Extraction and preparation of metalliferous ores
	Production and preliminary processing of metals
	Extraction of minerals other than metalliferous and energy-producing minerals; peat extraction
DN4	Manufacture of non-metallic mineral products
DN5	Chemical industry
	Man-made fibres industry
DN6	Manufacture of metal articles (except for mechanical, electrical and instrument engineering and vehicles)
DN7	Mechanical engineering
DN8	Electrical engineering
DN9	Manufacture of motor vehicles and of motor vehicle parts and accessories
DN10	Manufacture of other means of transport
DN11	Food, drink and tobacco industry
DN12	Textile industry
	Leather and leather goods industry (except footwear and clothing)
	Footwear and clothing industry
DN13	Timber and wooden furniture industries
DN14	Manufacture of paper and paper products; printing and publishing
DN15	Processing of rubber and plastics
DN16	Other manufacturing industries

Education Level Dummies

DE1	Low level
DE2	Medium level
DE3	High level

Country Dummies

DC1	Germany
DC2	France
DC3	The Netherlands
DC4	Belgium-Luxembourg

Year Dummies

DY1	1988
DY2	1989
DY3	1990
DY4	1991

Appendix 3.2: Definition of the variables in equations 3.2 and 3.3

Sectoral Dummies

DN1	Extraction of petroleum and natural gas
	Mineral oil refining
DN2	Extraction and preparation of metalliferous ores
	Production and preliminary processing of metals
	Extraction of minerals other than metalliferous and energy-producing minerals; peat extraction
DN3	Manufacture of non-metallic mineral products
DN4	Chemical industry
	Man-made fibres industry
DN5	Manufacture of metal articles (except for mechanical, electrical and instrument engineering and vehicles)
DN6	Mechanical engineering
DN7	Manufacture of office machinery and data processing machinery
	Instrument engineering
DN8	Electrical engineering
DN9	Manufacture of motor vehicles and of motor vehicle parts and accessories
DN10	Manufacture of other means of transport
DN11	Textile industry
	Leather and leather goods industry (except footwear and clothing)
	Footwear and clothing industry
DN12	Timber and wooden furniture industries
DN13	Manufacture of paper and paper products; printing and publishing
DN14	Processing of rubber and plastics

Country Dummies

DC1	Germany
DC2	United Kingdom
DC3	Denmark
DC4	Belgium-Luxembourg

Year Dummies

DY1	1981
DY2	1984
DY3	1988

Appendix 3.3: Coefficients of the sectoral dummies

Unemployment Equation (3.1)

Variables	Coefficients (*t*-statistics are in parentheses)
DN1	0.11 (3.60)
DN2	− 0.01 (− 0.23)
DN3	0.08 (6.52)
DN4	− 0.01 (− 0.48)
DN5	0.01 (0.51)
DN6	− 0.01 (− 1.23)
DN7	− 0.00 (− 0.17)
DN8	− 0.01 (− 0.97)
DN9	− 0.00 (− 0.17)
DN10	0.03 (1.20)
DN12	0.05 (1.94)
DN13	− 0.01 (− 0.77)
DN14	− 0.03 (− 2.50)
DN15	− 0.01 (− 0.93)
DN16	0.06 (2.07)

Employment and wage ratio equations (3.2 and 3.3)

Variables	Coefficients (employment equation)	Coefficients (wage equation)
DN1	−0.66 (−1.97)	−0.22 (−2.74)
DN2	1.24 (3.83)	0.13 (1.43)
DN3	1.40 (3.91)	0.05 (1.47)
DN4	−0.62 (−1.67)	−0.23 (−3.33)
DN5	1.31 (4.16)	0.16 (1.58)
DN7	−0.21 (−0.32)	−0.26 (−4.85)
DN8	−0.04 (−0.08)	−0.15 (−5.85)
DN9	1.52 (4.74)	0.20 (1.60)
DN10	0.22 (0.40)	−0.05 (−1.50)
DN11	2.46 (4.47)	0.24 (1.29)
DN12	2.64 (8.76)	0.43 (2.05)
DN13	−0.12 (−0.41)	0.00 (0.10)
DN14	1.00 (2.66)	0.07 (0.96)

4. Growing World Trade: Causes and Consequences

PAUL KRUGMAN

The rapid growth of NIE exports has more or less coincided with some disturbing trends in OECD labour markets: a sharp rise in wage inequality (especially in the USA) and a sharp rise in unemployment (mainly in Europe). It is widely believed that the unfavourable labour market trends and the growth of NIE trade are connected.

This belief has been expressed at greatly varying levels of sophistication. At one end there is the phenomenon of a self-made billionaire-turned-politician, who has declared himself an expert on economics and launched a campaign to warn his countrymen of the impoverishment they face as a result of free trade with low-wage nations. I refer, of course, to Sir James Goldsmith, whose book *The Trap* has been a European best-seller. While one might dismiss Sir James and his untitled Texan counterpart as marginal, milder versions of the same warning are found among highly respected and influential people. Even the European Commission, in its 1993 White Paper *Growth, Competitiveness, Employment*, attributed a major share of the rise in European unemployment rates to the fact that 'other countries are becoming industrialized and competing with us—even on our own markets—at cost levels which we simply cannot match' (Commission of the European Communities 1993:4).

Academic research has been far less supportive of the claim that NIE manufactures exports are a major source of problems in OECD labour markets. While there are some studies that do claim to find evidence for substantial pressure from low-wage imports on unskilled labour in advanced countries, it is probably fair to say that a preponderance of the research to date suggests that the impact of third world exports on first world labour markets has been small, or at least elusive. (See, in particular, Wood 1994; and Leamer 1993 and 1994 in support of the adverse effects of NIE exports, and Katz 1992–3; Bhagwati and Kosters 1994; and Sachs and Shatz 1994 for the alternative view.)

One thing that is conspicuously lacking in the literature to date, however, is a consistent picture of the *interaction* between labour market developments in the high-wage countries and the growth of exports from the low-wage countries. While some (though not all) of the studies are based on a consistent underlying model of employment and wages in the advanced countries, there does not seem to be any effort to show how wages and employment in the advanced countries, and trade with the third world might be simultaneously determined. That is, there do not seem to be any complete general-equilibrium stories out there.

In the remainder of this chapter I will try to fill that gap by developing a highly stylized model of global trade, employment and wages. This model simplifies reality too much to be estimated with or even calibrated to the data. It is possible, however, to use the results of other people's empirical work to assign a set of ball-park parameters to the model, allowing what amount to glorified back-of-the-envelope estimates of the impact of growing NIE trade.

4.1. Structure of the Model

In order to focus on the effects of NIE trade in manufactured goods, I assume a world consisting of only two economies: one that is intended to represent the OECD as a whole, the other to represent the aggregate of NIEs. All transactions within each aggregate are ignored, as is the existence of other types of countries, like oil exporters.

The aggregate OECD is assumed to produce and consume two goods, 1 and 2, with production of good 1 being skill-intensive. Demand is determined by a utility function in the consumption of goods 1 and 2,

$$U = U(C_1, C_2). \tag{4.1}$$

It will be convenient to assume that tastes are homothetic, so that marginal and average spending have the same composition.

Since the focus of this analysis is on labour market developments in the OECD, it is necessary to have some explicit treatment of the factor markets. I will make several strategic simplifications. First, the only productive inputs will be skilled labour(L_S) and unskilled labour(L_U); capital will be left out of the story. The main reason for doing this is that the distribution of income between capital and labour has neither changed a lot nor been a major source of controversy in the last two decades; the share of labour compensation in US national income, for example, has barely changed, actually rising from 73 to 74 per cent between 1973 and 1993. It is not clear that this is what one would have expected *a priori*, nor is it clear that capital will remain a sort of bystander factor indefinitely. For the purposes of this model, however, all income will be assumed to accrue either to skilled or to unskilled labour.

Second, production, Q, will be assumed to take place under constant returns to scale, with the production functions

$$Q_1 = F(L_{S1}, L_{U1}) \tag{4.2}$$

and

$$Q_2 = G(L_{S2}, L_{U2}) \tag{4.3}$$

Economies of scale are widely believed to be important in understanding both the causes and effects of trade within the OECD, but probably play a smaller role in NIE trade.

For the same reason, markets are assumed to be perfectly competitive. This is likely to raise some stronger objections. One common story about the effects of international trade on wages is that it has weakened the bargaining power of workers; this only makes sense if workers and employers are struggling over the division of some rent, presumably created by the market power of the firm. It is arguable whether such stories can be a larger part of the picture: they seem to predict a shift in the distribution of income between capital and labour, which has not happened, rather than between different types of labour, which has; and they apply only to those workers in traded-goods industries, whereas the rise in income inequality has been pervasive throughout the economy. In any case, for this model competition is assumed to be perfect.

The OECD's trade is the difference between its production and its consumption. Exports of the skill-intensive good, X_1, and imports of the less skill-intensive good, M_2, can be written as

$$X_1 = Q_1 - C_1 \tag{4.4}$$

and

$$M_2 = C_2 - Q_2 \tag{4.5}$$

How should the OECD's trade with the NIEs be modelled? It is common in trade theory to work with small economies that face given world prices; and some writers on the effects of changing world trade still use this assumption. For the OECD as a whole, however, this is a deeply unrealistic assumption; worse yet, it is analytically awkward, leading to excessively 'bang-bang' solutions in some cases. It thus makes sense to regard the OECD as having substantial market power relative to the NIEs. This can be represented by assuming that the OECD faces a rest-of-world offer curve.

$$M_2 = T(X_1) \tag{4.6}$$

I will not make any attempt to model the inside workings of the newly industrializing countries; they will simply be summarized by the offer curve given by equation 4.6. The growth and increased integration of the NIEs with the world economy are then captured simply by an outward shift in that offer curve. In fact, since their manufactured exports were negligible in 1970, the effects of their emergence can be approximated by contrasting an initial period in which the OECD has no external trade with a subsequent period in which it faces an offer curve that leads to the observed trade volumes. That is, the model analyses the effects of globalization by contrasting the current situation with one of autarky for the OECD as a whole.

That is the whole theoretical model. Before assigning ballpark parameter values, it may be useful to review some of the key mechanics of 2×2 production models.

The most important relationships are presented in Figure 4.1, which reproduces the familiar diagram introduced by Paul Samuelson (1949). Figure 4.1 summarizes the three-way relationship between goods prices, factor prices and factor proportions. The right panel shows that given the ratio of skilled to unskilled wages (W_s/W_u), each industry chooses a ratio of skilled to unskilled workers in production. The left panel shows the basic Stolper–Samuelson relationship between the relative price of the skill-intensive good (P_1/P_2) and the relative wage of skilled workers that prevails if both goods are produced.

4.1.1 Putting Numbers to the Model

Quantifying a model like this poses certain conceptual problems. That is a polite way of saying that it is somewhat difficult to know exactly how to assign numbers to a model that is, in important respects, blatantly untrue. Not only are there more than two kinds of labour, other factors besides labour, other regions besides the OECD and the NIEs; it is not even true that workers of apparently similar skill receive the same wages in exporting and import-competing sectors. Yet for the model to be used, it is necessary to assign a set of parameter values that fit together.

The following parameters are used in the trade model of the next two sections:

Initial ratio of skilled to unskilled wages	2
Share of skilled workers in industry 1 employment	0.5
Share of skilled workers in industry 2 employment	0.2
Share of skilled workers in labour force	0.4
Share of wages of skilled workers in industry 1 value added	2/3
Share of wages of skilled workers in industry 2 value added	1/3
Share of good 1 in total expenditure	5/7

Wage ratio

Adrian Wood, using his definitions, finds a wage ratio between skilled and unskilled workers in the North of 2.08 (Wood 1994: 403). I round this to 2.

Employment share in industry 1

Wood also estimates a share of skilled employment in export-oriented manufacturing of 50.24 per cent, which I round to 50 (Wood 1994: 403).

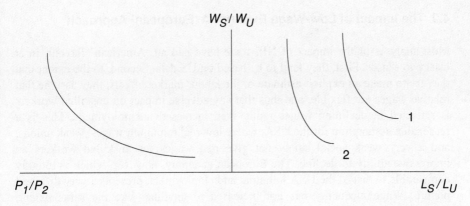

Source: Samuelson (1949).

Fig.4.1. Relationship between goods prices, factor prices, and factor proportions

Employment share in industry 2

Wood does not, for reasons explained below, estimate the employment composition of Northern import-competing production. Other sources, using different definitions, have produced estimates. However, in order to make the model internally consistent, one must meet a constraint that is not met in the actual data: the difference in average wages between export and import-competing industries must be fully accounted for by the difference in skill composition. Bela Balassa (1979) found that wages in US industries that export to developing countries were 28 per cent higher than those in industries competing with imports from those countries; by assigning the import-competing industry a 20 per cent skill fraction, I get an implied 25 per cent average wage ratio, which seems close enough.

Labour supplies

If the OECD is producing both goods, the ratio of skilled to unskilled workers in the labour force must be between the ratios in the two industries. The choice of 40 per cent skilled workers is arbitrary, but has little effect on the results below.

Remaining entries

These follow from the previous numbers. In particular, the share of industry 1 in expenditure is determined by the requirement that the derived demand for factors equal the supply.

This completes the stylized model of the interaction between NIE trade and OECD labour markets, together with some semi-realistic numbers that will allow back-of-the-envelope estimates of effects. The next step is to apply the model under two alternative assumptions about OECD labour markets.

4.2 The Impact of Low-Wage Exports: A 'European' Approach

Most analyses of the impact of NIE trade have had an 'American' flavour, in at least two senses. First, they tend to be based on US data. Second, to the extent that they try to make an explicit estimate of the labour market effects, they assume that relative wages are flexible, and thus that any adverse impact on unskilled workers is reflected in declining wages rather than increased unemployment. This is a reasonable assumption for the USA, where low real minimum wages, weak unions, and a very weak social safety net give real wages for unskilled workers an impressive ability to decline. The European economy, however, which is roughly comparable to that of the USA in output and employment, presents a very different picture. Wage inequality has not increased to anything like the same extent; meanwhile, unemployment has risen from less than 3 per cent at the beginning of the 1970s to double digits today.

This in itself would suggest that it is worthwhile to look at the impact of integration under 'European' assumptions, with relative wages rigid and the consequent reduced demand for less skilled workers reflected in unemployment. In addition, however, the European version of the story is revealing in other ways: it highlights the importance of a general-equilibrium approach, and (as the next section shows) there are some surprising quantitative contrasts between the effects of trade in a 'Europeanized' and an 'Americanized' model.

For the moment, then, assume that W_S/W_u, is fixed, so that any pressure on labour demand is reflected in employment rather than wages; and suppose that a previously autarkic OECD economy is now presented with an offer curve from a group of newly industrialized economies, which allows the OECD to export good 1 and import good 2.

The consequences may be analysed in stages.[1] First, note that with rigid relative wages, the skilled-to-unskilled ratio in each industry is fixed. These ratios are illustrated by the slopes of rays 1 and 2 in Figure 4.2, which shows employment in the economy. The point E represents the initial employment of the two factors. Since these levels of employment must be achieved using the factor proportions implied by the fixed relative wage, the resources employed in each industry are indicated by Q_1 and Q_2. Now suppose that there is a fall in the relative demand for the less skill-intensive good. This cannot be met by a change in relative wages, so it must be met with a reduction in unskilled employment. The employment point moves left to E'. And output obeys the Rybczynski theorem: the resources devoted to industry 2 fall to Q_2', while those devoted to industry 1 actually rise, to Q_1'.

Next, consider the implications for international trade. Figure 4.3 plots OECD exports against imports. Point O represents autarky (no trade in manufactures with the NIEs), and slope of the ray OA represents the relative price of good 1 in autarky. Now the NIEs arrive on the scene, with their presence summarized by the offer curve OC. What effect does this have on relative prices? As long as the

---

[1] This analysis was inspired by and closely follows the analysis in Brecher (1974).

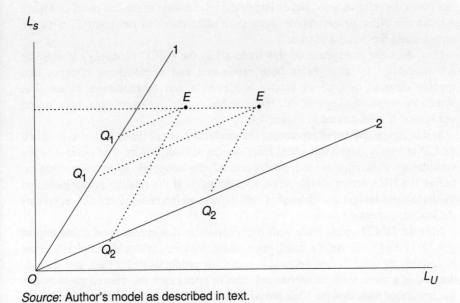

Source: Author's model as described in text.

Fig. 4.2. Adjustment of OECD employment under the 'European' model

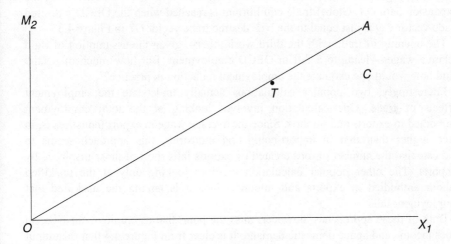

Source: Author's model as described in text.

Fig. 4.3. Adjustment of OECD exports and imports under the 'European' model

OECD continues to produce both goods, it has no effect: the fixed relative wage ties down the relative price, according to the relationship in the left panel of Figure 4.1. So the NIEs simply move along their offer curve to the point T, with OT representing the volume of trade.

How does the emergence of this trade affect the OECD economy? It must be accommodated by changes in both production and employment, changes that involve demand as well as supply and even a sort of multiplier effect. The somewhat surprising logic of this response has not, to my knowledge, been traced out before; it is illustrated in Figure 4.4.

In this figure, the curve represents the production possibilities of the aggregated OECD economy, given the initial employment of both factors. The point A is the equilibrium consumption and production of the economy in autarky—that is, before the NIEs arrive on the scene. Consumption at the relative prices indicated by the tangent budget line through A will depend on income; the ray OA represents the income expansion path.

Now the OECD opens trade with NIE economies that export good 2 and import good 1. If the OECD were a small, price-taking economy, it would completely cease production of good 2. But because it is not, its production of 2 falls and its production of 1 rises, with an unchanged relative price, until the desired trade equals the amount of trade that the NIEs are willing to do at that given relative price. Figure 4.4 allows that as employment of unskilled workers falls, the OECD's production moves down the 'Rybczynski line' AR, which corresponds to the kind of adjustment in production shown in Figure 4.2. The value of production falls, and therefore the budget line shifts in; consumption therefore also moves down along the expansion path OA. Global trade equilibrium is reached when the OECD's desired trade vector CQ is just equal to the NIE desired trade vector OT in Figure 4.3.

The opening of trade with the third world, then—given the assumption of rigid relative wages—leads to a fall in OECD employment. But how much of a fall? And how would one estimate the employment reduction in practice?

Interestingly, two popular calculations actually understate the employment effects of trade. One calculation involves looking at the total employment embodied in exports and imports. Since the average wage in export industries is, in fact, higher than that in import-competing industries, this approach seems to indicate that the number of jobs created by exports falls short of those displaced by imports. The other popular calculation involves looking only at the unskilled labour embodied in exports and imports, since it is among the unskilled that employment falls.

Both of these approaches, however, miss the point that as employment falls, so does income and hence domestic demand. It is clear from Figure 4.4 that the output of good 1 rises by less than the volume of exports, and that the output of good 2 falls by more than the volume of imports.

How, then, can the employment effects of trade be determined? One way is to calculate the new equilibrium and grind out the implied employment change. There is, however, a shortcut that is possible because there is no change in relative

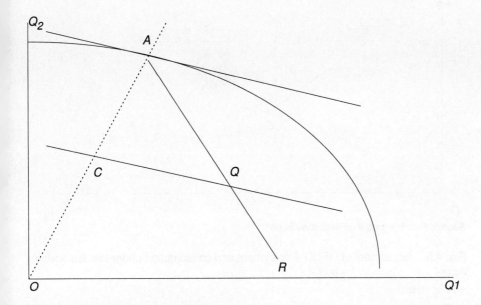

Source: Author's model as described in text.

Fig. 4.4. Adjustment of OECD production and consumption under the 'European' model

wages (by assumption) or relative prices (by implication). That approach is illustrated in Figure 4.5. As in Figure 4.2, we show the factor content of output, with A the initial employment. Figure 4.5, however, also shows OECD demand—the derived demand for factors embodied in production. In autarky this must be equal to the total supply. As income falls, this derived demand will fall along the expansion path OA. Meanwhile, employment of unskilled workers will fall to a point such as E. Through E, I have drawn a budget line, EC, whose slope is equal to W_s/W_u; employment and consumption of factors must both lie on such a line. Equilibrium involves a situation in which the production point, E, and the consumption point, C, are such that the implied trade in embodied factors, EC, equals the difference between the factors used to produce exports and those that would be needed to replace imports.[2]

---

[2] The relevant factor content of trade here is that in OECD import-substituting production; the factors used to produce the goods in the Third World are irrelevant. Wood (1994) has argued that developing countries produce 'non-competing goods' that are no longer produced in the high-wage nations, and that one must therefore try to estimate what it would have taken to produce these goods, rather than look at actual OECD industries. This assertion is, however, problematic. If these really are non-competing goods, how can one assess their impact without specifying how they substitute *in demand* for other goods? After all, in a two good model in which the OECD and the NIEs are specialized in producing different goods, an expansion of NIE exports would have no effect at all on equilibrium relative wages in the OECD.

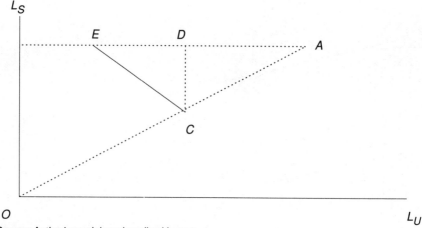

Source: Author's model as described in text.

Fig. 4.5. Adjustment of OECD employment and consumption under the 'European' model

It is immediately apparent that the decline in employment of unskilled labour is greater than the quantity of labour embodied in trade. The net 'import' of unskilled labour is the distance *ED*, but the actual fall in employment is measured by the full distance *EA*.

4.2.1 The Employment Effects of NIE Exports

As Figure 4.5 indicates, the effects of trade on employment in a rigid-wage economy may be estimated from the factor content of trade, together with an estimate of the general-equilibrium multiplier effect. Specifically, the fall in employment is

Net imports of unskilled labour + *(Net exports of skilled labour*
× Unskilled-to-skilled ratio in OECD economy)

Table 4.1 shows the results, using the World Bank's latest (1995) estimate of the share of NIE manufactures exports in OECD gross product and the parameters listed above.

This is a fairly large effect. It is still only a fraction of the actual rise in European unemployment, but it is far from negligible. And it therefore seems to suggest considerable reason for concern over the effects of low-wage manufactures exports on first world labour markets.

This fairly large estimate depends, however, on the assumption of rigidly fixed relative wages. Even in Europe, this is an exaggeration; and relative wages appear to be highly flexible in the USA. How do the results change if we 'Americanize' the model, allowing wages to be flexible and therefore assuming that the effects of trade manifest themselves in income inequality rather than unemployment?

Table 4.1. Employment effects of trade under 'European' assumption

Units as indicated	
Manufactures imports[a]	1.75
Net imports of unskilled labour[b]	0.82
Net exports of skilled labour[b]	0.41
Unskilled-to-skilled ratio in aggregate employment	1.5
Fall in employment[c]	1.43

Source: Author's calculations based on model described in text and World Bank (1995).

Note: [a] Percentage of GDP; [b] percentage of total employment; [c] per cent.

4.3 The Impact of Low-Wage Exports: An 'American' Model

With full employment of both skilled and unskilled labour maintained by wage flexibility, the effects of opening trade between the OECD and the NIEs can be represented by a figure so familiar that Ronald Findlay has dubbed it the 'sacred diagram' of international trade. Figure 4.6 shows how the pieces fit together when relative wages and hence prices can change. Point *A*, once again, represents OECD autarky. When trade is opened, the relative price of good 1 rises; the result is that production moves to *Q*, while consumption moves to *C*. If this is a global equilibrium, the NIE offer curve—drawn backward, with its origin at *Q*—must also pass through *C*, so that desired OECD exports equal desired NIE imports, and vice versa.

But how can we quantify this qualitative picture? At first, it might seem possible to begin in the same way as in the rigid-wage case, by calculating the factor content of trade; then asking how much these changes in effective supplies of skilled and unskilled labour affect relative wages, by making use of some estimated elasticity of substitution. This has in fact been the approach taken by some studies (see, in particular, Borjas, Freeman and Katz 1992). Unfortunately, it runs into serious conceptual difficulties. Even the concept of net trade in embodied services become hard to make sense of when relative factor prices change as a result of trade; and the elasticity of substitution between skilled and unskilled labour will change when an economy is opened, if it has any meaning at all. (It is possible to rescue the concept if the economy does not face given world prices, but rather faces a concave foreign offer curve—and this is certainly true for the OECD as a whole. So one should not be as harsh in condemning studies that attempt to make inferences from the factor content of trade as some critics, such as Leamer (1994), have been.)

Given these conceptual difficulties, several recent studies have attempted to infer the effects of trade on relative wages by looking at pieces of the mechanism by which the process should work. In particular, Robert Lawrence and Matthew Slaughter (1993) looked for evidence that the relative prices of less skill-intensive goods have indeed fallen, and that the industry mix within the USA has shifted toward skill-intensive sectors.

I offer here an alternative approach: with the addition of some further assumptions to the model already described, it turns into a tiny, computable general-equilibrium model of world trade. I can then ask the following question: *What changes in relative wages and prices would be consistent with the observed growth of trade?* The answer turns out to be surprisingly small—that is, the same model that predicts fairly large employment effects with rigid wages predicts quite small effects on relative wages when they are flexible.

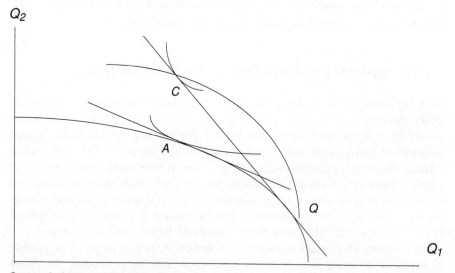

Source: Author's model as described in text.

Fig. 4.6. Adjustment of OECD production and consumption under the 'American' model

4.3.1 Making the Model Computable

In order to make the model computable in the face of flexible prices and wages, it is necessary to specify elasticities of substitution in production and consumption—in effect, to choose functional forms. Since this is a illustrative exercise rather than a full-fledged CGE modelling project, it is sufficient to go with the simplest case (which is not too far from most empirical estimates) of unitary elasticity. That is, the model will be made Cobb–Douglas throughout.

In stating the model, it is also convenient to make some simplifying choices of units. Letting unskilled labour be the numeraire, I choose units so that in autarky the prices of both goods are one. I also measure skilled labour in units of half a worker—a trick normalization that implies an autarky relative wage that is also one. To be consistent with this normalization, the economy's endowment is assumed to consist of 60 units of unskilled and 80 revised units of skilled labour.

Given these choices of units, and the parameter values listed above, output and factor markets in the OECD can be represented by the following equations:

First, letting w be the relative wage of skilled labour (one in autarky) gives expressions for average cost—which must equal prices if both goods are produced in the OECD.

$$P_1 = w^{2/3}, P_2 = w^{1/3}. \tag{4.7}$$

Next, expressions for the unit input choices for both factors in both sectors may be written

$$a_{s1} = \frac{2}{3}w^{-1/3}, a_{U1} = \frac{1}{3}w^{2/3}, a_{s2} = \frac{1}{3}w^{-2/3}, a_{U2} = \frac{2}{3}w^{1/3}. \tag{4.8}$$

Given these input coefficients, output is determined by the requirement of full employment of both factors. These conditions may be written

$$L_s = a_{s1}Q_1 + a_{s2}Q_2, L_u = a_{U1}Q_1 + a_{U2}Q_2, \tag{4.9}$$

which yield the output equations

$$Q_1 = D^{-1}[a_{U2}L_s - a_{s2}L_U], Q_2 = D^{-1}[-a_{U1}L_s + a_{s1} + L_U], \tag{4.10}$$

where

$$D = a_{s1}a_{U2} - a_{s2}a_{U1}. \tag{4.11}$$

Given the output and prices of the two goods, it is straightforward to calculate the implied trade vector. In fact, the relevant number is the share of OECD output; this is simply the difference between the share of good 1 in output and in consumption:

$$T = \frac{P_1Q_1}{P_1Q_1 + P_2Q_2} - \frac{4}{7}. \tag{4.12}$$

Equations 7–12, then, lead from an assumed relative wage to the implied relative prices and share of trade in output. It is also possible, therefore, to reverse the procedure, and ask how large a change in relative wages in the OECD might be associated with the emergence of NIE trade on the scale actually seen. And the answer is that trade on this scale should be associated with a fairly small wage change—and a very small change in relative prices.

Table 4.2 shows the implications of a 3 per cent rise in the relative wage of skilled workers from its autarky level. It turns out that this is large enough to imply NIE trade of 2.2 per cent of OECD gross product; which is more than the actual

Table 4.2. Implications of a 3 per cent rise in relative wages of skilled workers

Per cent

Share of NIE exports in OECD output	2.2
Change in relative price of good 1	1.0
Change in output of good 1	2.8
Change in output of good 2	−6.9
Change in real wages of unskilled workers	−1.43

Source: Author's calculations based on model described in text.

share of NIE manufactures in OECD spending. Yet this wage rise would be associated with a rise of only 1 per cent in the relative price of skill-intensive goods. Admittedly, this exercise is carried out not only with a highly stylized model, but also on the assumption of unitary elasticities of substitution in production and consumption. If these elasticities were lower, the implied change in relative wages would be larger. Nonetheless, the exercise helps to explain why studies that attempt to infer the effects of trade on income distribution by looking at prices have failed to find any clear-cut effects: for plausible parameter values, the change in relative prices associated with the growth of NIE trade should be well within measurement error.

4.3.2 The Limits to Factor Price Equalization

Some of those who worry about the effects of NIE exports on OECD labour markets might accept that these effects have been fairly small so far; but they would argue that these effects will become much larger, as industrialization spreads. It is possible to make a counterargument: As newly industrializing countries grow, their comparative advantage may shift away from products of very low skill intensity. Is it really likely that skilled labour will be a scarcer commodity in the world economy 20 years from now than it is today? But it is worth asking how large the potential effects of trade on OECD income inequality could be in a sort of worst case scenario.

An extreme view would be that growing international trade will lead to full factor price equalization: that wages for unskilled labour in OECD countries will be driven down towards their average levels in the world as a whole. Indeed, it might seem that this is precisely what conventional trade theory would predict: in the absence of any barriers to trade, is trade not a substitute for factor mobility?

This extreme view, however, neglects an important limitation to the factor price equalization theorem: it only works as long as a country remains non-specialized. If the change in relative prices is so large that the OECD no longer produces goods that compete with low-skill imports, any further reduction in the relative price of these goods will have no effect on income distribution. (This is why Wood's (1994) insistence that NIE exports are non-competing is so puzzling: surely this is exactly the case in which the tendency toward factor price equalization breaks down?)

In the context of my miniature CGE model, it is straightforward to find the limits of factor price equalization. At a relative wage of skilled labour 50 per cent above its autarky level, and a corresponding relative price of the skill-intensive good 14.5 per cent above its original level, the OECD economy becomes completely specialized in the skill-intensive good. Any further change in the relative price has no effect on relative wages.

Even this case, however, seems unlikely to occur because it implies unreasonably large trade volumes. At the point of OECD specialization, manufactured imports from the NIEs would reach 28.6 per cent of OECD gross product! In the context of this model, this is possible. If the model were modified to make a reasonable percentage (at least 60 per cent) of OECD expenditure fall on non-traded goods and services, the point of complete specialization in traded goods would be reached after a substantially smaller change in income distribution.[31]

The flexible-wage version of the model, then, suggests that NIE trade can explain only a fraction of the huge increase in income inequality that has occurred in the USA since the 1970s. And while it shows that larger effects from such trade could occur in the future, it also points out that there are limits to the change in relative wages that trade flows can produce.[4]

---

[3] For example, adding a non-traded sector that receives 60 per cent of expenditures, and assuming that this sector initially uses skilled and unskilled labour in the same proportions as the OECD endowment, the model says that NIE trade can raise the relative wage of skilled labour by at most 17 per cent.

[4] The comparison between the European and US cases may seem to suggest that a little bit of wage flexibility goes a long way, and to make one wonder whether even Eurosclerotic economies are really unable to adjust relative wages by a few per cent. It is important to be careful about making too much of this. First, the estimated impact of NIE trade in the European case amounts to roughly 20 per cent of the rise in European unemployment since the early 1970s, while the impact in the US case amounts to roughly 10 per cent of the rise in US wage inequality over the same period; given the number of *ad hoc* assumptions involved, this is not a major difference. Second, one should not fall into the fallacy of imagining that since any adverse shock can be decomposed into many smaller components, adjustment is always easy! (Achilles can, in fact, outrun the tortoise.) Rising European unemployment is presumably the result of a number of factors. Any one of these could have been offset by a small change in relative wages; but to offset them all would presumably have required something comparable to the massive growth in inequality that has occurred in the USA.

References

Balassa, B. (1966), 'Tariff Reductions and Trade in Manufactures among the Industrial Countries', *American Economic Review*, 56(3): 466–73.
—— (1979), 'The Changing International Division of Labour in Manufactured Goods', *Banca Nazionale del Lavoro Quarterly Review*, 130, 243–85.
Bhagwati, J., and Kosters, M. H. (eds.) (1994), *Trade and Wages: Leveling Wages Down?* AEI Press, Washington.
Borjas, G. J., Freeman, R. B. and Katz, L. F. (1992) 'On the Labour Market Effects of Immigration and Trade', in J. Borjas and R. B. Freeman (eds.), *Immigration and the Workforce: Economic Consequences for the United States and Source Areas*, University of Chicago Press, Chicago.
Brecher, R. A. (1974), 'Optimal Commercial Policy for a Minimum-Wage Economy', *Journal of International Economics*, 4(2): 139–49.
Commission of the European Communities (1993), *Growth, Competitiveness, Employment: The Challenges and Ways Forward into the 21st Century—White Paper*, Luxembourg Office for Official Publications of the European Communities.
Katz, L. F. (1992–3), 'Understanding Recent Changes in the Wage Structure', *NBER Reporter*, (Winter): 10–15.
Lawrence, R. Z. and Slaughter, M. J. (1993), 'International Trade and American Wages in the 1980s: Giant Sucking Sound or Small Hiccup?', *Brookings Papers on Economic Activity*, Microeconomics, 2: 161–226.
Leamer, E. E. (1993), 'Wage Effects of a US–Mexican Free Trade Agreement', in P. M. Garber (ed.), *The Mexico–US Free Trade Agreement*, MIT Press, Cambridge, Mass.
—— (1994), 'Trade, Wages and Revolving Door Ideas', Working Paper 4716, National Bureau of Economic Research, Cambridge, Mass. (April).
Sachs, J. D. and Shatz, H. J. (1994), 'Trade and Jobs in US Manufacturing', *Brookings Papers on Economic Activity*, 1: 1–69.
Samuelson, P. A. (1949), 'International Factor-Price Equalisation Once Again', *Economic Journal*, 59(234): 181–97.
Wood, Adrian (1994) *North–South Trade, Employment and Inequality: Changing Fortunes in a Skill-Driven World*, Clarendon Press, New York
World Bank (1995) *Global Economic Prospects and the Developing Economies*, World Bank, Washington.

5. The Labour Market Effects of International Trade: A Computable General Equilibrium Model

ALASDAIR SMITH

5.1 Introduction

Dramatic changes in relative wages that have taken place in the USA since the mid-1970s (documented, for example, by Krugman (1994), and by Freeman (1995), who writes 'an economic disaster has befallen low-skilled Americans, especially young men') and the almost as dramatic increases in European unemployment in the same period can be interpreted as different manifestations of a common phenomenon: the labour market misfortunes of the less skilled. (Alogoskoufis *et al.* (1995), for example, give data on the differential incidence of unemployment among unskilled workers as well as on the growth of European unemployment rates.) The period of these dramatic changes has also seen a very rapid growth of international trade in manufactured goods with developing countries, especially the 'tigers' of Southeast Asia and more recently China.

The standard textbook model of international trade, the two-good, two-factor Heckscher–Ohlin–Samuelson model, provides a means of interpreting these phenomena. Take the two factors as skilled and unskilled labour, suppose that the rapidly growing developing countries are abundant in unskilled labour (Wood (1994) notes that 'unskilled' in this context is to be interpreted as 'having only basic education', since workers without basic education do not generally engage in the production of traded goods), and the model predicts that growth of trade between developed and developing countries will in developed countries shift production towards skill-intensive products, drive down the relative price of unskilled-intensive goods, raise the real wages of skilled workers and reduce the real wages of the unskilled. The part of the Heckscher–Ohlin–Samuelson story that provides the link between relative goods prices and relative factor prices is the Stolper–Samuelson theorem. Add a story about downward rigidity of the real wages of the unskilled in socially-regulated labour markets and the model will generate unemployment rather than relative wage changes.

Faced with two striking empirical phenomena and a well-established theory that links the two, there is an almost overwhelming temptation to see the empirical phenomena as confirming the theory; and the perceived link between globalization and labour markets is politically influential in many quarters, particularly in France and in the USA.

However, the weight of academic opinion, at least among international economists, comes down against the view that there is a strong link between the growth of trade and the growth of labour market inequality. Freeman (1995) surveys the differing positions taken and notes the paradoxical fact that trade theorists are in the forefront of those denying the importance of trade in income distribution.

Lawrence and Slaughter (1993) made an influential contribution, with popularizing support from Krugman (1994) and Krugman and Lawrence (1994). Sachs and Shatz (1994) find more support for a link between trade and labour markets than Lawrence and Slaughter, but still fall short of confirming the popular view. Wood (1994) and Leamer (1995) are unusual among trade economists in finding evidence of strong links between trade and labour markets.

There is also a methodological dichotomy in the literature: some authors (including Wood, but also many of the labour economists who have written on the issue) have focused primarily on the effects of trade on the demand for labour, typically by estimating the factor content of trade; while others, such as Lawrence and Slaughter, have concentrated on the link between relative wages and the prices of traded goods.

The aim of this chapter is to investigate whether the use of a computable general equilibrium (CGE) model can contribute to our understanding of these issues, both substantive and methodological. Whether a price-oriented approach is superior to a demand-oriented one depends partly on general equilibrium considerations, such as whether trade-induced changes in factor demand can be absorbed by intersectoral shifts of production within the economy, and whether changes in world prices can generate changes in domestic factor prices without much change in trade flows. It also depends on the view one takes about the nature of the question being asked: as Deardorff and Hakura (1994) and Freeman (1995) have pointed out, both trade changes and labour market changes are endogenous phenomena, so attributing one set of effects causally to the other requires some care in the specification of what is the exogenous change being discussed. An advantage of the CGE approach is that it can bridge these methodological gaps by using the same model to produce results on the impact of trade both on labour demand, with factor prices unchanged, and on factor prices, when factor markets are allowed to clear; and by making explicit assumptions about exogeneity.

Specifically, the CGE methodology clarifies the nature of factor content calculations. Freeman (1995) notes two potential problems with such calculations (and Richardson (1995) raises the same problems in a different form): using a factor content calculation as the basis of an estimate of the impact of trade on the labour market does not take account of the role of domestic goods market adjustment in absorbing some of the impact of trade induced changes, or of the fact that labour market adjustment may already have taken place and affected the trade change being measured. CGE calculations can both clarify the nature and estimate the quantitative significance of such effects. A formal model can clarify the relation between factor content calculations and general equilibrium calculations.

Aggregation is another important methodological issue. Lawrence and Slaughter's failure to find the shifts in techniques of production towards less skill-intensity and in production patterns towards more skill-intensive products predicted by the Stolper–Samuelson theorem could reflect the fact that these shifts were present, but *within* sectors and not showing up at the level of aggregation of the data. Lawrence and Slaughter attempt to deal with this issue by showing the same phenomena at three levels of aggregation, of which the least aggregated is at four-digit SIC level. They suppose that disaggregation to this level will reveal the impact of vertical disintegration of production. However, even disaggregation to the four-digit level may fail to detect effects associated with quality and skill-content differences between similar products. Most CGE models operate at a quite high level of aggregation. For example, Gasiorek, Smith and Venables (1994) have 12 manufacturing sectors and one other, Cortes and Jean (1996) have 13 sectors of which 11 are manufacturing, Whalley and Wigle (1996) have nine sectors in total of which two are manufactures, and the WorldScan model described by Nahuis (1996) has only seven sectors of which three are manufactures. Such a level of aggregation limits the ability of a model to get to grips with the real issues in trade and labour. The present model operates at a level of disaggregation that is comparable to most non-CGE approaches to the issue.

On the substantive front, the CGE simulation results reported in this chapter seem to confirm the general conclusion in the literature that the labour market effects of trade are small, whether one looks at the effect on the demand for labour or on relative wages. Even an extraordinarily large shock—removing all EU trade with non-advanced countries—seems to have remarkably small impacts on labour markets, whether one measures the direct impact on factor demand via the labour content of trade flows, or the impact on factor demands with goods market adjustment but without labour market adjustment, or the impact on relative wages with all markets adjusting. However, from this I conclude not that the effects of trade in labour markets are really unimportant, but rather that the 'mainstream' empirical trade model of which the CGE model of this chapter is one version is ill-suited to provide good estimates of the labour market effects of trade, because its structure fails to provide an appropriate model either of the skill endowments of the economy or of the skill intensity of production.

5.2 The Structure of the CGE Model

In this section of the chapter, I outline the underlying structure of the CGE model. It is conventional in the sense of having intersectoral differences in intensities of two non-traded factors, manual and non-manual labour. This derives from joint work with Michael Gasiorek, and a fuller discussion of the underlying model is given in Allen, Gasiorek and Smith (1996).

The characterization of labour skills is different in this approach from that adopted in much of the American work on this issue, with labour being divided between non-manual and manual, as opposed to the US distinction between production and non-production workers. Richardson (1995) notes that production workers include non-manual categories such as supervisors, book-keepers and product development staff, while non-production workers include manual workers such as truck drivers. However, and this is a point to which I shall return in the concluding section of the chapter, the division between manual and non-manual labour is still a poor proxy for the division between unskilled and skilled labour.

The model is a computable general equilibrium (CGE) model calibrated to 1991 data, operating at the three-digit NACE level, and modelling producers as imperfectly competitive firms operating in markets with differentiated products. Technical details of the model are given in Gasiorek, Smith and Venables (1992), who use the same basic model, at a more aggregated level.

The model has 12 countries: the 1991 EU member countries (with Belgium–Luxembourg treated as a single country) with the rest of the world the twelfth country. Each country is endowed with three primary factors of production—capital, and manual and non-manual labour. Capital is assumed to be perfectly mobile internationally, and available at a constant price. The two labour inputs are internationally immobile, and their prices can adjust to equate demands to endowments. The commodity structure is defined by the three-digit NACE industries, with the rest of each economy aggregated into a single perfectly competitive composite which is taken as the numeraire. Each of the manufacturing industries is assumed to be imperfectly competitive, with a number of firms producing differentiated products with increasing returns to scale. All goods are tradeable.

Demand for differentiated products is modelled, following Dixit and Stiglitz (1977), as a two-stage process, where the demand for a product aggregate depends on a price index for that aggregate, while demand for an individual variety depends on the price of the variety relative to that of the product aggregate.

We assume that firms act as quantity competitors in segmented markets with differentiated products. Each firm chooses sales in each country market, taking as constant the sales of all its rivals in each market. Optimization requires the equation of marginal revenue to marginal cost in each market, where the slope of each firm's perceived demand curve depends on the extent of product differentiation, and on the share of the firm in that market. The key feature of the model is that price-cost margins thus depend on firms' market shares, and increased import penetration causes firms to behave more competitively, lowering their price–cost margins. An imperfectly competitive model is a natural way to model a real-world trade pattern in which intra-industry trade is significant, but the imperfectly competitive features of the model do not play a significant role in the analysis that is the focus of this chapter.

5.3 Model Calibration

The numerical calibration of the CGE model takes some key parameters, notably those describing demand elasticities and returns to scale, from literature estimates, and then calculates the values of remaining parameters and endogenous variables so that the base year observations are an equilibrium of the model.

The price elasticity of demand for the industry aggregates are assumed to be one. The price elasticities of demand for individual varieties depend on the elasticities of substitution in the CES aggregators. We assume that this elasticity of substitution is the same for all industries and is equal to 10.

For final products we assume that the base data set represents a long-run equilibrium in which profits are zero. Technology and firm scale imply a relationship between average cost and marginal cost, and, with the assumption of long-run equilibrium, this also gives a relationship between price and marginal cost. This price–cost margin is supported at equilibrium by the existence of market power deriving from product differentiation and from concentration and depending on the assumed nature of the competitive interaction between firms. We assume that the base case is a segmented-market Cournot equilibrium. The number of varieties and the output per variety are then chosen so that the degree of product differentiation implied by the assumed elasticity of substitution is compatible with the assumed scale economies. The final stage of calibration involves positioning demand curves so that consumption of products in each country is consistent with the matrix of production and trade.

Trade data come from the COMEXT database and production data from the VISA and INDE databases. Both trade and production data are available on the NACE three-digit classification, in which there are 118 manufacturing industries. However, to resolve some incompatibilities in the trade and industrial data and to deal with data limitations in certain sectors in small countries, this number is reduced by aggregation, and the model works with the 64 imperfectly competitive sectors listed in Table 5.1. These sectors constitute considerably less than half of the economy, so the greater part of each economy is modelled as being in the perfectly competitive sector. (It is clearly not accurate to model all non-manufactures, such as financial services, as perfectly competitive.) Even for 1991 the industrial data are not complete and various *ad hoc* procedures were adopted to fill the holes in the data.

Data on concentration are obtained from the study carried out by Davies and Lyons (1996). In a model based on imperfect competition, data on concentration are crucial, and compared with the work done by Gasiorek, Smith and Venables (1992), the availability of concentration data from Davies and Lyons collected on an EU-wide basis and in a way that is more satisfactory than national census data should considerably improve the reliability of the model. Indeed, the availability from Davies and Lyons of concentration estimates at the three-digit NACE level was crucial to the feasibility of the work reported here. For each sector, Davies and Lyons report a Herfindahl-equivalent number of firms in a Herfindahl-typical EU country, and it is the market share implied by this statistic that we have entered into our imperfectly competitive pricing equations in describing market concentration in the base equilibrium. The first column of numbers in Table 5.1 gives the average degree of concentration in that industry in Europe as reported by Davies and Lyons. The figure reported here is a Herfindahl index (HNAT in their terminology), the reciprocal of which gives the number of equivalent sized firms.

Other industry specific data required include the share of value added in production and the share of each factor in value added. Obviously, the sectoral labour input shares are most important to the exercise being undertaken here. The principal source for most of this data is the VISA database, with other data derived from supplementary sources such as INDE and published EUROSTAT data. In each case, we have taken UK sectoral data as representative. The second column of Table 5.1 gives the share of value added in each industry, the average share across all industries being 0.36. The third, fourth and fifth columns give the shares in value added of capital, non-manual labour and manual labour respectively in each industry. The ratio of non-manual to manual labour varies from 12 in computers and office machinery to just under 1 in footwear. In each sector, we assume there is a common elasticity of substitution between all three factors. The values assumed for this elasticity are based on Piggott and Whalley (1985) and vary between 0.59 in sectors 321 to 328 and 0.94 in sectors 481 to 483.

The last column of Table 5.1 lists the degree of economies of scale in each industry. In the majority of cases the percentage figure refers the increase in costs as a result of a 50 per cent reduction in output from the minimum efficient scale of output. For those industries with an asterisk the figure relates to the increase in costs arising from a 33 per cent reduction in output from the minimum efficient scale; and for those with a double asterisk a 67 per cent reduction. These estimates are engineering estimates for which the data source was Pratten (1988). Davies and Lyons also used Pratten's estimates of scale economies in their econometric work, although there are some minor differences for some sectors between the numbers we have derived from Pratten for the cost-disadvantage of sub-optimal scales of production and those used by Davies and Lyons.

5.4 Simulating the Labour Market Effects of Trade

The simulation undertaken is to suppose that all EU trade with non-advanced countries (NACs) ceases. For this purpose, 'non-advanced' countries were taken as the rest of the non-EU world, less the USA, Canada, Japan, Australia, New Zealand, and the EFTA countries. In the model, the whole of the rest of the world is treated as a single country. Technically therefore, such a change has to be simulated by raising sector-specific, country-specific non-tariff barriers to external trade until each EU country's external imports and exports in each sector are reduced to the level of their trade with 'advanced' non-EU countries.

Table 5.1. Industry characteristics

Industry		Conc.	VA Share	Shares in Value Added			Returns to scale
				Capital	NonMan labour	Manual labour	
22	Metals	0.17	0.28	0.25	0.48	0.27	1.11*
23	Mineral extraction	0.10	0.50	0.45	0.33	0.22	1.11*
241:244	Clay, cement, asbestos	0.04	0.44	0.37	0.45	0.17	1.25*
245:248	Stone, glass, ceramics	0.06	0.44	0.27	0.46	0.27	1.11*
251	Basic chemicals	0.07	0.31	0.38	0.53	0.10	1.15
255	Paint and ink	0.21	0.35	0.36	0.54	0.10	1.04*
256	Industrial/agricultural chemicals	0.11	0.39	0.40	0.50	0.09	1.15
257	Pharmaceuticals	0.07	0.41	0.40	0.50	0.09	1.15
258	Soap and detergents	0.06	0.30	0.39	0.52	0.10	1.02
259	Domestic chemicals	0.40	0.37	0.34	0.55	0.10	1.15
260	Manmade fibres	0.47	0.32	0.25	0.51	0.24	1.10
311:313	Metal manufacture	0.02	0.43	0.26	0.43	0.32	1.07
314:315	Metal structures, boilers	0.01	0.42	0.21	0.55	0.24	1.07
316	Tools and cans	0.01	0.40	0.30	0.47	0.23	1.07
321	Agricult. machinery	0.05	0.35	0.15	0.64	0.22	1.07
322	Machine tools	0.02	0.47	0.19	0.61	0.21	1.07
323	Textile machinery	0.04	0.41	0.16	0.63	0.21	1.07
324	Food and chemical machinery	0.03	0.43	0.27	0.55	0.19	1.07
325	Mining and constn. machinery	0.03	0.36	0.23	0.58	0.20	1.07
326	Transmission equipment.	0.05	0.47	0.20	0.60	0.20	1.09*
327	Paper and wood machinery	0.03	0.41	0.25	0.56	0.19	1.07
328	Other machinery	0.05	0.39	0.24	0.57	0.19	1.10
330	Computers and office machinery	0.27	0.44	0.34	0.61	0.05	1.07*
341	Insulated wires and cables	0.03	0.31	0.30	0.56	0.14	1.15
342	Electrical machinery	0.02	0.41	0.25	0.60	0.15	1.15
343	Electrical equipment	0.10	0.39	0.25	0.60	0.15	1.05*
344	Telecoms/measuring equipment	0.05	0.45	0.24	0.61	0.15	1.1*
345	Radio and TV	0.06	0.34	0.27	0.59	0.14	1.1*
346	Domestic electrical appliances	0.18	0.35	0.27	0.59	0.14	1.07*
347	Electric lighting	0.47	0.40	0.30	0.56	0.14	1.10
351	Motor vehicles	0.33	0.25	0.20	0.49	0.31	1.15*

Table 5.1. (cont.)

Industry		Conc.	VA Share	Shares in Value Added			Returns to scale
				Capital	NonMan labour	Manual labour	
352:353	Motor vehicle parts	0.08	0.36	0.22	0.47	0.30	1.15*
361:363,365	Ships, rail stock, cycles	0.15	0.36	0.17	0.50	0.33	1.08
364	Aerospace	0.29	0.40	0.19	0.69	0.13	1.15*
37	Instruments	0.09	0.48	0.27	0.57	0.16	1.15
411,420:423	Grains, pasta, bread	0.07	0.26	0.29	0.50	0.21	1.06**
412	Other foods	0.01	0.17	0.30	0.49	0.21	1.05**
413	Meat products	0.03	0.17	0.39	0.43	0.18	1.02**
414	Dairy products	0.02	0.25	0.40	0.42	0.18	1.08**
415	Fruit and vegetable products	0.08	0.23	0.31	0.49	0.21	1.05**
416:419	Fish products	0.05	0.27	0.44	0.39	0.17	1.08**
424:428	Drinks	0.08	0.40	0.48	0.39	0.13	1.07*
429	Tobacco	0.35	0.16	0.59	0.27	0.14	1.02*
43A,B	Wool, cotton, silk, flax	0.02	0.42	0.24	0.46	0.30	1.03
436	Knitting	0.01	0.37	0.28	0.41	0.32	1.03
438	Carpets	0.05	0.33	0.34	0.40	0.26	1.10
439	Misc. textiles	0.05	0.41	0.34	0.40	0.26	1.03
441	Leather tanning	0.01	0.26	0.32	0.38	0.30	1.03
442	Leather products	0.01	0.41	0.25	0.42	0.33	1.03
451	Footwear	0.01	0.38	0.25	0.36	0.39	1.01*
453	Clothing	0.00	0.34	0.25	0.43	0.32	1.03
455:456	Household textiles, fur	0.01	0.35	0.19	0.46	0.35	1.03
461:462	Wood boards	0.02	0.35	0.30	0.39	0.32	1.05
463:465	Other wood	0.01	0.40	0.23	0.43	0.35	1.05
466	Cork and brushes	0.03	0.41	0.25	0.41	0.34	1.05
467	Wooden furniture	0.00	0.37	0.25	0.41	0.34	1.05
471	Paper and pulp	0.03	0.33	0.40	0.37	0.23	1.10
472	Processed paper	0.02	0.33	0.31	0.46	0.23	1.10
473	Print and publishing	0.02	0.45	0.26	0.57	0.18	1.13
481:482	Rubber	0.16	0.45	0.31	0.45	0.24	1.05
483	Plastics	0.01	0.37	0.34	0.46	0.21	1.05
491	Jewellery	0.01	0.39	0.24	0.50	0.26	1.05
492:493	Musical instruments, photos	0.03	0.46	0.20	0.53	0.27	1.05
494	Toys and sports	0.06	0.37	0.35	0.43	0.22	1.05

Alternative assumptions may be made about market clearing. With no price adjustment in either goods or factor markets, the CGE degenerates to a factor-content calculation of the type standard in the literature. A CGE calculation with goods markets clearing but no adjustment of factor prices gives a more sophisticated estimate of the labour market impact of a trade shock, first by allowing intra-EU trade flows to adjust to absorb some of the effects of the changed extra-EU trade, and second by letting goods prices change so that changes in domestic consumption and production can respond to the changed trade. Finally, letting labour markets clear translates the effect of the trade change on the labour market into a pure price change. It is also possible to make alternative assumptions about entry and exit of firms and about goods market segmentation, but they are of no particular interest in this context.

Table 5.2 confirms that this is a large policy change that is being simulated. To save space only an arbitrary subset of sectoral results are shown. The percentage changes in external trade, shown in the second and third row for each sector, reflect the relative importance of 'non-advanced' countries in the total external trade of each EU country, so for example, French extra-EU imports of the products of sector 330 (computers and office machinery) decline by 47.7 per cent, this being approximately the share of NACs in total French extra-EU imports in this sector. Because the trade shock is large, the resulting sectoral output changes are non-trivial, with many of the resulting sectoral output changes, shown in the first row for each sector, being very substantial. Some concerns about the factor market effects of trade are at the sectoral level, and Table 5.2 implies that some of the sectoral employment effects are very large indeed. Even if aggregate employment effects are small, the jobs created by exports may be in different sectors from those lost to import competition. However, if we are considering the medium-run to long-run effects of trade on factor markets, it is appropriate to work with models that assume intersectoral labour mobility and that focus on economy-wide employment or income distribution. It is the results of such models that are presented here.

Table 5.3 uses a standard factor-content calculation to provide our first measure of the effect of the trade change on factor markets. Assuming that the ratio of inputs to output is the same in the production of exports and of import substitutes as in production in general, the table shows the percentage effect on the demand for labour in the manufacturing sector of eliminating both exports to and imports from non-advanced countries and replacing imports with domestic production with no other changes in goods or factor markets.

The fact that all the numbers shown in Table 5.3 are negative implies that trade with non-advanced countries has significant *positive* employment effects in all EU economies. This is a reflection of the positive trade balances, which each EU country has with the non-advanced countries. For the impact of trade on the relative fortunes of different types of labour, one should look at the differences between the last two rows of Table 5.3, which show that in all EU countries, trade with non-advanced countries has a bigger impact on the demand for non-manual than manual labour, as the Heckscher–Ohlin approach would imply. However, the effect is small—for all but one country, the increased demand for non-manual labour relative to manual labour is between 0.4 and 0.7 per cent.

Table 5.2. Sectoral impact on production, external imports, external exports of eliminating trade with NACs, selected sectors (% changes), labour markets clearing

France	Germ	Italy	UK	Neth	BelLx	Denm	Irelnd	Grce	Spain	Portgl
sector	311:313									
−0.4	−0.3	−0.7	−1.2	−0.2	−1.9	−0.4	0.6	0.3	−0.4	−0.1
−49.8	−37.6	−60.9	−54.9	−47.8	−76.6	−14.7	−8.4	−66.8	−66.8	−35.5
−31.8	−49.4	−41.1	−28.7	−45.5	−35.0	−22.4	−17.1	−53.5	−26.5	−32.8
sector	314:315									
−2.5	−1.3	−2.1	−2.0	−4.7	−2.3	−4.8	−1.0	−1.6	−1.4	−2.8
−83.6	−53.8	−82.7	−78.0	−63.7	−86.3	−47.0	−46.9	−96.9	−97.7	−99.3
−20.2	−42.2	−27.6	−25.5	−36.0	−19.2	−34.0	−27.7	−34.0	−27.6	−18.2
sector	316									
−2.5	0.0	−5.2	0.0	0.0	−0.1	−0.8	0.0	−3.9	−1.7	−1.3
−57.6	−40.6	−62.6	−49.6	−48.6	−56.6	−21.3	−30.5	−84.4	−75.1	−50.6
−53.5	−50.5	−45.4	−47.5	−51.6	−46.5	−27.8	−20.3	−60.7	−60.5	−58.6
sector	321									
−2.2	−8.0	−4.9	−18.6	−11.0	−14.1	−5.8	3.2	−8.9	−1.6	−0.3
−45.1	−40.4	−55.9	−46.6	−65.7	−58.2	−38.2	−31.1	−97.4	−92.0	−97.4
−6.4	−21.9	−16.7	−6.6	−17.9	−3.4	−9.6	−18.8	−44.6	−12.5	−9.5
sector	322									
−6.3	−10.1	−8.5	−10.5	−9.9	−3.2	−8.5	0.6	−13.5	−6.5	−8.9
−65.4	−56.8	−76.1	−53.9	−53.8	−66.3	−37.0	−37.7	−85.4	−75.1	−56.6
−12.7	−19.9	−20.9	−12.8	−21.1	−14.7	−11.7	−8.5	−37.5	−15.7	−44.5
sector	323									
−19.4	−35.1	−33.4	−29.9	−25.5	−1.3	−14.6	6.6	−16.7	−14.5	26.5
−62.8	−76.5	−83.4	−76.9	−85.6	−69.3	−54.6	−24.2	−75.7	−88.8	−52.1
−21.3	−31.5	−18.3	−20.4	−36.6	−7.6	−19.3	−5.8	−16.4	−23.2	−16.1
sector	324									
−12.7	−14.2	−20.9	−9.1	−16.6	−5.6	−12.7	1.2	−38.0	−18.1	−7.7
−68.9	−65.1	−75.8	−69.7	−65.2	−74.3	−54.4	−35.4	−87.4	−86.7	−42.5
−7.6	−13.8	−14.9	−7.5	−10.7	−14.8	−3.5	−2.4	−13.9	−8.7	−11.8
sector	325									
−14.4	−8.6	−12.9	−12.4	−3.4	−11.9	−17.2	−3.3	−24.1	−3.0	−0.7
−72.6	−64.8	−86.6	−58.2	−63.6	−57.2	−57.2	−55.8	−95.6	−91.1	−69.3
−12.7	−17.8	−23	−11.7	−10.6	−7.6	−4.6	−3.3	−12.8	−16.7	−10.6

Table 5.2. (cont.)

	France	Germ	Italy	UK	Neth	BelLx	Denm	Irelnd	Grce	Spain	Portgl
sector	326										
	−6.1	−9.7	−1.6	−7.3	−2.0	−15.3	−22.7	2.8	−49.3	−12.7	4.8
	−48.9	−45.2	−45.9	−46.0	−58.5	−47.3	−48.6	−9.1	−96.5	−50.1	−24.9
	−20.9	−19.9	−50.4	−18.9	−12.7	−9.6	−14.8	−23.0	−40.4	−11.6	−19.9
sector	327										
	−13.4	−10.3	−23.6	−12.1	−9.7	1.4	−7.6	2.2	−21.7	−12.5	2.1
	−58.2	−53.3	−70.1	−54.3	−69.5	−52.7	−35.4	−23.3	−90.1	−81.0	−28.3
	−4.5	−7.5	−11.9	−6.6	−4.5	−35.4	−8.6	−1.3	−8.7	−11.8	−9.5
sector	328										
	−17.6	−11.4	−24.5	−11	−25.3	−11.1	−19.8	−2.2	−41.1	−10	−0.7
	−61.6	−54.7	−77.8	−54.6	−68.6	−62.2	−53.0	−39.7	−94.8	−92.1	−82.7
	−7.7	−15.9	−16.0	−14.9	−12.9	−6.7	−6.7	−3.3	−25.4	−18.0	−17.9
sector	330										
	1.2	4.8	5.8	4.2	9.9	2.1	−3.5	3.2	−27.2	−1.3	−16.1
	−47.7	−36.5	−33.5	−26.4	−28.4	−42.7	−18.3	−32.5	−95.5	−53.7	−53.7
	−33.2	−39.5	−43.4	−34.6	−32.4	−27.0	−31.2	−31.8	−50.9	−37.6	−39.4

Table 5.3. Factor content calculation of effects of elimination of EU trade in manufactures with NACs (percentage changes)

	France	Germ	Italy	UK	Neth	BelLx	Denm	Irelnd	Grce	Spain	Portgl
capital	−5.8	−6.5	−5.7	−5.7	−4.8	−5.3	−6.5	−3.2	−4.7	−4.4	−3.0
non-manual labour	−6.0	−7.0	−6.5	−6.1	−5.2	−5.1	−6.7	−3.4	−4.4	−4.9	−2.9
manual labour	−5.5	−6.6	−6.1	−5.4	−4.9	−4.5	−6.3	−2.6	−3.0	−4.4	−2.2

Table 5.4 shows the results of the first true CGE simulation: the impact on demand for factors both in manufacturing and in the economy as a whole of the elimination of trade with non-advanced countries, but now with goods market adjustments. Changes in extra-EU trade will cause in goods markets imbalances between supply and demand which were ignored in the factor content calculation, but which now are allowed to give rise to two kinds of adjustment: in goods prices and in intra-EU trade. For many of the EU countries, particularly the larger economies, the results for the manufacturing sector are not wildly different from those obtained in the factor content calculation. However, the factor content results

Table 5.4. Effect on factor demands in manufacturing and in whole economy of elimination of EU trade with NACs (percentage changes)

	France	Germ	Italy	UK	Neth	BelLx	Denm	Irelnd	Grce	Spain	Portgl
Manufacturing											
Capital	−5.8	−7.2	−5.4	−4.0	−2.9	1.2	−4.2	13.4	1.0	−4.7	7.1
Non-manual labour	−5.6	−7.2	−6.7	−3.8	−3.2	1.2	−3.9	13.6	1.5	−5.3	7.8
Manual labour	−5.1	−6.0	−5.7	−2.6	−3.9	1.9	−2.0	13.0	3.4	−4.5	7.7
All economy											
Capital	−0.5	−0.8	−0.5	−0.3	−0.2	0.2	−0.3	2.8	0.1	−0.5	1.0
Non-manual labour	−1.2	−1.9	−1.4	−0.7	−0.7	0.3	−0.7	5.5	0.3	−1.1	2.1
Manual labour	−0.4	−0.6	−0.5	−0.2	−0.3	0.2	−0.2	2.1	0.2	−0.4	1.0

are reversed for Belgium–Luxembourg, Ireland, Greece and Portugal, where all factor demands increase as trade with the NACs is removed. This must be the result of intra-EU trade replacing trade with NACs. More subtly, the CGE calculation shows a fall in the relative demand for manual labour in Netherlands, Ireland and Portugal as trade with NACs is eliminated, so trade with NACs seems to increase the relative demand for manual labour in these countries, when we take account of changes in intra-EU trade.

The second panel of Table 5.4 presents the changes in relation to the whole economy—broadly speaking the percentage changes are five times smaller viewed in this way, though since the non-manufacturing sector itself adjusts and since the ratio of non-manual to manual labour in the non-manufacturing sector varies across countries, the all-economy changes are not in simple proportion to the changes in manufacturing.

Table 5.5 shows a different simulation of the same trade change, now with factor markets clearing, so that factor market effects show up as changes in wages rather than in factor demands. (Recall that capital is internationally mobile, so that its price does not change.) It is not only the endogenous response of the economy to a trade change that is different between Tables 5.4 and 5.5: the exogenous change itself is also different. The changes in external trade barriers that would generate the changes in external trade and the factor demand changes of Table 5.4, with factor prices fixed, are different from the changes in external trade barriers that would generate the same changes in external trade and the factor price changes of Table 5.5. This underlines the point made by Deardorff and Hakura (1994) and Freeman (1995) that care needs to be taken in the specification of what is exogenous when presenting arguments about the link between two endogenous phenomena.

Again recall that the change being modelled is the elimination of trade with NACs, so Table 5.5 shows that the wages of non-manual workers rise as a result of trade with NACs, though the impact on the level of wages of manual workers is more variable. Comparing the two rows shows that, except in Ireland, trade with NACs depresses the relative wages of manual workers, as one would expect from the Stolper–Samuelson theorem. (Observe that in this simulation, except in Ireland, we do not get the perverse effects that intra-EU trade seemed to have in the smaller countries in Table 5.4.)

Table 5.5. Effect on nonmanual and manual wages of elimination of EU trade with NACs (percentage changes)

	France	Germ	Italy	UK	Neth	BelLx	Denm	Irelnd	Grce	Spain	Portgl
Non-manual	−0.4	−0.5	−0.4	−0.4	−0.4	−0.4	−0.5	−0.1	−0.7	−0.3	−0.4
Manual	0.1	0.1	0.0	−0.1	−0.1	−0.1	0.0	−0.3	−0.4	0.0	−0.4

Table 5.5 shows that all the wage changes are remarkably small. Only one of the changes in wage levels shown in the table and none of the changes in relative wages exceeds 0.5 per cent. These are very small changes given that the experiment being modelled is a rather dramatic one.

The use of a single CGE model to compare the effects of trade with only goods markets clearing (Table 5.4) and with factor markets also clearing (Table 5.5) is somewhat similar to the exercise Krugman (1995) has conducted in comparing 'European' (rigid wage) and 'American' (flexible wage) versions of a numerical model of the effect of trade on labour markets. However, there are significant differences in the modelling undertaken in this chapter. Krugman's rigid wage model is one in which the wage of unskilled workers is fixed; here we consider in Table 5.4 the case in which no wages change in response to labour market disequilibrium, and this makes it difficult to compare my results with Krugman's. Second, the model here is a 'proper' CGE model calibrated to a substantial amount of more or less consistent data, whereas Krugman's model is, as he writes, a 'stylized' model, based on a small amount of data and a small number of given parameters. Finally, Krugman's is a traditional two-homogeneous-good model in contrast with the many-good differentiated-products model here.

This last difference is relevant to the interpretation of the wage changes here. The small effects on relative wages that emerge are in spite of the fact that the model seems to give more scope for such effects than the standard textbook Heckscher–Ohlin–Samuelson model. In the textbook model, so long as there is incomplete specialization, relative wages can change only insofar as 'world prices' change (and a change in the relative prices of goods traded between OECD and the newly industrializing economies (NIEs) is an essential component of the price changes Krugman analyses). With intra-sectoral product differentiation, relative goods prices and therefore relative factor prices can change within a country without specialization or changes in 'world prices' but we see that the Dixit–Stiglitz modelling of product differentiation followed here does not actually give much scope for large changes in relative prices.

This interpretation is reinforced by comparing the results presented here with two other CGE models that have been applied to analyses of the impact of trade on EU labour markets. Cortes and Jean (1996), in a model that is much more aggregated than the one presented here, but in which competition in goods markets is modelled using the same Dixit–Stiglitz approach I follow here, find results that are very similar to those displayed in Table 5.5: a doubling of the size of the rapidly growing emerging countries (that is to say a shock that is slightly smaller in size and opposite in direction to the one modelled here) implies a rise in the real wages of skilled workers in the EU by 0.7 per cent and a fall in the real wages of unskilled workers by 0.1 per cent. By contrast, Nahuis, in a model without imperfect competition, in which trade changes are therefore accompanied by large changes in the terms of trade, cutting off non-OECD trade (a shock very similar to the one modelled in this chapter) raises the relative wage of unskilled workers by almost 10 per cent. However, in the next section, I argue that the principal result of this chapter, that the labour market effects of market effects of EU trade with less advanced countries is modest, is less the result of how competition in world goods markets is modelled than of the basic structure of the modelling of markets.

5.5 Does the CGE Model Capture Skill Differences?

It is not too hard to understand why the model should have produced such small effects of trade on labour markets. Table 5.1 shows that the 'skill intensity' of production, as measured by the relative shares of manual and non-manual labour in value added, varies between sectors to only a modest extent. Table 5.6 shows that at this level of aggregation, even EU–NAC trade displays a fair degree of intra-industry trade. With only limited difference in the sectoral distribution of imports and exports and only limited variation in the sectoral difference in factor shares, it is arithmetically inevitable that trade will have small labour market effects. Intra-industry trade has no labour market effects in this model, because the effects of import changes in a sector are matched by export changes, while inter-industry trade has limited labour market effects because most sectors are fairly similar in their factor input proportions.

However, there are two major reasons to be sceptical about whether calculations at the level of aggregation and with the kind of data used in the model above are adequate to capture the real issues about the labour market effects of trade. This is not to suggest deficiencies in the CGE methodology *per se*, but in any calculations,

whether of factor content, or of the Stolper–Samuelson effects, or of general equilibrium effects, at this level.

The first doubt relates to the treatment of labour skills. Figure 1 in Lawrence and
Slaughter (1993) has a glaring but unremarked feature that should cast strong
doubt on whether their data can be interpreted within a two-factor Heckscher–
Ohlin approach. At the four-digit level, they show sectoral changes in the relative
wages of production to non-production workers that vary between − 55 and 130
per cent. This is wildly inconsistent with a model in which there are two kinds of
intersectorally mobile labour. Further evidence along the same lines is provided by
the data on which the present model is calibrated. If one makes a comparison
across sectors in the INDE data between wages per employee and the ratio of non-
manual to manual workers, one finds a positive association between the two
variables, but the relationship is not nearly close enough to justify a two-factor
interpretation of the data. For the large number of sectors with fewer non-manual
than manual workers, the relationship between the two variables in the graph is
quite weak: in the German 1991 data, for example, the average wage in a sector
can be as much as twice that in a sector with a comparable ratio of non-manual to
manual workers.

The second doubt relates to the treatment in the model of intra-industry trade as
trade in products that are identical in their method of production. At the three-digit
level, but excluding minerals and food production, the Grubel–Lloyd index of
intra-industry trade is 43 per cent for Italy–NAC trade in 1993 (not the same as the
figure shown in Table 5.6 because of different commodity coverage and year).
Thus, almost half of trade consists of offsetting flows of imports and exports
within three-digit sectors, that is to say flows that have zero effect in a factor
content or general equilibrium calculation. However, compare the statistics calculated at the eight-digit CN level. It is not possible to make an exact match between
the product categories chosen for analysis in the two classifications, but the 8,555
commodities in chapters 28 to 99 on the CN classification correspond reasonably
closely with the 83 NACE classes in the three-digit non-food manufacturing
sectors. Now the Grubel–Lloyd index is under 22 per cent, so half of the trade
excluded from the three-digit analysis as intra-industry trade is inter-industry trade
at the eight-digit level. Different eight-digit products with a three-digit sector can
have quite different factor requirements.

Furthermore, at the eight-digit level it is possible to use unit-values (the ratio of
value to weight) as a meaningful indicator of product quality, and to relate product
quality to skill-intensity or capital-intensity of production. (See Abd-el-Rahman
1991, Landesmann and Burgstaller 1997, Torstensson 1991, and others.) In
particular, differences between the unit values of imports and exports of products
in the same eight-digit class can be used to distinguish between horizontal and
vertical intra-industry trade. If the unit values of imports and exports diverge by
more than 15 per cent, this is taken as indicating that imports and exports are of
different quality so that there is vertical intra-industry trade (VIIT); while if
differences of less than 15 per cent indicate horizontal intra-industry trade (HIIT).

Table 5.6. Intra-industry trade in EU external trade, 1991

	France	Germ	Italy	UK	Neth	BelLx	Denm	Irelnd	Grce	Spain	Portgl
EU-NACs	0.49	0.44	0.50	0.53	0.49	0.66	0.43	0.49	0.53	0.47	0.54
EU-DCs	0.74	0.74	0.57	0.72	0.63	0.63	0.62	0.64	0.16	0.49	0.26
EU-ExtraEU	0.70	0.63	0.58	0.70	0.66	0.74	0.63	0.64	0.41	0.68	0.45

The statistics shown are Grubel–Lloyd indices calculated on three-digit NACE trade statistics. The DCs (developed countries) are the non-EU countries not included in the NACs—USA, Canada, Japan, Australia, New Zealand and EFTA countries.

One can further distinguish between VIIT+ trade, where the unit values of the export flow is greater (by at least 15 per cent) than the import unit value; while VIIT – trade describes the case where it is import unit values that are larger.

Of the 22 per cent of Italian–NAC trade that is IIT at the eight-digit level, only 5 per cent is HIIT, 14 per cent is VIIT +, and 3 per cent is VIIT − (the division between the two categories of VIIT reflecting the fact that Italy is more advanced than virtually all the NACs). Thus, whereas 43 per cent of trade is counted at the three-digit level as intra-industry trade that has no factor market impact, dis-aggregation to the eight-digit level suggests that only 5 per cent of trade is actually intra-industry trade in products of the same type and comparable quality. The remaining 38 per cent consists of matching flows of imports and exports, but the matching is either of different products in the same sector or of different qualities of the same product. These two rather different phenomena are what Wood includes in the term 'non-competing imports'; and both have the potential to have significant labour market effects. An attempt to model such labour market effects is made by Smith (1997).

5.6 Conclusions

I aimed in this chapter to explore both methodological and substantive issues in the use of a computable general equilibrium model to study the labour market impact of international trade.

The substantive results of the analysis are very much in line with the mainstream of work on this topic. The direction of the impact of trade on the relative position of manual and non-manual workers in European labour markets is as the Heckscher–Ohlin model would predict: trade with less advanced countries tends to raise the demand for and wage of non-manual workers with opposite effects on manual workers. However, the effects are of small size, suggesting, for example, that trade can explain only a small fraction of the change in European unemployment.

Methodologically, the CGE approach makes several contributions. By offering the possibility of conducting several different types of simulation experiments within one model, the relationship between different existing approaches may be clarified. For example, the results presented here suggest that a factor content calculation of the labour market impact of trade may in some cases be a good approximation to the full impact of trade on labour demands, but in other case may miss very significant effects. Running alternative experiments within a single model also helps clarify the nature of the assumptions being made in the different cases, in particular that the exogenous change must be different in a simulation of a trade change with factor prices fixed from a simulation of the same trade change with factor markets clearing.

The most important conclusion of the chapter, however, is that any model, whether or not of the CGE type, based on the assumptions that goods within a reasonably broad industrial classification are homogeneous and that there is a small number of homogenous factors of production, is likely to miss much of the impact of trade on the relative fortunes of skilled and unskilled workers in advanced economies.

References

Abd-el-Rahman, K. (1991), 'Firms' Competitive and National Comparative Advantages as Joint Determinants of Trade Composition', *Weltwirtschaftsliches Archiv*, 127: 83–97.

Allen, C., Gasiorek, M. and Smith, A. (1996), *Trade Creation and Trade Diversion, The Single Market Review*, Subseries IV: volume 3, Office of Official Publications, Luxembourg.

Alogoskoufis, G. *et al.* (1995), *Unemployment: Choices for Europe,* Monitoring European Integration, 5, Centre for Economic Policy Research, London.

Cortes, O. and Jean, S. (1996), 'Pays émergents, emploi déficient?', document de travail, no. 96–105, CEPII, Paris, March.

Davies, S. and Lyons, B. (eds.) (1996), *Industrial Organisation in the European Union*, Oxford University Press, Oxford.

Deardorff, A. V. and Hakura, D. S. (1994), 'Trade and Wages: What are the Questions?', in J. Bhagwati and M. H. Kosters (eds.), *Trade and Wages*, AEI Press, Washington DC, pp. 76–107.

Dixit, A. K. and Stiglitz, J. E. (1977), 'Monopolistic Competition and Optimum Product Diversity', *American Economic Review*, 67: 297–308.

Freeman, R. (1995), 'Are your Wages Set in Beijing?', *Journal of Economic Perspectives*, 9(3, Summer): 15–32.

Gasiorek, M., Smith, A. and Venables, A.J. (1992), '"1992": Trade, Factor Prices and Welfare in General Equilibrium', in L. A. Winters (ed.), *Trade Flows and Trade Policy after '1992'*, Cambridge University Press and Centre for Economic Policy Research, Cambridge, pp. 35–63.

Gasiorek, M., Smith, A. and Venables, A.J. (1994), 'Modelling the Economic Effects of Interpenetration between the European Community and the Countries of Eastern Europe', *European Economy*, 6: 521–38.

Krugman, P. (1994), *Peddling Prosperity: Economic Sense and Nonsense in the Age of Diminished Expectations*, Norton, New York.

—— (1995), 'Growing World Trade: Causes and Consequences', *Brookings Papers on Economic Activity*, 1: 327–77. Reproduced in this volume.

Krugman, P. and Lawrence, R. (1994), 'Trade, Jobs and Wages', *Scientific American*, 270(4, April): 44–9.

Landesmann, M. and Burgstaller, J. (1997), 'Vertical Product Differentiation in EU Markets: The Relative Position of East European Producers', *WIIW Working Paper*, 234a, Vienna.

Lawrence, R. and Slaughter, M. (1993), 'Trade and US Wages: Great Sucking Sound or Small Hiccup?', *Brookings Papers on Economic Activity*, Microeconomics, 2: 161–226.

Leamer, E. E. (1995), 'A Trade Economist's View of US Wages and "Globalization"', typescript.

Nahuis, R. (1996), 'Global Integration and Wages in a General Equilibrium World Model: Contributions of WorldScan', paper presented to conference on the impact of trade with low-wage economies on employment and relative wages in the EU at the European Institute for Asian Studies, December.

Piggott, J. and Whalley, J. (1985), *UK Tax Policies and Applied General Equilibrium Analysis*, Cambridge University Press, Cambridge.

Pratten, C. (1988), 'A Survey of the Economies of Scale', in *Studies on the Economics of Integration, Research on the 'Cost of Non-Europe': Basic Findings*, Commission of the European Communities, vol. 2, Brussels.

Richardson, J. D. (1995), 'Income Inequality and Trade: What to Think, What to Conclude', *Journal of Economic Perspectives*, 9(3, Summer): 33–55.

Sachs, J. D. and Shatz, H. J. (1994), 'Trade and Jobs in US Manufacturing', *Brookings Papers on Economic Activity*, 1: 1–69.

Smith, A. (1997), 'Quality Differentiation in Production and the Labour Market Effects of International Trade', presented to CEPR/CRENOS/CREI conference on growth, transfer of technology, capital and skills, September.

Torstensson, J. (1991), 'Quality Differentiation and Factor Proportions in International Trade: An Empirical Test of the Swedish Case', *Weltwirtschaftsliches Archiv*, 127: 183–94.

Whalley, J. and Wigle, R. (1996), 'Labour Standards and Trade: Quantitative Estimates', typescript, Warwick University, November.

Wood, A. (1994), *North–South Trade, Employment and Inequality: Changing Fortunes in a Skill-Driven World*, Clarendon Press, Oxford.

6. Trade with Emerging Countries and the Labour Market: The French Case

O. CORTES, S. JEAN AND J. PISANI-FERRY

6.1 Introduction

France is one of the countries in which the trade and unemployment issue emerged at the forefront of public debate in the early 1990s, following the publication of a parliamentary report by Senator Arthuis (1993), which claimed that relocation of manufacturing and service activities in low-wage countries was the cause of massive job destruction in France. In the debate that followed, it became clear that this view was shared by a significant proportion of the 'practical men' (especially among industrialists and trade unionists), but that it was at odds with the conventional wisdom held by most policy-makers and researchers.[1]

At that time, conventional wisdom was that trade with the LDCs had had a small but positive effect on French unemployment. It was mainly based on the results from factor content of trade (FCT) computations, like those carried out by Balassa (1986), Berthelot and Tardy (1978), and later confirmed by the more recent research of Vimont (1993). These results were rather intuitive, because French non-oil trade with LDCs was in surplus and because in the 1970s and the 1980s, this surplus had increased as a consequence of the oil shocks: in a standard FCT methodology, job losses arising from the product composition of trade were not significant enough to offset the overall impact of the surplus. However, they were also open to criticism, both on practical grounds and for theoretical reasons (Cortes and Jean 1995).

The debate around the Arthuis report stimulated further research on the employment impact of trade, with the aim of finding out whether the 'practical men' were right or wrong. Bonnaz, Courtot and Nivat (1994) attempted to take into account departures from the law of one price by assuming that goods produced in the LDCs substitute domestic products in quantity, rather than in value terms as assumed in the FCT methodology (basically, they assumed that shoes produced in the LDCs substituted French-made shoes one-for-one, instead of franc-for-franc). This resulted in an estimation of the effect of trade in manufactures with the LDCs to be a net job loss of 330,000, a figure considered by the authors to be an upper bound. Mathieu and Sterdyniak (1994) relied on a similar assumption for their model-

[1] Allais has, however, been a dissenting voice among the economists.

based calculations of the impact of the Asian NICs' trade emergence, which attempted to measure the medium term macroeconomic effects of this competition. Assuming that 1F of imports from the NICs would crowd out 2F of French production, they concluded that the rise of the Asian NICs had reduced employment in France by about 200,000 between 1973 and 1991.[2] Recent French research therefore reckons the impact of trade with LDCs to be less dramatic than assumed by 'practical men', but significantly more negative than previously estimated.

However, such calculations depend on *ad hoc* assumptions that may capture factors ignored in standard methodologies, but are neither theoretically neat nor empirically grounded. Substitution in quantity is clearly an extreme assumption for partial equilibrium calculations, as it ignores both income and substitution effects from a change in relative prices. Alternative approaches, like that of Neven and Wyplosz (1994), who rely on eclectic methodologies, tend to confirm the earlier view that trade with developing countries has not had an important effect upon wages and employment at the aggregate level, although it has had an impact on specific sectors. Furthermore, the modified FCT calculations undertaken for the French case do not distinguish between skilled and unskilled labour.

This chapter is an attempt to provide additional evidence on the labour market effects of French foreign trade. We begin in section 6.2 by sketching the French labour market situation, showing its peculiarities and comparing its evolutions with those of other industrialized countries. Section 6.3 is devoted to an analysis of French trade, in particular with emerging countries. Special attention is payed to the sectoral composition of trade with different kinds of partners, and therefore to the employment and skill content of the flows. We further link the two issues of trade and the labour market in section 6.4, where we discuss the employment and wage implications of trade in the case of France. Our approach consists of evaluating econometrically the impact of trade on productive structure. Conclusions are drawn in section 6.5.

6.2 Employment Trends and Labour Market Characteristics

The labour market impact of trade with developing countries obviously depends on the importing country's labour market characteristics. As the discussions in Europe and the USA have demonstrated, trade effects can show up in the importing country either as price or quantity changes. In what follows, we highlight a few stylized facts on the French labour market that are relevant for analysing the impact of trade. We then present some statistics on the evolution of employment.

The single most important indicator of labour market problems in France is obviously the unemployment rate, which has been steadily rising since the early

---

[2] Related research focused on the impact of trade with specific countries: using an eclectic methodology, Cadot and de Melo (1995) reckoned that the employment effect of French trade with the world lies between −3,300 and + 6,000 jobs (in comparison with 1990).

1970s and reached 12.5 per cent in 1994 (according to the OECD standardized definition). Although in 1994 a significant part of unemployment was cyclical, both available estimates of the NAIRU and the level of unemployment at the end of the previous expansion phase (8.9 per cent in 1990) suggests that it was mainly structural. Furthermore, a well-known characteristic of the French labour market is the high level of long-term unemployment. Exit from unemployment is especially difficult in comparison with other industrial countries: the monthly exit rate for unemployed persons was 3 per cent in France in 1994, against 37.6 per cent in the USA and around 9 per cent in Germany and the UK (OECD 1995). France therefore more than exemplifies the peculiarity of European labour markets recently stressed by CEPR (1995): although job-to-job movements are significant, outflows from unemployment are of a much smaller order of magnitude than in the USA This is likely to increase the cost of industrial restructuring arising from changes in the pattern of foreign trade, because sectoral job destruction frequently gives rise to long-term unemployment.

Turning to wage dispersion, the basic evidence is that unlike the USA, France has not experienced a widening of the wage differential between low-wage and high-wage workers. According to the OECD (1993), the wage dispersion among men measured by the ratio of the earnings of the fifth decile to that of the first one declined from 1.64 in 1975 to 1.56 in 1985 (and remained at that level thereafter), while in the USA the same ratio increased from 2.44 to 2.63 during the same period. There is a presumption that legal constraints on low wages played a role in reducing wage inequality. In fact, until the mid-1980s steady increases in the ratio of the legal minimum wage to the average wage fostered a narrowing of the wage differential at the bottom end of the wage scale, and the ratio of the average wage to the minimum wage remained roughly constant thereafter (Bayet *et al*. 1994).

A limited widening of the dispersion in the top half of the wage scale did happen during the same period (see the data in OECD 1993), but it was mainly the result of a rise in the level of education among high-wage employees. According to a recent study by Goux and Maurin (1995), the proportion of college graduates (persons with a minimum of two years of education after the *baccalauréat*) among employed men rose from 2.8 per cent in 1970 to 9.0 per cent in 1993. In fact, the same study shows that the return on education has significantly declined over the last two decades. For example, the ratio of the wage of men with more than two years of higher education to that of men without any degree dropped from 3.5 in 1970 to 2.6 in 1993. This evolution clearly contrasts with that of the USA, where the return on education has been rising in spite of a significant increase in the supply of university graduates (Murphy and Welch 1992).[3] As noted by Goux and Maurin, the US 'paradox', that is a rise in the return on education despite an increasing supply of skilled labour, does not appear in French data.

Trade with emerging countries is expected to drive a wedge between high- and

---

[3] It should, however, be mentioned that wage dispersion *within* skill categories increased in the 1980s, especially for managers (see CERC 1989).

low-skill labour. As this effect did show up on prices, we look at quantities. The evidence is that French low-skill workers have been especially hurt by unemployment. Figure 6.1 displays relative unemployment rates by education level for men (data for women exhibit a similar pattern). It is apparent that (i) unemployment is highest among low-skill workers, and (ii) the gap between the unemployment rate of low-skill and high-skill workers has widened over the last 20 years.

Differences in observed unemployment rates by education level can result either from differences in the cyclical responsiveness of employment or from diverging long-run trends. In order to separate the two components, we estimate simple equations of the form:

$$U_i = a_i + b_i t - c_i \text{GAP}(t-1) \quad i=1...6, t = 1971 \text{ to } 1995 \qquad (6.1)$$

where i is the index of the education category, t is a time trend and GAP is the output gap (difference between actual and potential GDP) measured by the OECD (1995).[4] The results of these regressions are given in Table 6.1. The cyclical responsiveness of unemployment and its trend increase are both negatively correlated with the level of education. The trend increase in unemployment is especially high for low-education workers (0.6 percentage points per year), while it is almost negligible (0.07 percentage points per year) for university graduates. (However, it is also apparent that a break occurred in the early 1990s, as the 1992–5 increase in unemployment among university graduates cannot be explained by the equation.)

Unemployment data therefore do indicate that, at least until the early 1990s, the labour market for high-skill workers was close to equilibrium, while low-skill workers suffered from rapidly rising unemployment.

This brief survey suggests that in order to investigate the possible effects of trade upon the French labour market, observations should concentrate on quantity rather than price changes, and on low- and medium-skill unemployment rather than total unemployment. This leads us to question the relevance in the French case of the standard objection to the FCT methodology, namely that trade flows are at best an indirect indicator of the labour market effect of trade. This objection stems from the fact that in a standard HOS setting, the channel of transmission from world product markets to the domestic labour market is essentially a price channel. Therefore, the FCT approach can possibly be totally misleading, if markets can be considered contestable (Leamer 1994).[5] Although this view has a considerable appeal in theory, we do not consider it very useful for investigating the impact of

---

[4] GAP $(t-1)$ is used in the equation instead of GAP (t) because unemployment by education level is measured in March of each year.

[5] Under HOS assumptions, the labour market effects of a rise in the intensity of foreign competition can fail to be fully reflected in the factor composition of trade if goods markets are contestable (which leads producers in rich countries to cut their price in response to foreign competition, without any prior change in trade flows) and the degree of substituability between factors in the production of goods is low. At the extreme, with Leontief technology and flexible labour markets, factor price equalization could take place without any change in trade flows.

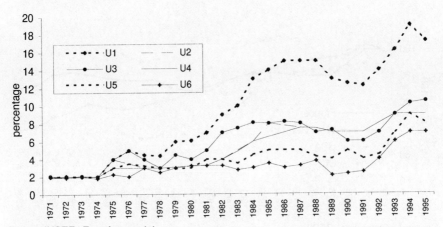

Source: INSEE, *Enquête emploi*.
Categories are ranked from 1 to 6 according to the level of education. Categories are: (1) without degree; (2) *Certificat d'études*; (3) BEPC; (4) CAP or BEP; (5) *baccalauréat*; (6) university degree.

Fig. 6.1. Relative unemployment rates by education level, men, 1975–95

Table 6.1. Cyclical responsiveness and trend increase of unemployment by education level, 1971–95

Education level	1	2	3	4	5	6
Cyclical responsiveness (c_i)	0.75	0.36	0.60	0.47	0.47	0.22
Trend (b_i)	0.61	0.28	0.23	0.26	0.18	0.07

Note: Equation for category 6 (university graduates) includes a dummy variable for 1992–5; without this dummy, the time trend increases to 0.12 and the cyclical responsiveness to 0.32.

Method: Ordinary least squares; all coefficients are significant at the 95 per cent level.

trade on an economy whose labour market is far from being flexible, and which has been for long protected from the low-wage countries' competition. We therefore turn to the analysis of the employment effect of trade.

The basic reason for investigating this effect is that employment in the tradables sector has been declining for two decades. As most industrial countries, France experienced a decline in manufacturing employment in the 1980s and 1990s. As shown in Figure 6.2, this decline was more pronounced than in the USA and in Germany, but less than in the UK. Job losses were especially significant in the steel industry, textiles and clothing, and the footwear industry: in these three branches, employment decreased by more than 50 per cent between 1973 and 1993 (Annex Table 6.1). As the last two of these industries have been facing increasing

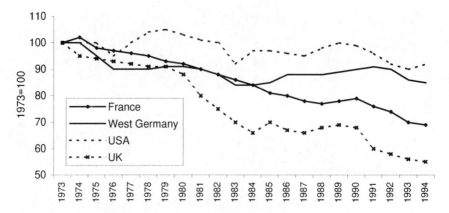

Source: National data, CEPII.

Fig. 6.2.   Employment in manufacturing, 1973–92

competition from LDCs, trade falls among the natural candidates for explaining the decline in manufacturing employment.

Changes also occured in the structure of employment. In accordance with the common pattern observed in industrial countries, the skill composition of employment rose in France during the last two decades. A standard way to evaluate the contribution to this rise of (possibly trade-induced) changes in the industrial structure is to decompose these shifts in the skill composition of labour demand into changes that occurred between industries, and those that occurred within industries.

To carry out this decomposition, we distinguish within each industry of the 'NAP100' industrial classification (100 industries) two skill categories: manual workers or employees ('unskilled workers' category), and employees with some responsibility or technicality (grouped in the 'skilled workers' category).[6] We decompose the changes in the skill composition of the employed labour force in the standard way, already used by Berman *et al.* (1993) for the USA, and by Machin (1994) for the UK. The principle is to break down the changes into a term

---

[6] The separation is based on the 'DE3' French classification of socio-professional categories. The 'unskilled workers' category is composed of: *agriculteurs, ouvriers qualifiés, ouvriers non qualifiés, employés qualifiés* et *employés non qualifiés*. The 'skilled workers' include: *ingénieurs, techniciens, cadres tertiaires moyens, cadres tertiaires supérieurs*. The source of the data is 'Structure de l'emploi', a survey made by INSEE. Nevertheless, the socio-professional categories classification used in the survey changed in 1984. Data after that year had then to be computed in the previous classification from the more detailed level, to preserve the homogeneity. Even proceeding this way, some trouble subsisted. We then had to make a global adjustment on the data prior to 1984 for each industry, to ensure that 1983's share of skilled workers corresponded to the 1984 to 1986 linear retropolation.

relating to the reallocation between industries and another corresponding to shifts in qualifications within each sector:

$$\Delta S = \sum_i \bar{l}_i \, \Delta S_i + \sum_i \bar{S}_i \, \Delta l_i \tag{6.2}$$

where S (for skill) is the share of skilled labour in total labour force, S_i is the share of skilled labour in industry i's labour force, and l_i is the share of industry i in total employment (a bar over a variable denotes the mean over time). The first term reflects changes in the skill composition of labour due to changes that occurred within industries. The second term corresponds to changes that can be ascribed to changes in the industrial structure. The results are reported in Table 6.2.

The within-industry component explains at least 55 per cent of total change, and up to 90 per cent for manufacturing. The significance of the 'between' component for the economy as a whole can be ascribed to the relative decline of employment in manufacturing and agriculture and to the rapid growth of several (non-traded) services, where average labour skill is far higher than in the other sectors: finance, insurance, telecoms, and services to enterprises. For manufacturing, where we could expect trade-induced adjustments to give rise to significant intersectoral effects, the 'between' component explains a very minor part of total change.

Similar decomposition was carried out by Berman *et al.* (1993) for the USA, and by Machin (1994) for the UK (Table 6.3), in both cases for manufacturing. The results are of similar orders of magnitude: in manufacturing industries, total rates of change in France and the USA are comparable (they are significantly lower in the UK). We also observe an acceleration of the phenomenon in the last period for both the USA and France. All three studies lead to the conclusion that the within-industry component is by far the most important in explaining the upgrading of skills in the manufacturing industry. The result is even more pronounced in our case: in the second period, the within-industry component reaches 90 per cent of total change. Nevertheless, we should stress that the comparison has an aggregation bias: a higher level of aggregation leads, *ceteris paribus*, to an increase in the share of the within-industry component. The number of manufacturing industries considered is 450 in the case of the USA, 100 for the UK, but only 33 for France. Although it is difficult to measure the magnitude of the bias, it could certainly contribute to explaining the differences between the results.

These calculations therefore give us two interesting pieces of information. First, changes in the skill composition of the manufacturing labour force has been rapid in France, specially during the 1980s, with a rhythm comparable to that of the USA. Second, like the UK and the USA, the changes have overwhelmingly taken place within industries. This does not suggest that trade has been a major force at work. Before investigating this issue further, we look at the magnitude and the structure of French trade with emerging countries.

Table 6.2. Decomposition of the increase in the share of skilled workers in the labour force (percentage per annum)

For the economy as a whole

Period	Within	Between	Total	Within/total (%)
1975–84	0.295	0.216	0.535	55.1
1984–93	0.452	0.231	0.610	74.1
1975–93	0.368	0.221	0.558	65.8

Note: Sectors S75 (telecommunications and post) and S90 (general administration) are excluded from the study.

For manufacturing industries only

Period	Within	Between	Total	Within/total (%)
1975–84	0.389	0.082	0.468	83.1
1984–93	0.552	0.065	0.614	89.9
1975–93	0.462	0.073	0.529	87.2

Source: INSEE, DARES, calculations of the authors.

Note: All calculations have been annualized, and all results are expressed in percentage points. Residuals are not reported.

Table 6.3. Decomposition of the changes in the share of skilled labour in manufacturing employment in the USA and the UK

United States (Berman *et al.* 1993)

Period	Within	Between	Total	Within/total (%)
1959–1973	0.078	− 0.009	0.069	113.0
1973–1979	0.187	0.112	0.299	62.5
1979–1987	0.387	0.165	0.552	70.1

United Kingdom (Machin, 1994)

Period	Within	Between	Total	Within/total (%)
1979–1990	0.301	0.066	0.367	82.0

Note: All calculations are annualized, and results are expressed in percentage points.

6.3 French Trade with Emerging Countries[7]

In comparison with other industrialized countries, France has not been experiencing an especially rapid increase in the penetration of products originating in low-wage countries (Figure 6.3). The rise of this new competition on the domestic market has been much less dramatic than for the USA, and the penetration ratio also remains below those of the UK or Germany. This can, at least in part, be ascribed to trade protection measures like those implemented in the framework of the Multi-Fiber Agreement.

A second significant difference with the USA is that French trade in manufactures with emerging countries (and more generally LDCs) remains in surplus. It has declined since the mid-1980s, in large part as a counterpart of the reduction in the energy surplus of oil-producing countries, but still represented 0.3 per cent of French GDP *vis-à-vis* emerging countries, 0.1 per cent of GDP for eastern Europe and the FSU, and 1.3 per cent of GDP for the other developing countries. This is why standard FCT calculations frequently exhibit a job-creating effect of trade with LDCs.

Over the last two decades, French imports of manufactured products from non-industrialized countries have grown from a negligible 0.5 per cent of GDP to 1.4 per cent (Figure 6.4). Most of this increase was due to the increased penetration of exports from the dynamic emerging countries of East Asia, Latin America and the Mediterranean region, while trade with other developing countries and the countries of central and eastern Europe has been stagnant. However, the bulk of French imports still originates from developed market economies, which amounted to 9.6 per cent of French GDP in 1993.

Standard trade theory leads to the expectation that trade with low-wage countries is predominantly of the inter-industry, rather than of the intra-industry type, as it is the case between industrialized countries. To test this hypothesis, we rely on a methodology initiated by Abd-El-Rahman (1986a, 1986b) and further developed by Freudenberg and Müller (1992) and Fontagné, Freudenberg, Péridy and Ünal-Kesenci (1995).[8] The principle of the method is to carry out a detailed analysis of French bilateral trade flows at the eight-digit level (10,000 products) and to decompose total trade with each partner into three categories:

- *one-way trade* if $X_{ij}^k < 0.1X_{ji}^k$ or $X_{ij}^k > 10X_{ji}^k$, where X_{ij}^k is the flow of product k from country i to country j, that is if the minority flow (for

---

[7] The 'emerging economies' category consists of the following countries: Brazil, Colombia, Mexico and Venezuela in Latin America; China, Hong Kong, Indonesia, Korea, Malaysia, the Philippines, Singapore and Taïwan in Asia; and Israel, Morocco, Tunisia and Turkey in the Mediterranean region. These countries were selected on the basis of their comparative export performance in world markets (see CEPII 1995).

[8] We are grateful to Michael Freudenberg for his assistance in the implementation of this method.

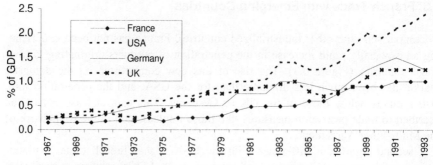

Source: CEPII, CHELEM Database.

Fig. 6.3. Imports of manufactures from emerging countries, selected countries, 1967–93

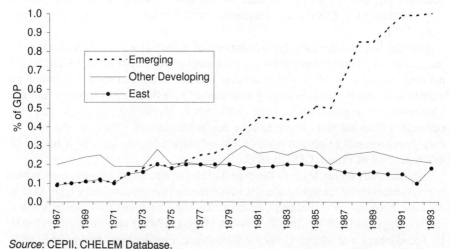

Source: CEPII, CHELEM Database.

Fig. 6.4. French imports of manufactures from emerging countries, 1967–93

example imports) represents at less than 10 per cent of the majority flow (for example exports);

- *two-way trade in similar products* if $0.1X_{ji}^k \leq X_{ij}^k \leq 10X_{ji}^k$ and $0.85p_{ji}^k \leq p_{ij}^k \leq 1.15p_{ji}^k$, where p_{ij}^k is the unit value of X_{ij}^k, i.e. if export and import unit values differ by less than 15 per cent;
- *two-way trade in vertically differentiated products* otherwise.

This method improves standard measures of the intensity of intra-industry trade, by taking into account the similarity of products (as measured through prices) as well as the overlap of trade, as when using a Grubel–Lloyd index. In fact, the degree of the overlap of trade is captured by the share of one-way trade in total trade, which is highly correlated with the Grubel–Lloyd index.

Table 6.4 displays the composition of French trade in manufactures[9] with emerging as well as with industrialized countries. As expected, trade with emerging countries is overwhelmingly of the one-way type, while such trade represents only one-third of total trade with industrialized countries.[10]

Looking at the structure of trade with individual partners, theory suggests that the share of intra-industry trade between France and any partner country depends positively on (i) the degree of development of the partner country, and (ii) its size. We therefore regress the share of one-way trade in French trade on the GDP per capita of the trading partner, measured at PPP exchange rates, and on its GDP:

$$OW_j = -0.21 \log(y_j) - 0.1 \log(Y_j) - 0.29 \ eu_j \qquad n = 50, R^2 = 0.67 \qquad (6.3)$$
$$(3.5) \qquad\qquad (3.1) \qquad\qquad (12.2)$$

where y_j is the PPP GDP per capita of country j and eu_j is a dummy variable for countries participating in the European union.

Equation (6.3) implies that doubling the GDP per capita of a partner country reduces the share of one-way trade by six percentage points, and that doubling its absolute size reduces it by three percentage points. Participation in the EU (which may capture a distance factor, rather than a specific feature of European integration) reduces the share of one-way trade by almost 30 percentage points. According to equation (6.3), the share of one-way trade with emerging countries whose GDP per capita is 15 per cent of the French level is almost 50 percentage points higher than for a developed European country. This broadly confirms the view that trade with low-wage countries is of a different nature than trade with developed countries.

The next step in the analysis is to examine whether French foreign trade conforms to comparative advantage by carrying out a decomposition of trade flows by type of trade partner and by skill composition of products. For this purpose, we follow a method experimented by Sachs and Schatz (1994) for the analysis of US trade. We rank the trade partners of France according to their 1992 GDP per capita

---

[9] Trade in 'other transportation equipment' is excluded because it includes a large part of inward–outward processing. The sample is limited to the first 50 trade partners of France in order to avoid giving an excessive weight to smaller countries for which trade flows are quantitatively insignificant.

[10] The relationship between the two measures is captured by a simple equation:

$$GL_j = -0.61 OW_j + 60.5 \qquad n = 50, R^2 = 0.99$$
$$(66.2) \qquad (83.1)$$

where GL_j (resp. OW_j) is the Grubel–Lloyd index of (respectively the share of one-way trade in) bilateral French trade in manufactured goods with country j, for the 50 major exporters of manufactures to the French market.

Table 6.4. Structure of French Trade in Manufactures, 1994 (in percentages)

	Trade with Industrialized Countries	Trade with Emerging Countries	Total Trade
One-way trade	33.8	87.4	41.0
Two-way trade in vertically differentiated products	47.0	11.2	42.3
Two-way trade in similar products	19.1	1.3	16.8
Total	100.0	100.0	100.0

Source: Based on EUROSTAT data.

(measured at PPP exchange rates), and we group them into rough groups. The first group comprises 'relatively poor' countries, whose GDP per capita was below 80 per cent of the French level in 1992. It includes all LDCs, plus some industrialized countries like Ireland, Portugal and Spain. The remaining countries are split into two categories, depending on the level of their per capita GDP compared with that of France: we label 'intermediate' countries those whose 1992 GDP per capita was below that of France, and 'rich' countries the remaining ones.

We also rank industries according to the skill composition of the labour force and group them into nine categories, each of which represents one-ninth of French foreign trade. We then use the resulting matrices X_{ik} and M_{ik} to compute the contribution of each category to the French trade balance as follows:

$$CS_{ik} = \frac{1000}{GDP}\left((X_{ik} - \frac{Q_k}{Q}X_i) - (M_{ik} - \frac{D_k}{D}M_i)\right) \qquad (6.4)$$

where
X_{ik} are exports of product category k to country group i
M_{ik} are imports of product category k from country group i
Q_k is French production of good k
D_k is French demand of good k
Q is total French manufacturing production
D is total French demand for manufactures

The first term on the right-hand side of equation (6.4) can be regarded as a difference between two indicators: a contribution to exports which represents the difference between actual French exports of good k to country i and the hypothetical value of the same flow in world without comparative advantage. This indicator is measured in tenth of thousandths of GDP. Note that by definition, $\Sigma_k CS_{ik} = 0$.

The results of these calculations are presented in Table 6.5. As expected, trade with relatively poor countries exhibits deficits in low-skill industries and surpluses in high-skill industries. Thus, trade with these countries broadly conforms comparative advantage. Furthermore, the trade deficit is concentrated in the first sector which includes clothing, wearing apparel, wood and some food products. A similar pattern emerges with intermediate countries, with which French trade exhibits deficits for all low-skill industries and surpluses for all high-skill industries. However, the degree of specialization as measured by the contribution to the trade balance CS_{ik} is less pronounced. Finally, trade with the rich countries does not confirm a clear pattern of comparative advantage. It should be noted, however, that this group consists of countries (especially Germany) whose GDP per capita is very close to that of France.

Since trade seems to follow comparative advantage, we now present the employment and skill contents of French trade flows with major trade partner categories.[11] To measure the factor content of imports, we assume that domestic products and imports are perfect substitutes within any given product category; therefore, 1FF of imports displaces 1FF of domestic production. We do not differentiate between average and marginal employment coefficients either. We do agree with that these are heroic assumptions, and furthermore we are ourselves critical of the FCT method (Cortes and Jean 1995). Nevertheless, we consider it a useful benchmark.

Table 6.6 gives the results of the calculations for three different years (1977, 1985 and 1993), the same two categories of labour as before (skilled and unskilled), and two categories of trade partners (relatively poor countries, and intermediate and rich countries—we do not distinguish between the latter two). We also report the results of the same calculations for the 'emerging countries' group.[12]

In 1993, the net employment balance was positive for total trade, as well as for trade with 'relatively poor' countries, while it was negative for 'intermediate and rich' countries and close to zero for emerging countries. This result, which is consistent with that of other studies (Bonnaz *et al.* 1994; Vimont 1993), essentially reflects bilateral surpluses and deficits, which are not offset by small differences in employment coefficients between trade partner. It is worth noting that our 'relatively poor countries' category is quite large, as it includes for instance eastern and southern European countries (including Spain, Portugal and Greece, as well as Ireland). Therefore, French trade with the 'other countries' is not very specialized, and not always in the way predicted by the factor proportion theory: the main French imports from these countries consist of clothing and leather goods, but also of automobiles, electronics or basic chemicals.[13] For emerging countries, however, the employment coefficient of exports is clearly inferior to the employment content

---

[11] We use the method of the total employment content of trade, taking into account not only the employment embodied in the value added, but also inter-industry linkages represented by the input–output matrix, and we carry out the calculations at the 'NAP100' level.

[12] See footnote 7 above.

[13] This lack of specialization was obvious in 1977, and has been weakening ever since.

Table 6.5. Contributions to the French trade balance in manufactures, 1992

Industry groups	Country groups		
	relatively poor	intermediate	rich
1	− 67	− 5	27
2	− 4	− 19	9
3	1	− 20	− 8
4	− 10	− 3	8
5	7	32	− 5
6	14	8	− 17
7	16	4	− 1
8	9	4	8
9	33	− 2	− 22
Share of French trade	13%	45%	42%

Source: authors' calculations based on CHELEM-CEPII trade data and INSEE employment and production data.

of imports. Therefore, a balanced trade of the order of magnitude of one percentage point of GDP (FF 80bn) with this trade partner should result in a net 'loss' of 25,000 jobs, a significant number but hardly a major cause of unemployment.

Turning to the skill content of trade, the pattern of comparative advantage is apparent in trade with emerging countries and 'intermediate and relatively poor countries', as the relative skill content of exports significantly exceeds that of imports: the average employment content of a FF 1bn (balanced) trade with emerging countries is nil for skilled labour, but a negative 330 jobs for unskilled labour; this confirms that unskilled labour suffers from that trade, while skilled labour does not. The pattern is also apparent but less pronounced for the 'intermediate and relatively poor countries' group, for which the average employment contents are respectively + 50 and − 160.

Finally, Table 6.6 shows the evolution over time of the factor content of trade. Three remarks can be made. First, the net employment content of total trade declined from +385,000 persons per year to + 122,000 between 1977 and 1993. This loss was concentrated in unskilled labour (− 245,000), whereas the net skilled labour content of trade remained roughly constant. Second, the most significant cause of this loss was the worsening of the trade balance with the 'relatively poor countries' group (that can be in part ascribed to the drop in OPEC imports of manufactures), which resulted in a 'loss' of 350,000. Finally, it is worth noting that the average skill content of trade with emerging countries has been deteriorating over time, as the skill content of imports (relative to total trade) has risen, while the skill content of exports has declined.

As noted above, part of the decrease in the employment content of trade can be

Table 6.6 Factor content of foreign trade, various partners, 1977–93

	Total Labour			Skilled labour			Unskilled labour		
	1977	1985	1993	1977	1985	1993	1977	1985	1993
Factor content of trade (thousands)									
Total trade	385	274	122	75	81	58	310	193	65
Trade with intermediate and rich countries	− 226	− 154	− 136	− 47	− 28	− 42	− 180	− 127	− 94
Trade with relatively poor countries	612	428	259	121	109	99	490	319	159
Trade with emerging countries	73	55	14	17	20	14	567	36	0
Employment content of FF1bn exports (thousands)									
Total trade	8.85	3.19	2.29	1.51	0.71	0.68	7.34	2.48	1.61
Trade with intermediate and rich countries	8.83	3.13	2.28	1.46	0.69	0.67	7.37	2.44	1.61
Trade with relatively poor countries	8.89	3.32	2.33	1.60	0.75	0.70	7.29	2.57	1.62
Trade with emerging countries	8.61	3.18	2.24	1.61	0.79	0.72	7.00	2.38	1.52
Employment content of FF1bn imports (thousands)									
Total trade	8.87	3.21	2.33	1.48	0.69	0.67	7.39	2.53	1.66
Trade with intermediate and rich countries	8.76	3.18	2.30	1.49	0.69	0.68	7.27	2.49	1.62
Trade with relativerly poor countries	9.45	3.37	2.43	1.39	0.66	0.65	8.06	2.70	1.78
Trade with emerging countries	10.53	3.65	2.56	1.57	0.74	0.71	8.97	2.91	1.85
Relative employment content of imports (%)									
Total trade	100.2	100.7	101.6	97.6	96.5	98.5	100.7	101.9	103.0
Trade with intermediate and rich countries	99.3	101.7	101.0	102.3	99.9	101.3	98.7	102.2	100.9
Trade with relatively poor countries	106.2	101.4	104.5	86.9	88.6	92.0	110.5	105.1	110.0
Trade with emerging countries	122.4	114.9	114.2	97.3	93.2	98.0	128.1	122.2	121.8

Source: Authors' calculations based on INSEE, DARES, and CHELEM-CEPII data.

ascribed to changes in the overall or the bilateral trade balance(s). Economists do not tend to consider such developments as being an effect of trade. Rather, they emphasize (i) that changes in the global trade balance result from macro, rather than micro causes, and (ii) that bilateral balances are irrelevant. Practical men, however, generally consider job losses that result from changes in the trade balance (globally or *vis-à-vis* a given country) as an effect of trade. To a certain extent, the figures in Table 6.6 help to understand why the practical man's view of the issue differs so much from that of the economists: for the latter, the main lesson from the table is that employment coefficients do not differ widely, and therefore that the labour market impact of a balanced increase of trade can be considered minor; for the former, that trade did result in significant job losses, especially for low-skill labour.

The evidence presented in this section highlights the intersectoral nature of trade with relatively poor countries, whereas trade with rich countries is rather of the intra-industry type. But the pattern of specialization with relatively poor countries concerned only a limited number of industries: only the least-skill intensive industries exhibit a high import penetration ratio. Furthermore, some inter-industry trade takes place with rich countries, especially with the least developed among them.

6.4 Trade and Employment: Further Evidence

As French trade with emerging countries is overwhelmingly of the inter-industry type, the basic framework for analysing the labour market effects of this type of trade is provided by the Heckscher–Ohlin–Samuelson approach. In the standard HOS model, the removal of barriers to trade between rich that is well endowed with human capital) countries and poor (that is relatively endowed with unskilled labour) countries results in an upward change in the relative price of skill-intensive versus non-skill-intensive goods, in a rise in trade of skill-intensive for non-skill-intensive goods, and in a drop in the relative price of unskilled labour in the rich countries—or in a rise in unemployment of this category of labour if prices are prevented from clearing the market.

As a number of authors have argued (see for example Lawrence and Slaughter 1993; Leamer 1993, Sachs and Schatz 1994, Wood 1994), this framework is the appropriate one to carry out an empirical analysis. As the ongoing debate on the trade effects of employment shows, it however requires some qualifications and adjustments, and empirical implementations are fraught with difficulties (see Cortes and Jean 1995 for a detailed survey).

A first difficulty arises from the implicit competitive labour markets assumption. Assume for example that skills are industry-specific, or that industries are geographically concentrated and that interregional labour mobility is low, and that wages are set by a negotiation between employers and unions. A rise in the intensity of foreign competition could result in a decrease in the industry's relative wage, rather than in a decrease in the industry's employment. As stressed by Krugman (1995), another downward bias that can be especially significant for Europe could result from permanent unemployment: if laid-off workers end up in long-term unemployment, the effect of trade is to increase the NAIRU, that is to lower the economy's aggregate supply. This affects the measured effect of trade upon the labour market.

Data limitations have prevented us from testing for the existence of industry-specific wage adjustments. They may have played a role, but the existence of a general minimum wage puts a limit on industry-specific downward wage adjustments. We suspect that trade-induced increases in the NAIRU may have been a more significant cause of underestimation of the employment effects of trade. Survey data (*enquête emploi*, INSEE) indicate that two years after losing their job, about 50 per cent of former employees remain either unemployed or inactive. The proportion varies depending on the industry, and it can reach 70 per cent in certain industries. But it does not seem to be related to the sectoral trade variables. This could be a promising route for further research, although it is not easy to establish the link between the entry–exit model of the labour market of a given sector and its trade performance.

A second difficulty arises from aggregation bias. A good way to present the related methodological hurdles is to compare the results of standard FCT calculation with the controversial figures provided by Adrian Wood (1994). To that end, Table 6.7 therefore presents both measures for French trade with developing countries.[14]

Table 6.7 highlights the most obvious difficulty arising from FCT measurements, namely aggregation bias. A classical limitation of the standard methodology is that it ignores employment effects of trade within industries. While the HOS framework implicitly relies on a clear definition of what a product is, FCT computations make use of trade and especially industrial classifications, which frequently aggregate different goods in a single category. As comparative advantage leads to the expectation that the goods exported by low-wage countries are more labour-intensive than those exported by high-wage countries, this introduces a downward bias in the measurement of the employment effects of North–South trade. As stressed by Wood (1994), FCT computations confuse non-competing imports (for example T-shirts from East Asia) with proximate products from rich countries (for example fashion polo shirts), although their respective labour and skill contents differ widely. If this is the case, an increase in the import penetration of non-computing products leads to an increase in the skill intensity of the industry. The purpose of Wood's 'non-competing imports' method is to correct for this bias, however his calculations involve some heroic assumptions too.

Finally, traditional FCT computations can also be challenged because they generally assume perfect competition on the product markets. This may lead one to

---

[14] Wood does not provide calculations for France. In Table 6.7, it is assumed that the ratio of Wood's to standard FCT coefficients for the OECD as a whole can be applied to French trade.

Table 6.7. Alternative measures of the employment content of French manufacturing trade with developing countries,1993

	(1) Standard FCT	(2) Non competing imports
French Exports (FFbn)	194	194
French Imports (FFbn)	126	126
Balance (FFbn)	68	68
Employment content of FF1bn exports (thousands)	2.29	2.29
Employment content of FF 1bn imports (thousands)	2.33	7.90
Ratio	101.6%	29.1%
Employment content of exports (thousands)	444.2	444.2
Employment content of imports (thousands)	293.6	995.8
Employment balance (thousands)	+150.6	−551.6

Sources: (1) Authors calculations, with some more sectors for the trade flows as in the Table 6.7, which explains that the employment balance is a bit larger in this case (2) Authors calculations using the ratio of Wood's employment content coefficient to the standard FCT employment content coefficient for the OECD as a whole; see Wood (1994), Table 4.9.

underestimate the labour market effects of trade as changes in the demand for labour within industries are neglected. For example, Driver *et al.* (1988) consider that companies are heterogeneous, and that foreign competition eliminates the least productive ones;[15] therefore, the marginal factor content of trade differs from the average FCT; Wood (1995) raises the more general issue of defensive innovation in response to increased competitive pressures; there is significant anecdotal evidence that supports these views.

Summing up, FCT calculations suffer from a downward bias if trade results in:

1. a shift towards skilled labour in industries where imports are non-competing products, or where the data are biased by aggregation (Wood 1994); or
2. an increase in labour productivity because of non-competing imports or aggregation bias, or if firms are heterogeneous and trade forces the least productive firms to exit the market, or more generally due to imperfect competition on the product markets.

---

[15] Possible reasons for persistent heterogeneity between firms in the same sector include capital market imperfections, lack of competition in the goods market, and protection ('cultivating lame ducks' has for long been used by efficient firms to justify their demand for protection). We are not aware of systematic empirical studies on this subject.

To test for the presence of such additional trade-induced changes in labour demand, we run cross-industry regressions for the manufacturing sector, and test for the impact of trade-related variables upon the industries' labour demand. A more detailed description of these estimates, together with similar regressions for Germany and the USA, are given in Cortes and Jean (1997).

The data correspond to a disaggregation of the French economy into 100 sectors (NAP 100 classification), but we limit our analysis to manufacturing industries. After eliminating services, the primary sector and some problematic industries (armaments, tobacco products, and the energy sectors), we are left with 33 manufacturing industries. Ideally, we would wish to estimate time series x cross-section factor demand equations for the various industries, and to test for the additional effect of trade variables. Given our will to make afterwards similar estimates for Germany and the USA, material constraints and data limitations prevent us from using this methodology; we therefore work on medium-term periods. We were also unable to gather satisfactory capital stock and investment data at this disaggregation level.[16]

No variable relating to labour cost was included. Based on the example of Berman *et al.* (1993), this variable was held not to be exogenous. To be sure, certain categories of labour may be specific to certain sectors, and the relative wages may vary, but the corresponding information seems fairly limited. On the other hand, including such variables may be problematic: trade may have an influence on the level of wages in each sector (see Oliveira-Martins 1993), and differences in average wages are most likely to be linked to differences in skills, even when several categories of labour are identified. It was thus decided not to include labour cost variables in the estimation. However, the estimates were carried out so as to ensure the consistency of the results, with respect to the introduction of a labour-cost variable.

We first estimate test the influence of trade variables on productive efficiency. We run cross-section estimates of the apparent labour productivity. Estimated equations are of the form:

$$\Delta\ln(\frac{L_k}{Y_k}) = a + b\Delta\ln(Y_k) + c\mathrm{TRADE}_k + d\mathrm{RD}_k + u_k \qquad (6.5)$$

where L_k and Y_k are employment and value added at 1980 prices of industry k, RD_k is the share of research and development spending in value added, TRADE_k stands for trade variables, and u_k is the residual. We run separate estimates for the periods 1977–85, 1985–93 and 1977–93, and test for the influence of trade

---

[16] Our database covers employment, share of skilled workers in the labour force, value added and production (at constant and current prices), prices of value added, ratio of import penetration and export intensity. We split trade partners between 'rich' and 'other' countries. Nevertheless, to take into account the fact that we cover here a quite long period, we based the definition on the year 1980: the rich countries are those whose per capita PPP GDP exceed 80 per cent of the French one in 1980. This group includes: the 15 members of the EU less France, Spain, Portugal, Ireland and Greece; Switzerland, the USA, Canada, Australia, Norway, Japan and New Zealand.

penetration ratios (in level and in variation) from various country groups and of export ratios.[17] Results are presented in Table 6.8, where we only report estimates for which all variables are significant at the 90 per cent level.

Table 6.8. Cross-section estimates of logarithmic variation of labour productivity, France

Period	Const	$\Delta\ln(Y)$	$\Delta(MR)$ all	$\Delta(MR)$ rich	$\Delta(MR)$ poor	Dummy 'computers'	R^2aj.	SCR
(8.a) 77–93	0.24	0.50	0.68				0.51	1.359
	(4.32)	(5.83)	(1.83)					
(8.b)	0.21	0.59	1.05			−0.64	0.61	1.050
	(4.04)	(7.19)	(2.98)			(−3.07)		
(8.c)	0.21	0.62		0.49	1.76	−0.70	0.62	0.981
	(4.25)	(7.44)		(0.95)	(2.96)	(−3.37)		
(8.d) 77–85	0.16	0.51	0.30				0.41	0.598
	(3.76)	(5.16)	(0.59)					
(8.e)	0.12	0.62	0.91			−0.51	0.60	0.397
	(3.39)	(7.20)	(2.06)			(−4.02)		
(8.f)	0.12	0.63		0.57	1.68	−0.54	0.60	0.388
	(3.44)	(7.21)		(0.98)	(1.67)	(−4.09)		
(8.g) 85–93	0.11	0.60	0.65				0.55	0.432
	(4.26)	(6.34)	(1.92)					
(8.h)	0.11	0.64		0.03	1.20		0.56	0.398
	(4.29)	(6.58)		(0.06)	(2.35)			

Notes: *t*-statistics are in parentheses. The equation estimated corresponds to the general form given in equation (6.5). The number of observations is 36. '$\Delta(MR)$' is the variation of the import penetration rate respectively for 'all' partners, for the 'rich' ones and for the 'poor' ones, 'Dummy computers' is a dummy variable for the office machinery industry (including mainly computers). These results concern goods producing industry, except energy, mining and quarrying.

Source: DARES, INSEE, calculations from the authors.

The basic equation includes a constant term (which may be interpreted as representing autonomous labour productivity gains). It is always positive, and corresponds to an increase in the labour productivity of 1.9 per cent per annum in the first period and 1.3 per cent in the second period. We also introduced a dummy variable for computers industry, given the very particular evolution of this industry and the difficulty to measure it correctly, especially at constant prices.

The coefficient of the growth rate of value added ($\Delta\ln(Y_k)$) is always negative

---

[17] We only report estimates for direct employment. Alternative estimates have been run with total (direct and indirect) employment in place of direct employment and/or production in place of value added. This worsens the quality of the estimates.

and of the order of magnitude of 0.5 to 0.6. This reflects the well-known fact that productivity gains are higher in high-growth industries.

The coefficient of the intensity of R&D spending (with respect to value-added) is only weakly significant when a variable for the rate of value-added growth is not introduced into the equation, and not significant at all when this variable is introduced, as in the estimates reported here. It seems that the growth of value-added permits better control of the characteristics of each sector, especially as far as the pace of endogenous technical progress is concerned.

Our main purpose was to assess the impact of trade variables. We have not been able to find any significant effect for export ratios. However, the coefficient of the variations in the total imports penetration ratio[18] by sector is significant and consistent. It means that a one percentage point increase in the import penetration rate induces a 0.65 per cent to 1.05 per cent increase in labour productivity. This corresponds to an important effect, especially given that the total import penetration ratio in the French goods-producing industry rose by more than ten point between 1977 and 1993.

We then tried to investigate whether this effect may differ with the nature of the trade partner. In estimations (8.c), (8.f) and (8.h), two penetration rates are distinguished, according to whether imports come from rich[19] or poor countries.[20] The results are not very clear-cut, because of the lack of precision, most of all concerning the coefficient for rich countries. However, they seem to indicate that the effect could be more pronounced for the imports coming from poor countries, even if this would have to be confirmed with a larger sample (see Cortes and Jean 1997).

This result provides support to the hypothesis that imports do influence efficiency in manufacturing production, as suggested by the non-maximizing behaviour hypothesis, by the firms heterogeneity hypothesis, or by the non-competing imports hypothesis.

We then turn to estimating changes in the labour skill. Estimated equations are of the form:

$$\Delta\ln\left(\frac{S_k}{U_k}\right) = \alpha + \beta\,\Delta\ln(Y_k) + \gamma\,\text{TRADE}_k + \delta\text{RD}_k + \omega_k \qquad (6.6)$$

where S_k (U_k) is the share of skilled (unskilled) labour in industry k, ω_k is the residual, and the other notations are as before. As in the previous estimates, we test for various trade variables, in level and in evolution. The results are reported in Table 6.9.

---

[18] The rate of penetration is given by the ratio of imports to apparent final demand (production + imports − exports).

[19] See note 16.

[20] We also tried to distinguish between emerging and rich countries, but it gives less consistent results.

Table 6.9. Cross-section estimates of the logarithmic variation of skilled to unskilled ratio, France

	Period	Constant	$\Delta\ln(Y)$	$\Delta(MR)$	R^2 aj.	SCR
(8.a)	1977–93	0.35 (8.21)	0.27 (4.05)	0.82 (2.88)	0.40	0.808
(8.b)	1977–85	0.15 (4.93)	0.17 (2.36)	0.98 (2.70)	0.23	0.320
(8.c)	1985–93	0.20 (8.96)	0.30 (3.69)	0.81 (2.79)	0.36	0.321

Notes: Notations are the same as in Table 6.8. *t*-statistics are in parentheses. The equation estimated corresponds to the general form given in equation (6)

Source: DARES, INSEE, calculations from the authors.

The constant term is positive and significant: it points out the independent trend to the rise in skill levels in industrial employment. The growth of value-added stands out in a significant manner, indicating that the skill upgrading has been faster in fast-growing industries. This may result from the existence of skill-biased endogenous technical change, although other interpretations are possible. As before, the coefficient of the intensity of R&D spending is never significant.

The only trade variable that has a significant and robust effect is the variation in the total import penetration ratio. The results show that a one percentage point increase in this ratio is accompanied by a 0.8 per cent to 1 per cent increase in the skilled to unskilled ratio. This may provide support to the non-competing imports hypothesis. However, distinguishing imports from poor and rich trade partners, or from emerging countries, does not provide consistent results, as would be predicted by the non-competing imports hypothesis. This point would therefore need further research.

6.5 Conclusions

Due to the characteristics of the French labour market, the impact of trade regards employment rather than wages. Our FCT calculations show that from 1977 to 1993, developments in trade with countries whose GDP per capita is inferior to that of France have resulted in a job loss of about 350,000 jobs, almost entirely among low-skill workers. However, this 'loss' was in large part due to changes in the trade balance, rather than in the factor content of trade, that is it was due to macroeconomic rather than specifically trade factors. Trade factors alone seem to have played a minor role.

However, we share the doubts of those who claim that the standard estimates of the employment effects of trade suffer from a downward bias. In this study, we have therefore attempted to test some reasons why this standard estimates may be overly optimistic. Our estimates show that, indeed, trade does impact upon the industries' productive efficiency and upon the average skill of their labour demand. The effect on labour skill seems to be rather weak. But our results suggest that the pressure of foreign trade explains 20 to 30 per cent of apparent labour productivity growth observed in French industry between 1977 and 1993. This may have significant consequences on the labour market, but the evaluation of the final impact in terms of employment lies outside the scope of this study. In particular, it would require knowing in what way productivity gains arising from productivity growth are distributed throughout the rest of the economy.

As far as our estimates are concerned, these effects do not seem to be specific to trade with developing countries. Intra-industry trade with developed countries seems to play also an important role in fostering efficiency.

We see at least two possible explanations for this phenomenon. As we saw, trade with rich countries mainly follows a pattern of intra-industry trade, but some inter-industry features are also present: countries whose GDP per capita was between 80 and 100 per cent of the French one benefit from non-negligible comparative advantages in some low-skilled industries. But the main explanation is probably that in the 1980s, external pressures pushed firms to their efficiency frontier and affected their mark-up, and led them to innovate and to introduce new processes. It is also possible that new entrants carried with them new technologies of production. In that game, competition from highly developed countries like Japan, the USA and Germany was certainly instrumental.

There are obviously additional channels that are not taken into account in this study. For example, it does not take into account foreign direct investment. We also mentioned that possible trade-induced increases in equilibrium unemployment should be investigated. But we must also stress that actual trade flows between France and emerging countries are of a very limited size. Indeed the penetration of products originating in emerging countries has so far been limited to some very specific sectors, whose share in the French economy is quite small, and for which adjustments to a large extent already belong to the past. (It becomes more and more difficult to lose jobs in industries like clothes and footwear.) Imports coming from the LDCs may exert a larger pressure on the French economy in the future, but only if their competition turns to concern a wider range of products.

We therefore end up emphasizing a rather obvious conclusion: globalization, in its wider sense, rather than just the insertion of emerging countries into world trade, plays an active role in the changes affecting labour markets.

References

Abd-El-Rahman, K. (1986a), 'Réexamen de la definition et de la mesure des échanges croises de produits similaires entre les nations', *Revue économique*, 1.

—— (1986b), 'La 'difference' et la 'similitude' dans l'analyse de la composition du commerce international', *Revue économique*, 2.

Arthuis, J. (1993), *Rapport d'information sur l'incidence économique et fiscale des délocalisations hors du territoire national des activités industrielles et de services*, Sénat, Paris, June.

Balassa, B. (1986), 'The Employment Effects of Trade in Manufactured Goods Between Developed and Developing Countries', *Journal of Policy Modelling*, 8(3): 371–90.

Bayet, A., Bisault, L. Destival, V. and Goux, D. (1994), *Emploi et chômage des non-qualifiés en France*, INSEE, Paris

Berman E., Bound, J. and Griliches, Z. (1993), 'Changes in the Demand for Skilled Labour with US Manufacturing Industries', *NBER Working Paper Series*, 4255.

Berthelot, Y., and Tardy, G. (1978), *Le défi économique du Tiers-monde*, Report for the Commissariat général du Plan, Paris.

Bonnaz, H., Courtot, N. and Nivat, D. (1994), 'Le contenu en emplois des échanges industriels de la France avec les pays en développement', *Economie et Statistique*, 279–80.

Cadot, O., and de Melo, J. (1995), 'France and the CEECs: Adjusting to Another Enlargement', in R. Faini and R. Portes (eds.), *European Union Trade with Eastern Europe: Adjustement and Opportunities*, CEPR, London.

CEPII (1995), *Concurrence des pays émergents et emploi*, CEPII, Paris.

CEPR (1995), *Unemployment: Choices for Europe*, CEPR, London.

CERC (1989), *Les Français et leurs revenus: le tournant des années quatre-vingt*, Centre d'étude des revenus et des coûts, Paris.

Cortes, O., and Jean, S. (1995), 'Echange international et marché du travail: une revue critique des méthodes d'analyse', *Revue d'économie politique*, 3.

—— —— (1997), 'Quel est l'impact du commerce extérieur sur l'emploi? Une analyse comparée des cas de la France, de l'Allemagne et des Etats-Unis', *Document de travail*, 97–8, CEPII, and *Document d'études*, 13, DARES, French Ministry of Labour, Paris.

Driver C., Kilpatrick, A. and Naisbitt, B. (1988), 'The Sensitivity of Estimated Employment Effects in Input-Output Studies', *Economic Modelling*, 5(2).

Fontagné, L, Freudenberg, M. Péridy, N. and Ünal-Kesenci, D. (1995), 'Intégration européenne et échange de biens intermédiaires', *Document de travail CEPII*, Paris.

Freudenberg, M. and Müller, F. (1992), 'France et Allemagne: quelles spécialisations commerciales?', *Economie prospective internationale*, 52(4).

Goux, D., and Maurin, E. (1995), 'Les transformations de la demande de travail par qualification en France', INSEE, Direction des études et synthèses économiques, *Document de travail*, G9803, June.

Krugman, P. (1995), 'Growing World Trade: Causes and Consequences', *Brookings Papers on Economic Activity*, 1. Reproduced in this volume.

Lawrence, R. and Slaughter, M. (1993), 'International Trade and American Wages in the 1980s: Giant Sucking Sound or Small Hiccup?', *Brookings Papers on Economic Activity*, Microeconomics, 2: 161–226.

Leamer, E. (1993), 'Wage Effects of a US–Mexican Free Trade Agreement', in P. Garber (ed.), *The Mexico-US Free Trade Agreement*, MIT Press, Cambridge, Mass.

—— (1994), 'Trade, Wages, and Revolving Door Ideas', *NBER Working Paper*, 4716.

Machin, S. (1994), 'Changes in the Relative Demand for Skills in the UK Labour Market', *CEPR Discussion Paper Series*, 952.

Mathieu, C. and Sterdyniak, H. (1994), 'L'émergence de l'Asie en développement menace-t-elle l'emploi en France?', *Revue de l'OFCE*, 48.

Murphy, K. M. and Welch, F. (1992), 'The Structure of Wages', *The Quarterly Journal of Economics*, CVII(February).

Neven, D. and Wyplosz, C. (1994), 'Trade and European Labour Markets', unpublished manuscript.

OECD (1993), *Employment Outlook*, OECD, Paris.

—— (1995), *Employment Outlook*, OECD, Paris.

Oliveira-Martins, J. (1993), 'Market Structure, International Trade and Relative Wages', *OECD Working Paper*, 134.

Sachs, J. D. and Shatz, H. J. (1994), 'Trade and Jobs in US Manufacturing', *Brookings Papers on Economic Activity*, 1: 1–69.

Vimont, C. (1993), *Le commerce extérieur de la France: créateur ou destructeur d'emplois?*, Economica, Paris.

Wood, A. (1994), *North–South Trade, Employment and Inequality*, Clarendon Press, Oxford.

—— (1995), 'How Trade Hurt Unskilled Workers', *Journal of Economic Perspectives*, Summer.

Annex Table 6.1. Skill structure and employment in manufacturing, 1977–93

		Share of skilled labour			Employment		
		1977	1985	1993	1977	1985	1993
10	produits de la siderurgie	12.7	20.8	34.6	138 500	91 200	51 300
11	produits de la premiere transform-ation de l'acier	9.3	12.6	15.7	59 600	42 400	26 800
13	metaux et demi produits non ferreux	16.3	20.7	25.9	63 900	55 700	43 600
15	materiaux de construction et ceramique	10.3	13.6	17.1	195 400	136 200	117 500
16	industrie du verre	12.3	11.8	14.1	73 600	58 100	55 000
17	industrie chimique de base	22.4	25.6	33.9	142 000	124 900	103 600
18	produits de la parachimie	30.3	35.2	40.8	116 900	104 000	106 300
19	produits pharmaceutiques	38.2	44.3	57.5	62 200	70 300	79 300
20	produits de la fonderie	11.4	11.5	12.9	106 100	87 100	87 700
21	produits du travail des metaux	12.1	14.8	17.1	456 600	347 200	335 700
22	machines agricoles	16.7	17.9	22.1	56 100	41 500	30 600
23	machines outils	19.7	23.4	27.1	74 500	50 700	41 500
24	equipement industriel	21.3	24.4	28.6	267 000	237 600	211 600
25	materiel pour les travaux publiques et la siderurgie	22.4	27.3	30.8	85 600	64 300	55 300
27	machines de bureau et informatique	7.7	8.8	9.7	4 300	2 400	55 100
28	materiel electrique	18.8	25.7	29.4	201 100	189 400	178 400
29	fabri. de mater. electronique	29.0	39.3	50.9	271 200	254 800	223 600
30	equipement menager	9.6	12.9	18.0	67 800	49 700	39 400
31	automobiles, cycles et motocycles+ferrov	12.7	16.1	21.9	543 000	435 100	360 700
32	construction navale	14.3	16.6	19.1	68 200	54 600	32 900
33	construction aeronautique	38.9	46.3	54.2	114 300	122 000	102 200
34	instruments et materiels de precision	15.8	20.4	25.1	93 000	71 200	67 600
41	boissons et alcools	21.5	23.7	26.9	57 200	50 700	43 200
43+44	fils et fibres artificiels et synthetiques+art.fil+fils nat	8.6	10.7	13.2	351 500	266 300	180 500
45+46	cuirs et peaux+chauss+art. cuir	7.1	8.6	9.5	120 800	90 900	61 300
47	articles habillement+bonnetterie	7.2	8.8	11.0	301 600	195 800	130 600
48	travail du bois	7.9	9.4	11.0	125 800	99 400	94 600
49	meubles	10.1	11.9	13.0	134 000	111 200	95 900
50	papier, carton	10.9	13.2	15.3	132 500	109 900	102 600
51	presse et produits de l'imprimerie et de l'edition	23.8	29.4	34.6	217 900	228 400	234 700
52	pneumatiques et autres produits en caoutchouc	13.6	17.1	21.0	111 800	90 500	86 300
53	produits de la transformation des matieres plastiques	12.1	14.3	16.4	110 400	109 200	121 900
54	produits des industries diverses	14.5	18.3	19.7	121 500	112 200	97 500
	Moyenne	15.9	20.9	26.2	5 077 877	4 206 885	3 656 793

Source: INSEE, DARES, author's calculations.

7. Wage and Mobility Effects of Trade and Migration

JOHN P. HAISKEN-DE NEW AND
KLAUS F. ZIMMERMANN

7.1 Introduction

The persistently high level of unemployment in Europe and the increased share of the working poor have caused considerable concern in industrialized economies. There is also the observation that the relative wages of skilled workers have increased. While there is much debate, there is no agreement on the major causes of these phenomena affecting the European labour markets (see OECD 1994a and 1994b, for a review of the labour market problems in the European context). Recently, two new potential determinants that involve international economic relations have attracted particular attention, namely labour migration and trade. Burtless (1995) and Zimmermann (1995b) provide an overview of major parts of both strands of this literature. However, both debates are largely unrelated to each other.

Labour economists have examined the hypothesis that immigration is causing a decline in wages and increases in unemployment among natives, and that low-skilled workers are being hit the hardest. As reviewed by Borjas (1994) for the USA and Zimmermann (1995a) for Europe, there is not much evidence that supports this conjecture. De New and Zimmermann (1994) found the strongest negative wage effects (for Germany) in the European context, but even they conclude that the response remains in an acceptable range. While Winkelmann and Zimmermann (1993) obtained in their analysis that a larger share of foreign labour had increased the frequency of unemployment of Germans in the 1970s, Mühleisen and Zimmermann (1994) have found no effects for the 1980s.

One of the hottest debates is on trade and the labour markets. While economists like Minford, Riley and Nowell (1995), Revenga (1992), Sachs and Shatz (1994) and Wood (1991 and 1994) strongly support the negative labour market consequences of trade, especially from the Third World, other authors like Baldwin (1995), Berman Bound and Griliches (1994), Bhagwati (1994 and 1995) and Lawrence and Slaughter (1993) are opposed to this idea and claim that the labour market problems were caused by technical progress, among other factors.

There are few studies, such as those of Freeman and Katz (1991) and Borjas, Freeman and Katz (1992), that combine both trade and migration. It is the objective of this chapter to follow this line of reasoning and to combine the two strands of literature. It uses West German micro panel data on employed male earnings and various measures of labour mobility for investigation. A novel feature here is that we are able to differentiate job changes by occupation, inter-firm and intra-firm movements. We further study earnings and mobility of various subgroups of the male labour force, namely blue- and white-collar workers, and low-skilled and high-skilled workers defined by work experience and job status. In this way, we obtain a detailed pattern of the effects of trade and migration on the labour market. We are also able to deal with the important issue of labour market flexibility, and how it relates to trade and immigration.

The chapter is organized as follows: Section 7.2 provides an introduction to trade, migration and the labour market in Germany. Section 7.3 explains the micro data set used in the subsequent section. Section 7.4 reports the findings of the econometric investigations. Section 7.5 concludes.

7.2 Trade, Immigration and the German Labour Market

This section discusses the relevance of trade and immigration for the German labour market. International trade is of substantial importance for Germany, and the relevance has strongly increased over the last decades. Measured in 1991 prices, the share of exports of gross national product of West Germany was 13.7 per cent in 1960 and the respective import share 10.5 per cent. In 1994, the real export share was already 36.1 per cent, and the real import share was 29 per cent. While the trade balance was always positive, its size varied largely with the business cycle. Figure 7.1 demonstrates this for the real trade balance in per cent of gross national product for the 1965–94 period. Unification in 1990 changed this picture significantly in that a large part of the exports was absorbed by East Germany. Figure 7.1 exhibits a declining trade balance for unified Germany, which becomes even negative, while the trade balance for West Germany is developing more strongly than ever. This has implied increased demand for goods produced by West German firms. A 'quick and dirty' conclusion from this is that trade cannot be responsible for the recent problems on the West German labour market.

Figure 7.2 provides a sectoral breakdown of the trade deficit ratio and its evolution over time from 1984 to 1992. The trade deficit ratio is defined as imports minus exports in per cent of the output of the sector, all measured in real terms. (Note that this is minus the trade balance ratio used in Figure 7.1.) As Figure 7.2 shows, this ratio is largely stable in many industries, and this confirms the message provided by Figure 7.1 for the period 1984 to 1992. Only a few industries (mining, textiles, food and banking) have experienced a positive trend in the trade ratio, indicating an increased pressure on the labour market. Some had adjustment problems after unification (food and railways) and some were unstable (education, sport and the public sector). These pictures may suggest that no major problems were caused by trade. However, this is not the right way to evaluate the potential

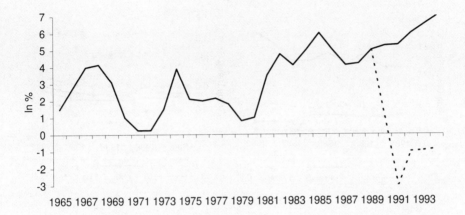

Source: Sachverständigenrat (German Council of Economic Advisors, Annual Report 1994, pp. 360–1. *DIW-Wochenbericht*, various issues. Dashed line is unified Germany, solid line is West Germany only.

Fig. 7.1. Trade balance (exports–imports) in % of GNP

threat of trade for the labour market. If there is enough variation in the data, one may infer from a regression analysis what will happen if imports receive a larger weight holding other relevant factors constant. It is also clear that the real issues are the major changes in the labour market, say from the late 1960s to the 1970s and 1980s and then to the 1990s. However, for such an analysis we would need a larger time-series of micro data, which is not available.

A different way of approaching the subject is to investigate the regional structure of trade and its changes. Table 7.1 provides a picture for the 1990s differentiated according to major regions of trade, including the European Union, the EFTA countries, central and eastern Europe, the USA and Canada, Japan, central and South America, as well as the dynamic Asian economies. It is very clear that by far the most of the trade is with western Europe and North America, although trade with central and eastern Europe, central and South America and the dynamic Asian economies is growing substantially. Nevertheless, it is hard to belief that trade with those emerging markets can be held responsible for the decline of the West German labour market. In 1995, their share of total exports was 16.9 per cent, and their share of total imports was 16.8 per cent.

Trade flows induce demand effects for production of goods and affect native wages and employment. A relative increase in the import pressure may cause rising unemployment rates and declining (relative) wages. A new trade debate associates especially the large increase in the unemployment of unskilled workers (predominantly in Europe) and their declining relative wages (predominantly in the

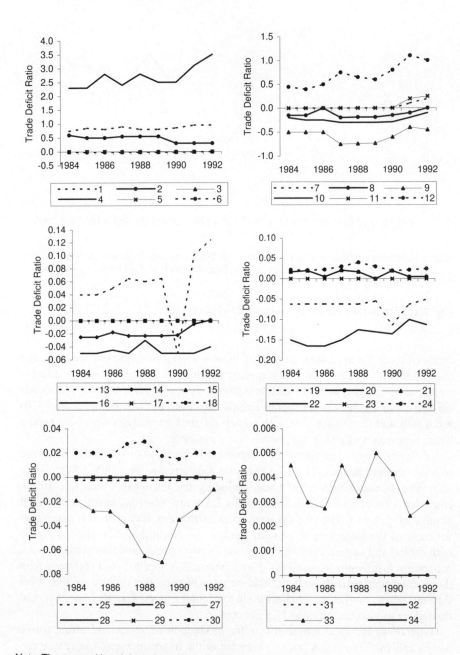

Note: The sectoral breakdown is explained in the Appendix.

Fig. 7.2.   Sectoral trade deficit ratios

Table 7.1. Germany's trade by region, annual growth rates (%)

	1991	1992	1993	1994	1995	Share of total in 1995
Exports (F.o.b.) to						
EU	1.8	0.8	−13.3	9.0	3.3	56.7
EFTA	−2.7	−4.3	−5.5	10.1	6.9	6.3
Central and Eastern Europe	−5.3	−4.6	12.0	13.1	13.3	8.6
United States and Canada	−10.0	0.3	7.6	16.0	0.6	7.9
Japan	−5.4	−11.2	4.9	14.0	6.3	2.5
Dynamic Asian economies	12.3	4.3	15.3	23.3	13.0	5.8
Central and South America	6.2	5.4	6.0	10.7	10.9	2.5
Other	7.0	−7.9	9.2	1.5	4.0	9.7
Total	0.6	0.6	−5.8	10.0	5.3	100.0
Imports (F.o.b.) from						
EU	15.9	−0.7	−16.2	8.5	0.3	54.4
EFTA	7.6	2.3	−4.0	9.8	6.2	6.0
Central and Eastern Europe	20.3	2.1	0.2	21.8	16.3	9.0
United States and Canada	10.4	0.2	−5.3	8.8	4.2	7.7
Japan	22.6	−5.6	−9.2	−0.9	3.3	5.6
Dynamic Asian economies	24.5	−6.0	4.3	8.1	7.6	5.7
Central and South America	3.4	−5.7	−15.5	13.1	3.9	2.1
Other	13.4	−2.7	12.2	4.9	3.2	9.5
Total	15.6	−1.2	−10.0	8.7	3.0	100.0

Source: OECD (1996).

USA) to the increased competition from developing countries' imports. Since trade with developing countries is limited, its relative contribution must be limited. But this ignores the additional impacts of defensive labour-saving innovations, substitution effects in favour of high-qualified labour, and the displacement of labour in services and non-traded-goods sectors that provide goods and services that are needed in manufacturing industries. So far, we know of no emprical study that evaluates the labour market effects of trade for Germany.

Let us now turn to the migration issue. After the Second World War, West Germany became a *de facto* country of immigration (see Zimmermann 1995a and 1995b for a more detailed analysis). First, this was due to the large inflow of ethnic Germans, mainly as a consequence of forced resettlements caused by the war. Second, in the manpower recruitment phase from 1961 to 1973, a shortage of labour, which since the construction of the Berlin wall in 1961 was no longer compensated by the inflow of people of German origin from East Germany, induced a search for foreign workers. A 'guest worker system' was established by means of recruitment treaties with Italy (1955), Spain and Greece (1960), Turkey (1961),

Morocco (1963), Portugal (1964), Tunisia (1965) and Yugoslavia (1968). Whereas the engagements offered were thought to be of a short-term nature, they in fact became largely long-term committments. This process stabilized even after 1973, when in the face of the first oil crisis and a recession, active recruitment policies ended. With this in mind, it is no surprise that the share of foreign labour has typically been about 8 per cent in West Germany in recent years.

West Germany is the most prominent immigration country in Europe. This is supported by Table 7.2, which shows the 1992 breakdown of residents in the member states of the European Union according to nationality. This also offers some clues as to the existence of ethnic networks. About five million people from the EU live in other member states, most of them ending up in Germany, France or the United Kingdom. In 1992, about ten million people or 2.9 per cent of the total EU population was from outside the EU. About 3.2 million are from Turkey and the former Yugoslavia, 2.8 million from Africa, 1.6 million from Asia and 0.7 million from central and eastern Europe. People from areas outside the European Union predominantly go to Germany, and even Asia has a larger group in Germany than the UK. (Many Asians, however, carry UK passports.) Among the major European immigration countries, Germany attracts Turks and people from the former Yugoslavia, France receives Africans, and the UK attracts mainly migrants from the EU member states.

According to Table 7.2, about 74 per cent of all immigrants from central and eastern Europe are in Germany, followed by France, the UK and Greece. Due to historical connections with Hungary, the former CSFR and Bulgaria, Austria seems to be another important receiving country for east European emigrants.

However, the numbers in Table 7.2 do not include immigrants of German origin (ethnic Germans) from eastern Europe called *Aussiedler*, because they automatically become German citizens. As a consequence of the collapse of the socialist regimes, the inflow of *Aussiedler* in West Germany jumped from 78,498 in 1987 to 202,645 in 1988, 377,042 in 1989 and 397,067 in 1990. Consequently, the German government altered the entry procedures for *Aussiedler* in 1990, requiring them to apply for entry before arrival. This measure led to a reduced immigration flow: 221,974 in 1991, 230,489 in 1992 and 218,882 in 1993. In the period 1988 to 1993, 51.2 per cent of the *Aussiedler* came from the former USSR, 35.7 per cent from Poland and 12.2 per cent from Romania. At the end of 1992, 3.5 million ethnic Germans were still living in central and eastern Europe.

It is also true for the German employment statistics that it is impossible to separate out the group of ethnic Germans. Nevertheless, it is instructive to study the level of foreign employment according to ethnic sources and their developments over recent years. Such an analysis is provided by Table 7.3, where we obtain the numbers of foreign workers for 1989 to 1995 for major areas, for example Africa, America, Asia, Australia and, most important, Europe, with a breakdown for the European Union, former Yugoslavia, Poland, Turkey and other Europe. The 1995 share in per cent (column 8 in Table 7.3) exhibits that less than 12 per cent of foreign employment in Germany is from outside Europe. The largest

Table 7.2. Stock of foreign population in 1992 (in thousands)

	Total	EU	Africa	Asia	Central and East Europe	Poland	Romania	former USSR
Belgium	922.5	554.6	188.6	24.1	6.9	4.8	–	0.9
Denmark	169.5	28.4	8.2	40.0	7.3	4.9	0.9	0.6
France	3596.6	1311.8	1633.1	227.0	63.0	47.1	5.1	4.7
Germany	6066.8	1487.3	236.4	553.4	550.4	271.2	92.1	51.4
Greece	213.3	61.5	20.9	39.1	35.7	11.4	4.6	12.1
Italy	537.0	111.2	170.2	85.8	20.8	9.1	5.2	2.3
Netherlands	732.9	176.1	197.7	56.8	10.2	4.6	2.0	1.2
Portugal	114.0	30.0	48.0	4.5	0.6	0.1	0.0	0.2
Spain	360.7	158.3	62.9	32.3	3.1	3.1	–	–
UK	2012.4	800.5	195.4	500.1	49.3	29.4	–	14.8
EU	10041.9	–	2762.6	1564.1	747.3	385.8	109.9	88.2
Austria	517.7	77.5	8.5	25.7	62.3	18.3	18.5	2.1
Finland	37.6	5.5	3.2	4.0	12.1	0.7	0.2	10.5
Sweden	493.8	72.5	22.5	83.0	31.8	16.1	5.5	3.4

Source: EUROSTAT (1994), own calculations. Numbers for France are for 1990.

Table 7.3. Employment of foreigners in Germany

	1989	1990	1991	1992	1993	1994	1995	1995 Share in %	Increase since 1989 %
EU	592,295	601,760	608,306	595,998	680,559	686,287	679,892	31.9	13.8
Former Yugoslavia	300,934	312,974	325,258	375,082	417,548	420,934	418,668	19.7	33.0
Poland	25,383	35,106	45,615	56,477	72,326	67,546	66,193	3.1	95.9
Turkey	561,806	594,586	632,324	652,097	631,837	605,147	600,434	28.2	6.7
Other Europe	40,070	48,366	66,990	100,756	114,719	106,632	108,315	5.1	99.4
Africa	40,438	44,683	52,320	63,183	65,292	64,098	66,218	3.1	49.3
America	34,798	38,448	42,197	45,172	46,428	44,303	41,849	2.0	18.5
Asia	73,921	85,836	103,839	123,574	127,991	125,997	126,958	6.0	54.1
Australia	2,244	2,464	2,807	2,909	2,908	2,903	2,744	0.1	20.1
No passport	17,410	18,030	18,884	20,906	23,971	16,685	17,451	0.8	0.2

Source: Sachverständigenratsgutachten (1996). Own calculations.

share is from the European Union (32 per cent), which is followed by Turkey (28 per cent), former Yugoslavia (19 per cent) and Poland (3.1 per cent).

Foreign employment in Germany has increased substantially over the last few years, but the distribution of the increase from 1989 to 1995 has been rather uneven. As the last column in Table 7.3 shows, the largest increase (excluding ethnic Germans) came from Poland (96 per cent) and other Europe (99 per cent), what is mostly eastern Europe. The inflow from Turkey was the smallest (7 per cent) apart from the group of people with no passport (0 per cent). Further areas of significance were Asia (54 per cent), Africa (49 per cent) and former Yugoslavia (33 per cent). As is well known, the migration flow within the European Union is low. Hence, the small increase in the stock of EU workers of about 14 per cent comes as no surprise.

There have always been concerns about the labour market consequences of immigration. However, most economists support the position that, for allocative reasons, free international movements of labour are beneficial, as is the free movement of capital and goods, at least for the economy as a whole. Labour may suffer in part, but its relevance is an empirical issue. The key issue for the evaluation of the wage effects of immigrant labour is whether foreigners are substitutes or complements to natives. A reasonable simplification is that high-qualified and low-qualified workers are complements and that immigrants tend to be substitutes for low-qualified natives and complements to high-qualified natives. Hence, increased immigration may depress wages and increase unemployment among low-income workers and may induce the reverse effects for the high-qualified. This is supported for German wages by De New and Zimmermann (1994). Winkelmann and Zimmermann (1993) found that a larger share of foreign labour increased the frequency of unemployment of Germans in the 1970s, while Mühleisen and Zimmermann (1994) found no such effects for the 1980s.

If migration and trade are related to labour market performance, different patterns of trade and migration for the indutrialized countries should be correlated with differences in the patterns of wages and unemployment. As, for instance, Bean (1994) wants us to believe, the European Community countries (as of 1994) are significantly different from the USA, the northern (Nordic) European countries (and also Austria and Switzerland), and Japan in that they have experienced a strong increase in the unemployment rate since the early 1970s. This reflects popular beliefs. In Bean's analysis, this is due to a decline in the outflow rate from unemployment in these European Community countries. However, as an update of the numbers (see Figure 7.3) shows, the 'Nordic model' has disappeared in the meanwhile— unemployment rates there are just as high as in other parts of OECD Europe.

Anyway, the US model was never unique to Northern America: Canadian unemployment rates have also been increasing together with the European ones in recent decades (see again Figure 7.3). And the USA has experienced a significant widening of inequality and a rise in the working poor (see Blank 1995). Furthermore, even Japan is not innocent: there is substantial labour-hoarding in large Japanese firms and considerable measurement problems of unemployment. Therefore, 'true' unemployment seems to be much higher, and there is a perspective for rising unemployment rates in the near future.

This all suggests a different explanation. There seem to be fundamental shifts in labour demand within Western countries, which is causing a decline in unskilled workers. Consequently, countries with regulated labour markets react with rising unemployment, while those with more flexible labour markets experienced rising wage inequality. So there is a general problem that calls for a common explanation, but it does not necessarily have one common cause.

Could migration or trade be regarded as common causes? From our analysis so far we remain sceptical about the potential of both mechanisms to contribute significantly. Nevertheless, we wish to investigate more formally how migration and trade are related to wages and labour mobility. Our particular approach is to employ a micro-econometric excercise using a large-scale panel data set for West Germany on wages and labour mobility, which we merge with sector- and region-specific variables measuring trade and migration. Identifying various subgroups in the labour market, we are investigating the relative effects of trade and migration indicators while controlling for other relevant variables. The next section will detail the data issues.

7.3 The Data

Hereafter, we will concentrate on West Germany only. This decision is guided by the available data. The micro data we are using is primarily from the 1980s, and most periods are before German unification (in 1990). This study employs data of the first nine waves (1984–92) of the German Socio-economic Panel (SOEP) for West Germany. The data consist of a large household panel survey produced by Deutsches Institut für Wirtschaftsforschung (DIW), Berlin. An introduction to the data set is provided by Wagner, Burkhauser and Behringer (1993).

The SOEP is a rich and unique data source in various ways. It is the longest time-series of cross-sections available in Europe and provides a large number of questions. For instance, it explicitly asks employed individuals whether they have changed their employer or changed their position inside the firm. It also requests respondents to describe their job in detail. Based on this description, two occupational variables are created by the DIW, which follow the one- and three-digit levels of the International Labour Office's international standard classification of occupations, the so-called ISCO code. We have cleaned this data and followed the individuals up through the years to study occupational changes. We also combine the information on changes of position between firms and within firms with the occupational changes on the one-digit and three-digit levels. The SOEP also provides data on monthly gross labour earnings. A more detailed description of the variables used in the analysis is given in Appendix 7.1. Here we provide an overview only.

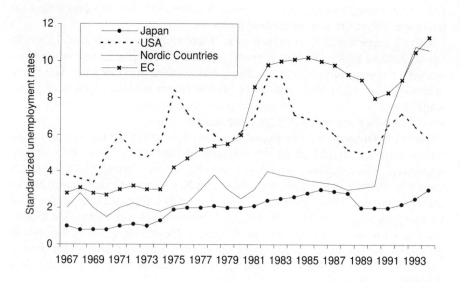

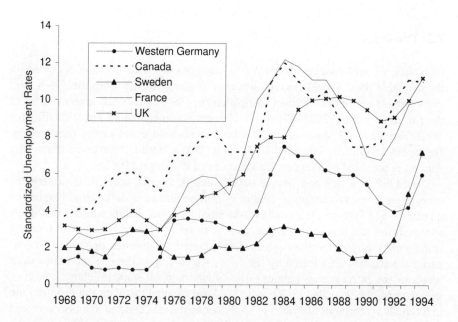

Source: OECD Employment Outlook, various issues.

Fig. 7.3. Standardized unemployment rates

We will investigate an earnings regression and various regressions on job mobility. Labour earnings is used as log real earnings. Real monthly earnings, in contrast to real hourly wages, is used here to avoid potential complications in calculating an hourly wage with more unprecise data on hours worked. This decision seems not to be too problematic, since we concentrate on males only. The change variables capturing labour mobility (or job positions) are coded as (0,1) dummies. They measure year-to-year changes of occupation (at the ISCO 1 or ISCO 3 level) and year-to-year changes of the work-place within the firm (intra-firm changes) and or between the firm (inter-firm changes). The full sample size for the earnings regressions is 17,137 and for the mobility analysis is 12,855. The different number of observations are the result of different data requirements and data availability in both cases. For instance, the earnings regressions cover period 1985–92, while the labour mobility regressions only period 1985–91.

The following variables are used as regressors: Individual characteristics, including a dummy for carrying a foreign passport (foreigner), marriage and union membership (1,0) dummies, age, age squared, years of education, education squared, firm tenure, tenure squared, percentage handicapped, size of the community, firm size, unemployment experience (number of months unemployed in the last ten years), and number of previous jobs (in the last ten years). Regional or industry level information like industry dummies, regional unemployment, sectoral growth, union density (measuring the strength of the union in the particular sector), a trade deficit ratio, and the regionally and sectorally differentiated foreigner share in the labour force. The semi-aggregated data were merged by us using official sources with the micro data.

Since the number of observations available is large, we are able to split the data in various subsamples. A possible differentiation is between blue- and white-collar workers, which is a standard differentiation of the two major groups of workers. While such a split is straightforwardly executed, it is not necessarily the most convincing strategy to obtain two homogeneous samples. Both groups contain skilled and unskilled workers. Since the proposition is that trade and migration are a major threat to low-skilled workers, one better combines the skilled and unskilled individuals from both groups. We, however, also keep the subgroups separated. This leaves us with seven regressions: (i) the total sample, (ii) four regressions for skilled and unskilled blue-collar and skilled and unskilled white-collar workers, and (iii) two regressions for skilled (blue- and white-collar) workers and unskilled (blue- and white-collar) workers.

The definition of 'skilled' is up for debate. We investigated two alternative strategies, which are explained in detail in Appendix 7.1. Following De New and Zimmermann (1994), we defined persons to be skilled if they had 25 or more years of work experience. A different concept used here for the first time has been to define people as skilled if they have a 'qualified' job. Blue-collar workers were considered to exhibit high job qualifications if they had a vocational training, or are foremen or *Meister* (master). White-collar workers were considered to exhibit high job qualifications if they were classified as 'very qualified' or were a manager. The analysis was carried out using both measures. This results in 13 different regressions for wages and 52 regressions for labour mobility.

There are various econometric problems with which to deal. The panel nature in the earnings regressions is exploited by applying a random effects panel model. The mobility variables are (0,1) dummies. We, therefore, use probit estimates with time-specific fixed effects using Pseudo-R^2's suggested by Veall and Zimmermann (1992). Both the trade deficit ratio and the foreigner share variable are potentially endogenous. We, therefore, have instrumented these variables using growth of industry value added, industry dummies, time dummies and industry-specific time-trends as instruments. The R^2 for the migration regression is 0.4, for the trade regression 0.8. A standard argument against a simple merging of group-specific variables with continuous micro data derived from Moulton (1990) is that under certain conditions t-ratios are upward biased if the group structure is not appropriately specified. Note, however, that due to the panel structure we are able to deal with this problem by employing industry-specific fixed effects.

This chapter has some relationships with previous studies. While De New and Zimmermann (1994) have examined the wage effects of immigration and Zimmermann (1995c) has dealt with labour mobility as discussed in this chapter, they both do not address the trade issue. Also, De New and Zimmermann (1994) use a substantially different sample by including fewer waves and creating different sub-samples. They also concentrate on natives only, employ different specifications and use wages instead of earnings. The migration data used in this chapter are far more detailed, containing the region-specific foreigner share by industry, provided by the Bundesanstalt für Arbeit (German Labour Office). In this data set, some smaller states are grouped (with neighbouring larger ones) by the Bundesanstalt für Arbeit, namely (i) Schleswig-Holstein and Hamburg, (ii) Niedersachsen and Bremen, and (iii) Rheinland-Pfalz and Saarland. The net effect is an eight times increase in detail in comparison with the previous studies.

7.4 Results

How are the earnings of the various groups affected by trade and migration? We study this question in the well-established framework of an earnings regression. The model specification is given in Appendix Table A7.1. Foreigners receive lower earnings. Among the standard human capital variables, tenure obtains the lowest statistical support. Married men earn more, large firms pay more, and individuals living in smaller cities receive lower payment. Union membership does not pay, previous job flexibility has a positive impact, previous unemployment experience has a negative effect on earnings. Regional unemployment also depresses wages. This all confirms earlier studies in the literature, and is fairly stable across the subsamples. Therefore, the more detailed findings are not discussed here to conserve space.

The trade deficit ratio exhibits a negative (and statistically significant) effect on wages in all model specifications of Appendix Table A7.1. However, the estimated coefficients are not larger (in absolute terms) for low-skilled workers than for high-skilled workers as one may wish to obtain. This is true for both approaches to measure skill levels. These findings are also listed in Table 7.4 and compared with the results of the more detailed sample specifications. If one separates blue- and white-collar workers, the same message prevails: Blue- and white-collar low-skilled workers do not have stronger wage effects than the comparable high-skilled workers. In contrast, high-skilled workers seem often to experience stronger effects. This seems also to be true if we compare blue-collar workers with white-collar workers. White-collar workers seem to be affected more strongly.

Table 7.4 contains also all estimates concerning the effects of the foreigner share in the labour force. Overall, the finding is that the relative size of foreigners exhibit a complementarity effect. A larger share has a positive effect on wages, at least in the full sample. The general finding occurs because migrants seem to be complements to high-skilled individuals while there is no effect on low-skilled wages. Migrants do not affect wages of white-collar workers much, but have a positive impact on high-skilled blue-collar workers.

Appendix Table A7.2 exhibits the model specification for the mobility probit estimates. Mobility is measured in terms of occupational changes at a more aggregated (ISCO1) or largely disaggregated (ISCO3) level, intra-firm and inter-firm changes. Among the findings are: foreigners are less flexible, age has a negative effect on occupational and inter-firm mobility, and education exhibits a U-shaped relationship. Handicapped people are more mobile within a firm, and union members have a lower inter-firm flexibility. Regional unemployment and industry growth are hardly important, but union density has a negative impact on occupational flexibility and inter-firm changes.

What are the effects of trade and migration on mobility? A detailed summary can be found in Table 7.5. We do not report the results differentiated for white-collar and blue-collar workers since these findings do not add much additional information. The trade deficit ratio indicates that increasing competition reduces occupational mobility and intra-firm flexibility but stimulates inter-firm flexibility. The inter-firm mobility effect shows up across all skill groups. The negative effect on intra-firm mobility appears only for low-experienced workers. Occupational mobility is affected more negatively for lower job levels and wider experience. The impacts of immigrants are less pronounced. Intra-firm mobility is affected negatively in the full sample, and this seems to be driven by individuals with a low job level and/or low experience. All other impacts are negligible.

Table 7.4.   Wage effects of trade and migration[a]

	Trade Deficit Ratio	Foreigner Share	R^2/Observations
Full sample	− 0.111	0.613	0.37
	(5.1)	(2.8)	17,137
Job level			
Low−all	− 0.118	0.203	0.28
	(− 5.1)	(0.8)	8,682
High−all	− 0.131	1.260	0.41
	(− 3.2)	(3.4)	8,398
Blue−low	− 0.040	0.738	0.17
	(− 1.9)	(1.8)	5,602
Blue−high	− 0.093	1.442	0.15
	(− 2.3)	(3.9)	5,916
White−low	− 0.351	0.995	0.43
	(− 3.4)	(1.2)	3,080
White−high	− 0.355	0.330	0.27
	(− 5.0)	(0.5)	2,482
Experience level			
Low−all	− 0.065	0.207	0.48
	(− 1.7)	(0.6)	8,155
High−all	− 0.095	0.511	0.29
	(− 3.5)	(1.8)	8,982
Blue−low	− 0.049	0.663	0.25
	(− 1.0)	(1.5)	5,154
Blue−high	− 0.046	0.851	0.10
	(− 1.5)	(2.4)	6,364
White−low	− 0.052	− 0.559	0.49
	(− 1.4)	(− 1.7)	3,001
White−high	− 0.242	0.114	0.20
	(− 7.4)	(0.4)	2,618

[a] Random effects panel models. t-values in parentheses. Full specification of variables is contained in Table A7.1. Precise definitions of variables are given in the Appendix. Both variables are instrumented.

Table 7.5. Mobility effects of trade and migration[a]

	Trade Deficit Ratio	Foreigner Share	R^2_{MZ}/R^2_{VZ}	Observations
Full sample				12,855
Occupation				
ISCO 1	−3.357 (−4.3)	−0.029 (−0.2)	0.19 (0.18)	
ISCO 3	0.726 (1.0)	−0.147 (−1.5)	0.22 (0.22)	
Intra-firm	−2.091 (−1.7)	−0.597 (−2.8)	0.12 (0.08)	
Inter-firm	3.214 (3.3)	0.168 (1.3)	0.18 (0.14)	
Job level				
Low–all				6,565
Occupation				
ISCO 1	−2.923 (−2.8)	0.073 (0.5)	0.20 (0.18)	
ISCO 3	0.756 (0.8)	−0.077 (−0.6)	0.24 (0.23)	
Intra-firm	−0.975 (−0.6)	−0.732 (−2.5)	0.11 (0.08)	
Inter-firm	3.205 (2.2)	0.123 (0.6)	0.26 (0.19)	
High–all				6,266
ISCO 1	1.849 (1.4)	0.181 (0.9)	0.32 (0.30)	
ISCO 2	2.068 (1.8)	−0.234 (−1.4)	0.23 0.23	
Intra-firm	−1.653 (−0.9)	−0.348 (1.1)	0.22 (0.12)	
Inter-firm	3.308 (2.3)	0.280 (1.5)	0.15 (0.11)	
Experience level				
Low–all				6,035
Occupation				
ISCO 1	1.376 (1.3)	0.203 (1.3)	0.19 (0.17)	
ISCO 3	3.281 (3.5)	0.031 (0.2)	0.17 (0.16)	
Intra-firm	−2.059 (−1.3)	−0.832 (−2.7)	0.14 (0.09)	
Inter-firm	2.122 (1.8)	0.158 (1.0)	0.12 (0.09)	
High–all				6,820
ISCO 1	−5.637 (−4.2)	−0.028 (−0.1)	0.31 (0.29)	
ISCO 2	−2.358 (−2.0)	−0.307 (−1.9)	0.30 (0.31)	
Intra-firm	−0.557 (−0.3)	−0.233 (−0.8)	0.12 (0.06)	
Inter-firm	6.698 (3.1)	0.128 (0.5)	0.17 (0.10)	

a Probit estimates; *t*-statistics in parentheses. Full specification of variables is contained in Table A7.2. Precise definitions of variables are given in the Appendix. Both variables are instrumented.

7.5 Conclusions

This chapter has used micro panel data for Germany to study the effects of migration and trade on the labour market. Germany is an excellent case for such a study since (i) it provides a good data base, the German socio-economic panel, (ii) it is substantially involved in international trade, and (iii) it has experienced a large inflow of immigrants. Trade and migration flows are related. There is evidence that those sectors that compete mostly with imports also employ a larger share of immigrant workers. However, strong export-oriented sectors hire fewer migrants.

This correlation suggests that regressions concentrating on one of both variables only may suffer from misspecification.

Our findings imply that trade is the more relevant variable for the German labour market, and also the more dangerous threat. Our earnings regressions suggest that male wages are negatively affected by the trade deficit ratio. If the trade deficit ratio defined as net imports divided by the output of the sector increases, this will reduce wages, or if wages are not downwardly flexible, will cost jobs. Perhaps somewhat surprising, this affects skilled workers at least as much as unskilled workers. In contrast, immigration has no effect on low-skilled workers, but a positive effect on the wages of the high-skilled. Hence, negative employment effects for natives are unlikely, and this is quite independent of the case of downward-inflexible wages.

Similarly, labour mobility is much more affected by trade than by immigration. Mobility is measured by occupational changes and intra- and inter-firm changes of the workplace. A larger share of immigrant workers reduces intra-firm flexibility only. A relative increase in imports has a negative effect on occupational mobility and intra-firm flexibility but encourages inter-firm flexibility.

Has trade caused wage pressure and reduced labour market flexibility in West Germany? Not recently. Due to unification, output-weighted net imports have declined in West Germany. This was caused by the increase in demand from East Germany. However, the mechanism confirmed in this analysis was tested in a period (1985–91) with no pronounced trend in trade. It may also well be that, seen in a longer time-perspective, trade had caused labour market problems. These implications are worthy of further study.

References

Baldwin, R. E. (1995), 'The Effect of Trade and Foreign Direct Investment on Employment and Relative Wages', *NBER Working Paper*, 5037.

Bean, C. R. (1994), 'European Unemployment: A Survey', *Journal of Economic Literature*, 32: 573–619.

Berman, E., Bound, J. and Griliches, Z. (1994), 'Changes in Demand for Skilled Labour within US Manufacturing: Evidence from the Annual Survey of Manufactures', *Quarterly Journal of Economics*, 109(2): 367–97.

Bhagwati, J. (1994), 'Free Trade: Old and New Challenges', *The Economic Journal*, 104: 231–46.

—— (1995), 'Trade and Wages: A Malign Relationship?', unpublished manuscript, Columbia University.

Blank, R. M. (1995), 'Changes in Inequality and Unemployment over the 1980s: Comparative Cross-National Responses', *Journal of Population Economics*, 8: 1–21.

Borjas, J. G. (1994), 'The Economics of Immigration', *Journal of Economic Literature*, 32: 1667–717.

Borjas, J. G., Freeman, R. B. and Katz, L. F. (1992), 'Labour Market Effects of Immigration and Trade', in J. G. Borjas and R. B. Freeman (eds.), *Immigration and the Work Force:*

Economic Consequences for the United States and Source Areas, University of Chicago, Chicago, pp. 213–44.

Burtless, G. (1995), 'International Trade and the Rise in Earnings Inequality', *Journal of Economic Literature*, 33: 800–16.

De New, J. and Zimmermann, K. F. (1994), 'Native Wage Impacts of Foreign Labour: A Random Effects Panel Analysis', *Journal of Population Economics*, 7: 177–92.

EUROSTAT (1994), 'Ausländer machen über 4 per cent der Gesamtpopulation der Europäischen Union aus', *EUROSTAT Schnellberichte: Bevölkerung und soziale Bedingungen*, 7: 1–11.

Freeman, R. B. and Katz, L. F. (1991), 'Industrial Wage and Employment Determination in an Open Economy', in J. M. Abowd and R. B. Freeman (eds.), *Immigration, Trade, and the Labour Market*, University of Chicago Press, Chicago, 235–60.

Lawrence, R. Z. and Slaughter, M. J. (1993), 'International Trade and American Wages in the 1980s: Giant Sucking Sound or Small Hiccup?', *Brookings Papers on Economic Activity*, Microeconomics, 2: 161–226.

Minford, P., Riley, J. and Nowell, E. (1995), 'The Elexir of Growth: Trade, Non-Traded Goods and Development', *CEPR Discussion Paper*, 1165.

Moulton, B. R. (1990), 'An Illustration of a Pitfall in Estimating the Effects of Aggregate Variables on Micro Units', *Review of Economics and Statistics*, 72: 334–8.

Mühleisen, M. and Zimmermann, K. F. (1994), 'A Panel Analysis of Job Changes and Unemployment', *European Economic Review*, 38: 793–801.

OECD (1994a), 'The OECD Jobs Study, Part I', OECD, Paris.

OECD (1994b), 'The OECD Jobs Study, Part II', OECD, Paris.

Revenga, A. L. (1992), 'Exporting Jobs?: The Impact of Import Competition on Employment and Wages in US Manufacturing', *Quarterly Journal of Economics*, 107(1): 225–84.

Sachs, J. D. and Shatz, H. J. (1994), 'Trade and Jobs in US Manufacturing', *Brookings Papers on Economic Activity*, 1: 1–69.

Veall, M. R. and Zimmermann, K. F. (1992), 'Pseudo-R^2's in the Ordinal Probit Model', *Journal of Mathematical Sociology*, 16: 333–42.

Wagner, G., Burkhauser, R. V. and Behringer, F. (1993), 'The English Language Public Use File of the German Socio-Economic Panel', *Journal of Human Resources*, 28: 429–33.

Winkelmann, R. and Zimmermann, K. F. (1993), 'Ageing, Migration and Labour Mobility', in P. Johnson and K. F. Zimmermann (eds.), *Labour Markets in an Ageing Europe*, Cambridge University Press, Cambridge, pp. 255–83.

Wood, A. (1991), 'The Factor Content of North–South Trade in Manufactures Reconsidered', *Weltwirtschaftliches Archiv*, Band 127: 719–43.

—— (1994), *North–South Trade Employment and Inequality*, Oxford University Press, New York.

Zimmermann, K. F. (1995a), 'European Migration: Push and Pull', in Proceedings volume of the World Bank Annual Conference on Development Economics, supplement to the *World Economic Review and the World Bank Research Observer*, pp. 313–42.

—— (1995b), 'Tackling the European Migration Problem', *Journal of Economic Perspectives*, 9: 45–62.

Zimmermann, K. F. (1995c), 'German Job Mobility and Wages', in I. Ohashi and T. Tachibanaki (eds.), *Employment Adjustment, Incentives and Internal Labour Market*, Macmillan Publishing Company, London.

Appendix 7: Data Construction

The survey data used in this study are the first nine waves for 1984–92 of the German Socio-Economic Panel (SOEP) for West Germany. The panel is provided by the Deutsche Institut für Wirtschaftsforschung (DIW, Berlin), and a general introduction can be found in Wagner, Burkhauser and Behringer (1993). The group of foreigners is slightly oversampled. Since our analysis involves changes, the first wave is lost. For the Probit mobility analysis, the last wave is lost as well due to missing information. Hence, we study the period 1985–91. We concentrate on males only. The definition of the variables is as follows:

(i) Data from the SOEP:

General background information:

Foreigner	(0,1) dummy for foreigner (Turk, Yugoslav, Greek, Italian, Spanish)
Age	Year–year of birth
Married	(0,1) dummy for marriage
Union member	(0,1) dummy for union member in 1985
Handicapped	Percentage handicapped
Firm size (med)	200–2000
Firm size (large)	more than 2000
City (small)	< 100,000 inhabitants

Industry breakdown:

Sector	Potentially available are 34 sectors

Human capital variables:

Years education	Own calculation on the basis of individual degrees
Experience	Experience = Age – (Years Education) – 6
Tenure	Current year – first year in current firm

Job Type and Mobility variables:

ISCO1	Change in ISCO one-digit: eight job categories
ISCO3	Change in ISCO three-digit: 224 job categories with observations available
Intra-firm	Change of workplace within firm (0,1)
Inter-firm	Change of firm (0,1)

Job groupings	By job qualification		By work experience
Blue collar	LOW	1: no training	LOW <=25 yrs experience
		2: some training	HIGH >25 yrs experience
	HIGH	3: vocational training	
		4: foreman	
		5: Meister	
White collar	LOW	1: Werkmeister	LOW <=25 yrs experience
		2: simple job	HIGH >25 yrs experience
		3: qualified job	
	HIGH	4: very qualified	
		5: manager	
Months unemp	Number of months unemployed in last 10 years, asked in 1984		
Num prev jobs	Number of employers in last 10 years, asked in 1984		

(ii) Data merged by us from other sources:

The merging process was undertaken by connecting the industry code in the various sources with the industry code in the SOEP.

Foreigner Share (Migration):

The share of foreigners by industry, state and year is taken from the published issues of the Amtliche Nachrichten (1985–93) der Bundesanstalt für Arbeit. Specifically, of those workers covered by the federal mandatory social insurance programme, it is the share of workers with nationalities other than German as of 30 September in each year. Thus, depending on the individual micro level indicators for industry, state and year, the macro data have been appropriately merged into the micro data at the SOEP two-digit level (34 values).

Trade Deficit Ratio:

The real DM value (1991) of exports, imports and output (Bruttowertschöpfung, gross value added) by industry and year have been taken from published issues of the Volkswirtschaftliche Gesamtrechnungen FS18,R1.3 (1986–93) from the Statistisches Bundesamt. 'Trade Deficit Ratio' is calculated as (imports–exports)/output.

Unemployment:

Unemployment rate, detailed by year and German state (*Länder*).
Source: Statistisches Bundesamt, Statistisches Jahrbuch, various issues.

Growth:

Industry growth calculated as the growth rate of gross value added. Detailed per year and industry according to the Statistisches Bundesamt, *Statistisches Jahrbuch*, various issues.

Union Density:

Union density, share of union members to total workers in that industry.
Source: Statistisches Bundesamt, *Statistisches Jahrbuch*, various issues.

(iii) GSOEP industry classification

(1) Agriculture and forestry
(2) Fishery
(3) Energy and water
(4) Mining
(5) Chemical/coal processing/oil

(6) Plastics/rubber/asbestos
(7) Stone/ore/ceramics/glass
(8) Iron/foundries/processing

(9) Steel/machine/vehicle assembly
(10) Electro/fine mechanics
(11) Wood/paper/printing
(12) Leather/textile/clothing
(13) Food and sundries
(14) Construction: main
(15) Construction: subsidiary

(16) Wholesale
(17) Trade middlemen
(18) Retail
(19) Railway
(20) Post/telephone/postbank

(21) Other transport/communication
(22) Banks/savings banks
(23) Insurance
(24) Hotels/restaurants
(25) Personal service

(26) Cleaning/garbage disposal
(27) Education/sport
(28) Health
(29) Legal advice
(30) Other service

(31) Churches/organizations
(32) Private households
(33) Municipalities
(34) Social insurance

Table A7.1. Wage effects of trade and migration: full specification

Variables	Full sample	Job qualification		Work experience	
		Low	High	Low	High
Foreigner	− 0.080	− 0.086	− 0.076	− 0.081	− 0.063
	(− 8.4)	(− 8.0)	(− 5.9)	(− 6.6)	(− 4.7)
Experience	0.034	0.030	0.034	0.055	0.017
	(35.6)	(26.3)	(21.5)	(24.8)	(4.4)
Experience^2	− 0.000	− 0.000	− 0.001	− 0.001	− 0.000
	(− 27.3)	(− 20.9)	(− 16.9)	(14.5)	(3.2)
Years of education	− 0.015	− 0.011	− 0.013	0.008	− 0.021
	(− 3.5)	(− 2.4)	(− 2.1)	(0.9)	(− 4.0)
Years of education^2	0.003	0.003	0.003	0.002	0.004
	(17.1)	(10.8)	(11.8)	(6.2)	(13.3)
Tenure	0.000	0.002	− 0.000	0.000	0.001
	(0.7)	(2.4)	(− 0.1)	(0.079)	(1.1)
Tenure^2	0.000	0.000	0.000	0.000	0.000
	(2.1)	(1.6)	(1.5)	(0.1)	(1.9)
Married	0.016	0.016	0.027	0.025	− 0.007
	(2.8)	(2.3)	(2.9)	(3.3)	(− 0.7)
Union member	− 0.003	0.006	− 0.025	0.003	− 0.012
	(− 0.3)	(0.6)	(− 2.3)	(0.2)	(− 1.1)
Firm size (medium)	0.011	− 0.001	0.025	0.018	0.007
	(3.0)	(− 0.2)	(4.1)	(3.1)	(1.5)
Firm size (large)	0.017	0.017	0.025	0.027	0.008
	(4.8)	(3.8)	(4.1)	(4.7)	(1.8)
Number of previous jobs	0.015	0.012	0.011	0.005	0.009
	(5.0)	(3.8)	(2.8)	(1.4)	(2.0)
Months unemployed	− 0.006	− 0.005	− 0.006	− 0.007	− 0.006
	(− 7.9)	(− 6.2)	(− 5.2)	(− 7.8)	(− 5.0)
City (small)	− 0.023	− 0.033	− 0.027	− 0.020	− 0.031
	(− 4.0)	(− 4.7)	(− 3.3)	(− 2.3)	(− 4.1)
Unemployment	− 0.024	− 0.023	− 0.021	− 0.019	− 0.018
	(− 23.2)	(− 19.1)	(− 13.6)	(− 12.1)	(− 12.2)
Trade deficit ratio	− 0.111	− 0.118	− 0.131	− 0.065	− 0.095
	(− 5.1)	(− 5.1)	(− 3.2)	(− 1.7)	(− 3.5)
Foreigner share	0.613	0.203	1.260	0.207	0.511
	(2.8)	(0.8)	(3.4)	(0.6)	(1.8)
Constant	7.449	7.548	7.457	7.186	7.621
	(204.8)	(192.1)	(137.1)	(105.2)	(95.8)
N	17,137	8,682	8,398	8,155	8,982
R^2	0.37	0.28	0.41	0.48	0.29

Note: Full sample using SOEP micro data 1984–92. Random effects panel models. *t*-statistics in parentheses. All regressions include 15 industry dummies and a constant.

Table A7.2.   Wage effects of trade and migration: full specification

Variables	ISCO 1	ISCO 3	Intra-Firm	Inter-Firm
Constant	−0.801	0.245	−1.803	−0.001
	(−2.1)	(0.803)	(−3.3)	(−0.0)
Foreigner	−0.178	0.021	−0.152	−0.182
	(−3.1)	(0.5)	(1.9)	(−2.8)
Married	−0.145	−0.078	0.112	−0.078
	(−2.5)	(−1.5)	(1.3)	(−1.2)
Age	−0.037	−0.078	0.011	−0.052
	(−2.2)	(−5.5)	(0.5)	(−2.5)
Age^2	0.000	0.001	−0.000	0.000
	(1.4)	(4.2)	(−1.4)	(0.9)
Years of education	−0.015	−0.074	−0.032	−0.065
	(−0.5)	(−3.9)	(−0.9)	(−2.3)
Years of education^2	0.002	0.004	0.003	0.003
	(2.3)	(5.1)	(2.3)	(3.0)
Handicapped (%)	−0.001	0.000	0.005	0.001
	(−0.4)	(0.2)	(2.3)	(0.5)
Union member	−0.106	0.040	0.026	−0.105
	(−2.3)	(1.0)	(0.4)	(−1.9)
Number of previous jobs	0.040	0.038	−0.064	0.071
	(−2.8)	(2.9)	(−2.3)	(4.8)
Months unemployed	0.008	0.013	−0.008	0.006
	(2.3)	(4.4)	(−1.0)	(1.4)
Unemployment (−1)	−0.003	−0.004	−0.005	0.000
	(−0.3)	(−0.6)	(−0.4)	(0.0)
Growth (−1)	0.223	0.049	1.576	0.316
	(0.4)	(0.1)	(2.0)	(0.5)
Union density (−1)	0.050	−0.370	0.241	−1.004
	(0.4)	(−3.2)	(1.4)	(5.6)
Foreigner share (−1)	−3.357	0.726	−2.091	3.214
	(−4.3)	(1.0)	(−1.7)	(3.3)
Trade deficit ratio (−1)	−0.029	−0.147	−0.597	0.168
	(−0.2)	(−1.5)	(−2.8)	(1.3)
N	12,855	12,855	12,855	12,855
R^2_{MZ}	0.20	0.22	0.12	0.19
R^2_{VZ}	0.18	0.22	0.08	0.14
LRT	646.84	1057.51	146.73	373.66

Note: *t*-statistics in parentheses. Probit regressions. All regressions include time dummies. SOEP micro data 1985–91.

8. Brief History of the Social Clause in Trade Policy

PAUL BAIROCH

8.1 Introduction: What it is and Where it Came From

We shall begin this chapter with a succinct—and, therefore forcibly incomplete—definition of the term 'social clause'. The body of the chapter will provide the remainder of our definition. A social clause is a clause that may be included in a customs tariff (or other commercial instrument) and which sets forth sanctions to be applied against the importation of products from countries that do not enforce a minimum standard of working conditions. The idea that the differences in social conditions from one country to the next can influence international trade is quite an old one. It can be traced at least as far back as the end of the eighteenth century. Testifying to this is the text written in 1788 by the renowned French financier and statesman, Jacques Necker. In chapter 9 (*Consideration of another objection: the day of rest*) Necker points out that 'the country which, out of barbarian ambition, would abolish the day of rest prescribed by religion, would probably attain a certain degree of superiority if it were the only country to do so; but as soon as other nations follow the lead, this advantage would be lost, and shares in sales would return to what they had been prior to the change. The same reasoning demonstrates that countries where days of rest are multiplied beyond the norm will have a disadvantage with respect to countries that have selected as days of rest only the holy days imposed by the church.' Let us point out here that Necker is considered by certain historians of the ILO—and, in particular, by André de Maday (1921)—as one of the precursors of the organization. In an article published in 1935, de Maday esteems Necker even to be a precursor of social policy in general. We say that the idea that social policy affects the competitiveness of a country on the international scale has been around since *at least* the end of the eighteenth century; in fact we are convinced that it can be traced back even further than Necker, not only in Western economic and social philosophy, but also in that of other civilizations.

On a more tangible level, the social aspect became part of the economic debate in the 1830s during lively discussions concerning the new English commercial policy introduced in 1815. But it was not until the 1870s and the development of the USA that pressure really grew for what would be called, a century later, the social clause.

Indeed, it was towards the end of the 1870s that the American trade unions began pushing for customs laws that would protect them against imports originating in countries having low salaries. Traditionally, the McKinley Tariff Act of 1890 is seen as the first application of the social clause to American tariffs. The McKinley Act was a direct response to the pressure of the trade unions and was intended to give 'to American industry a full and complete protection against cheap foreign labour'. Despite popular reference to the McKinley Act, however, it is actually in 1880 that the social clause was first used, forbidding the importation of products manufactured by prisoners. This interdiction, moreover, is still in place; it was recently used by the USA against China. Other countries followed the US example with similar legislation: United Kingdom (1897), Canada (1907), New Zealand (1908), and South Africa (1913).

It is not by accident that American pressures rose just as the USA had become the richest country in the world. In terms of real GNP, the arrival of the United States as the richest country occurred, according to our calculations, around 1877/8. Such precision may be illusory, but what is certain is that, around 1870, the GNP per capita of the usa was about 10 per cent lower than that of the UK, whereas in 1880, it was 3 per cent higher.

Of course, there was not yet any reference to a social clause. The use of this term is quite recent. It was probably only introduced a century later, towards the mid-1970s. My preliminary bibliographical research has shown that this term was apparently used for the first time in 1976 during a meeting (in February) of the International Metalworkers Federation. During a Third World Congress, held in Vienna in October 1980, the International Textile Garment and Leather Workers Federation presented a document (1980), the third section of which was entitled 'The Social Clause'. An important development was the publication in 1981 of Göte Hansson's book *Social Clauses and International Trade*. It is symptomatic that Gus Edgren's article on 'Equitable Standards of Work and Trade Liberalization' should not use the term social clause. At this point I would like to thank Gijsbert van Liemt of the International Labour Organization, whose suggestions contributed much to the preliminary stages of this work.

8.2 Reasons for the Late Appearance of a Concern for Salary Inequalities

While today's economists may regard the events of 1870/80 to have been ahead of their time, historians would consider them overdue since they take place more or less a century and a half after the beginning of the agricultural revolution in England, and about a century after the beginning of its industrial revolution, which was to usher in the modern era of economic development. In an attempt to explain the delay in this concern for salary inequalities, we suggest that the following six factors be considered:

1. For a long time the differences in levels of development were only very small. Towards 1830, some 70 years after the beginning of the industrial revolution, the GNP per capita of the UK was only about 46 per cent greater than that of continental Europe (excluding Russia) and only about 98 per cent greater than that of Russia whose level was then approximately equivalent to that of the future Third World.

2. The initial stages of the industrial revolution (in fact until 1880–90) were characterized by a growing inequality in income distribution. This suggests that salaries did not keep pace with the majority of other income sources nor, therefore, with the GNP per capita. Consequently, the increase in the international distribution of salaries lagged behind that of development levels. While such a generalization of the trend in income distribution is debatable, it is nevertheless highly likely that inequalities did emerge in this way.

3. The spread of social legislation was more rapid than the rate of development. The Factory Act of 1833, for example, was the first English law to limit working hours and to have been effectively enforced. It forbade children below the age of nine from working and fixed a 48 hour working week for children between the ages of nine and 13. Similar measures were introduced elsewhere, notably in Germany (Prussia) from 1839, in France from 1841, in Austria-Hungary from 1884 and in Belgium from 1889 (but not until 1917 in the United States).

4. The appearance of political parties representing the working classes was a late development. The following are the years in which socialist parties were created in various countries: Germany (1875); Denmark (1876); Spain and France (1879); Switzerland (1880); Italy (1882); and Belgium (1885). As for the United Kingdom, the Labour Party was founded in 1877, although its political colour was quite different from that of the socialist parties in continental Europe. In this sense it should be noted that the first welfare state was not the UK of the post-Second World War period, but the Germany of Bismarck. As part of his *realpolitik*, Bismarck implemented several important social measures (from 1883) to counter the rise of the socialist party. Sickness insurance dates from 1883, accident insurance from 1884 and, the most important, old age and invalidity insurance, was introduced in 1889.

5. Transportation costs provided a natural barrier to foreign competition. It should be remembered that before the steam revolution (railways and ships) the cost of transportation was very high. The turning point came during the period 1860–70. These high transportation costs even had repercussions on lightweight manufactured products (textiles). With reference to the commercial history of the nineteenth century, we have calculated the relative transportation costs of five products: wheat, iron ore, cotton thread, manufactured iron and cotton products, taking into account internal transport (road, river and rail) over a distance of 800 km. The weighting has, of course, been varied according to the means of transport. We have also taken into account international maritime transportation. The following results of our

calculations and estimations for iron ore and manufactured cotton and iron products illustrate the sudden change that took place. The figures represent the cost of transportation as a percentage of the price of the product:

	Around 1830	Around 1880
Iron ore	115–20	60–5
Manufactured iron	32–8	16–20
Manufactured cotton	8–11	4–5

6. England's economy was predominant until 1870–80, despite the fact that it was largely influenced by liberal thinking. It was not until 1880 that a new power, protectionist this time, began to overtake England: the United States. Needless to say that, in general, the social clause found more favour with the protectionists than with the free traders.

8.3 But a 'Social' Element Began to Appear Much Earlier in Modern Tariff History

Although the social clause may seem very recent to the historian, this does not mean that social aspects had always been absent from tariff history. In fact, these aspects were already present in the first modern ddiscussions about trade policy, not to mention the reflection that had already been given to such problems, as we suggested in the introduction. Modern tariff history began with the debate surrounding the decision to implement the first tariff (after the Napoleonic Wars) in the country that became the cradle of the industrial revolution: England. Before this point, the predominant practice had been mercantilist, in which social considerations do not appear to have played an important role. We can even pinpoint the precise date at which these discussions began: 1815, the year of the 1815 Corn Laws (so-called in order to distinguish them from other laws of the same name). This law effectively forbade the importation of cereals, and was to launch a long, far-reaching and bitter debate, particularly virulent during the 1830s.

The peasants and the gentry tended to support the Corn Laws. Opposition came mainly from textile industrialists but also, of course, from economists. The spearhead of opposition to the Corn Laws was the Anti-Corn Law League, founded in 1836 and led by Richard Cobden. A strong advocate of free trade, Cobden was the driving force behind this league, which rapidly became an active pressure group and the main protagonist in the struggle for the introduction of free trade. If it was not the first then it was certainly one of the first modern economic pressure groups. It organized conferences, published articles and even had its own premises. One of the main propaganda messages claimed that the abolition of the Corn Laws would improve the standard of living of workers by reducing the price of bread. This, of course, assumed the maintenance of salaries at low levels, which would protect and expand exports and also allow cereal exporting countries to purchase greater quantities of British manufactured goods.

Besides these major socio-economic factors, there were significant implications for international policy-making highlighted by the Anti-Corn Law League, which saw free trade as a powerful means of promoting international peace through increased prosperity and, particularly, the interdependence of nations. Richard Cobden waxed lyrical on this subject and went as far as to dream of the 'commune'. During his speech in Manchester in 1846, he declared: 'I take a wider view; I believe the principle of free trade has the same effect as the principle of gravity in the universe—to bring men together, to reject antagonisms based on race, belief and language; and to unite us all in everlasting peace.'

It wasn't until 1846 that the Anti-Corn Law League's crusade was victorious. The abolition of the Corn Laws, marking the beginning of British liberalism, was initially undertaken as an emergency measure in exceptional circumstances. Indeed, it was due to the bad weather conditions of 1845, together with the disastrous potato harvest in Ireland, that on 6 June 1846, the law was passed to abolish the Corn Laws. As J. Morley (1882) wrote in his biography of Richard Cobden, 'It was the rain that rained away the Corn Laws.'

8.4 The Position of the Working Classes in the Nineteenth Century

With reference to the welfare of the working classes, it is virtually impossible to identify any real doctrine in the area of customs and trade policy (except for the USA from 1870 to 1880). The great debate between free traders and protectionists presented working class partisans with a dilemma: free trade, which implied a reduction in agricultural prices and, therefore, in the cost of living, carried with it the risk of job losses, protectionism, while safeguarding jobs, could provoke an increase in agricultural prices and consequently a decline in the standard of living.

In general, those unions with socialist sympathies tended to position themselves nearer to free trade than to protectionism. We may assume that the same could be said for the socialist political parties, without it being one of their major preoccupations. In fact, they intervened seldom in debates on this question. During the discussion on the 1881 amendment to the French tariff, for example, the socialist deputies (admittedly few at this time) did not intervene at all. When interventions were made, later and in other circumstances, they were more a reflection of opposition to agricultural protectionism. During the discussion of the French tariff in 1892, all the socialist deputies (now in greater numbers) spoke against this protectionist tariff. Nevertheless, between 1907 and 1914, the unions—particularly in the sectors where unemployment was relatively high (cabinet-making, glass-making, weaving, glove-making, mining)—were opposed to importing from countries where salaries were lower.

A few French-speaking socialist thinkers did in fact speak out against the protectionism associated with nationalism. As the work of M. Hollande demonstrates (1913), they included Jules Guesde (in 1887) and Emile Vandervelde (in 1892). We shall now move on to other linguistic spheres and other political landscapes, limiting our study to the two most important among them: Germany and the Anglo-Saxon world.

The position of the German social democrats was initially one of indifference. The Congress of Gotha (in 1876) included the declaration 'The socialists of Germany are indifferent to the controversy which currently rages among the landowning class over protectionism and free trade.' But later, especially after 1890, they were to become very much in favour of free trade.

In Great Britain, the Labour Party embraced free trade. Even during the great controversy in 1906 over Joseph Chamberlain's 'fair trade'—advocated by the Tariff Reform League—the party took the side of the opposition. To avoid confusion, it should be noted that the term 'fair' had no social connotation whatsoever, even if Joseph Chamberlain is considered to be one of the precursors of the welfare state. It was the view of the Tariff Reform League that, in the face of the Europeans who were not abiding by the unwritten rules of good practice, it was necessary to oppose *fair* trade to *free* trade. Moreover, we note that the proposals of the fair trade partisans were only very moderately protectionist. At a time when the customs duties on goods in continental Europe were around 20 per cent (about 40 per cent in the USA), Joseph Chamberlain's project was proposing 10 per cent. And, in 1932, when free trade was abandoned, only a breakaway minority of the Labour Party, the National Labour Group, voted in favour of the law (February 1932). When the Labour Party was in power (June 1929 to August 1931) Viscount Philip Snowden, as Chancellor of the Exchequer, published a tract entitled 'The Truth about Protection: The Worker Pays'. Staying in the Anglo-Saxon world, we should also mention the publication in 1886 of the work of the influential American publicist and politician, Henry George, 'Protection or Free Trade: An Examination of the Tariff Question with Special Regard to the Interest of Labour', translated into French in 1888.

8.5 Predecessors of the ILO and the Social Clause

We can of course link the emergence of the social clause to the movement towards the creation of an international labour organization. Indeed, Göte Hansson has taken this approach. Certainly the work in this direction has included discussions of certain aspects associated with the social clause. Leaving aside the precedent set by Necker, referred to in the introduction, we shall take a look at the historian John W. Follows (1951) who, in his work on the origins of the ILO (which has since become a classic), suggests that the predecessor was in fact Robert Owen. Indeed, Owen delivered a memorandum on this subject to the Congress of Aix-la-Chapelle in 1818. This congress settled the conditions for peace after the Napoleonic Wars and was, in a sense, equivalent to the congress which, after the First World War, was to culminate in the Treaty of Versailles which, in turn, gave rise to the ILO. Robert Owen's memorandum proposed that meetings should be held in order to adopt social measures on an international scale. He concluded that the congress offered the 'best opportunity ... to establish a framework for lasting peace ... and charity'.

The first person to have openly advocated an international labour organization was Edouard Ducpétiaux. Moreover, in his book of 1843 *(On the Physical and Social Condition of Young Workers and the Means to Improve It)*, he wrote: 'Which argument is most often used against projects for social reform? The tyranny of competition.' He too, therefore, was a precursor of the social clause. Born in Brussels in 1804, Ducpétiaux was, at the age of 24, already writing pamphlets on the prison system and the death penalty. With Belgian independence (1830) he was appointed inspector general of prisons and of the Institut de Bienfaisance. His work of 1843, one of many publications, is in fact an analysis of international social legislation. He is considered to be one of the precursors of the concept of the ILO.

But the ILO was actually only created after the First World War. And, as we shall see later, its creation (1919) was met with a British proposal that sought to make the social clause one of the principal means of promoting the spread of the social standards that were to be adopted by the institution. During the 1920s there were a few moves in this direction, which of course were hindered during the years of depression due to the general reinforcement of protectionism.

The first international convention in favour of a social clause would seem to be that of the Conference on Hygiene in the Workplace, held in Bern in 1906. A motion was adopted forbidding the manufacture, introduction (that is imports) and sale of matches containing white phosphorus in an attempt: to prevent the terrible phosphorus necrosis of the maxillary.

8.6 A Word on Migration

Before going into greater detail on the post-First World War situation, mention must be made of an aspect of the social clause debate between the Third World and developed countries. Whenever representatives of the developed world put forward the idea of a social clause, representatives of the Third World reply by pointing out the problem of obstacles to migration. It is in this area that trade union activity in the developed world has been the most advanced, albeit in a negative way: attempting to curb immigration. Of course, such a movement was not confined to the trade unions. The most notorious and probably the earliest case is that of Australia where the federal law of 1902 limiting immigration benefited from union support (and was even partly a result of union pressure). But this law is the culmination of a long series of measures taken by the states that were to form the future Commonwealth of Australia. In 1855, for instance, in the most heavily populated of these states (Victoria) measures were taken in this area. Before disembarking, immigrants were required to perform a 50-word dictation in a European language which, of course, had the effect of limiting the influx of Chinese and other non-Westerners.

In the USA the first obstacles to immigration were decreed in 1882 and concerned essentially those immigrants with a criminal record, the mentally ill, the sick or those likely to be a burden on the community. Refusal criteria were subsequently broadened, particularly to include polygamists. From 1917, entrance was refused to the Chinese, a measure preceded in 1907 by an agreement with the Japanese government to limit the emigration of Japanese citizens to the USA. In 1921, the USA installed a system of quotas (by country of birth), resulting in a dramatic reduction in immigration. The quota was fixed at 3 per cent of the number of foreigners present in the USA at the 1910 census. In 1924, the system was again strengthened, the limit being fixed at 2 per cent and this time in relation to the census of 1890. Moreover, the total annual number of immigrants was fixed at 150,000. This was to be divided pro rata among the various countries of birth, which meant that the immigration quota was not fulfilled for certain nationalities. These measures were taken as a result of increasing opposition from the US population to the scale of the migratory movement in general, and to the geographical origin of the new waves of immigrants in particular.

Here we can point out that New Zealand followed the Australian example from 1881, and more clearly in 1896 with a measure targeted primarily at the Chinese. One person of Chinese origin was accepted for every 200 tonnes 'of shipping'. South Africa (in 1913) also took measures to limit the arrival of immigrants from Asia, targeting the Indians more than the Chinese.

8.7 The ILO and the Social Clause

This brings us to the First World War, which marks not only a political but also a social turning point, foreshadowing that which was provoked later on by the Second World War. The reasons that these two wars, which were the first total wars, should lead to social advances lie essentially in the *rapprochement* between social classes, in the army as well as among the political authorities. To establish social peace, necessary for the great industrial effort behind this type of war, governments tended to promise social benefits once peace had returned.

As far as this chapter is concerned, the most important development of the post-First World War era is the creation, in 1919, of the ILO (International Labour Organization) by the Peace Conference meeting in Versailles. In fact, the Treaty of Versailles, which brought to an end the First World War, not only led to the foundation of the ILO but also, in a sense, paved the way for the social clause, since part of the preface to section XIII of this treaty declared: 'Given that the non-adoption by a particular country of a truly humane labour regime presents an obstacle to other nations in their efforts to improve the conditions of workers in their own country'.

During the interwar period, at least 67 international social conventions were adopted by the ILO during the course of international conferences on working conditions. These conferences soon began to be held annually. The first of these conventions dates from 1919 and dealt with working hours, which were fixed at 48 hours a week (already advocated in 1833 by the English precursor of socialism, Robert Owen).

The adoption of these conventions soon gave rise to the idea of exercising pressure through trade as a means of promoting their enforcement. And the Labour Party played an important role in this trend. From 1919 this party suggested that the League of Nations could withdraw the principle of the most favoured nation clause from those countries in breach of the obligations of international labour conventions. In 1925, there was another suggestion from the Labour Party that ILO members should undertake to refuse to import goods from a country in breach of the terms of a convention, whether or not they had ratified it (Steve Charnovitz 1987). The principle of 'cost balancing' was included in the 1922 and 1930 tariff laws of the USA. As S. Charnovitz points out, according to the law of 1930: 'The President had the authority to adapt the customs duties in order to balance the differences in production costs between an article manufactured in the United States and a similar article originating in the main competitor country. This measure applied to all factors of production and not just to labour, but the legislation aimed to address the problem of foreign products manufactured by poorly paid workers at a time when labour costs represented a large proportion of production costs. The measure, which was initially widely applied at the beginning of the 1930s, later ceased to be applicable to imports arising from trade agreements.' These measures were followed by that of 1934 in Spain. We should remember that the Republican Party had been in power from 1931 and that a decree had been adopted offering the first definition of 'social' dumping: the practice of price reductions resulting from 'the non-compliance with international social regulations governing aspects such as salaries and working conditions'.

On the whole, the 1930s being a period of generalized protectionism, few measures dealing with social clauses seem to have been taken. On the other hand, this was a period when systems of unemployment compensation were becoming more widespread and being consolidated, a factor contributing to demobilization. It should be noted here that the preoccupation with the Third World among working class circles and their representatives was virtually non-existent until the post-Second World War period.

8.8 From the End of the Second World War to Today

At the international level, despite a real spread of the welfare state, it is important to highlight the failure of the Havana Conference of March 1948, which provided for the creation of a world trade organization to cover all questions of international trade and in which the idea of a social clause would be clearly defined. The so-called Havana Charter, which was therefore never implemented, stated that members recognize that all countries have a common interest in the establishment and the maintenance of good working conditions in relation to productivity, as well as in the increase of salaries and the improvement of working conditions, insofar as productivity will allow. Members recognize that unfair working conditions, particularly in production for export, create obstacles to international trade and that each member should therefore take the appropriate practicable measures to abolish such conditions on their territory.

The world trade organization was, to a certain extent, replaced by the GATT. This organization was very liberal in inspiration, which partly explains the eclipse of the social clause over the next 30 years. We will be a lot more brief on this more familiar period for which we can refer to the works of W. Adamy (1994), S. Charnovitz (1987), G. Hansson (1981), W. Sengenberger and D. Campbell (1994), J.-M. Servais (1989), and G. van Liemt (1994), among others.

It was not exactly by chance that interest in the social clause should reappear in the mid-1970s with the re-emergence of greater structural unemployment and also, as Gijsbert van Liemt (1994) notes, at a time when awareness of the unfavourable social conditions existing in those countries exporting to the developed world was increased through television.

Here too we can identify a few precedents. For example, one can consider article 68(2) of the ECSC Treaty (European Coal and Steel Community) which outlined sanctions against those companies using a reduction in salaries as a means to increase their competitiveness. Then there was the United States' proposal (which was rejected) to the GATT in 1979 for a minimum labour standard aimed at 'certain working conditions posing a risk to the life and health of workers irrespective of the level of development'. For a long time the European Union—which began in 1958 as the Common Market and which was the direct successor to the ECSC—tended to neglect social aspects of policy-making. As André Sapir (1996) notes in his review of social policy in the process of European economic integration, the years 1958–73 were a period of 'benign neglect' in this field. And it is only after 1992 that discussions began on the question of 'social dumping'. This problem became all the more pressing with the adhesion to the EU of southern European countries (Spain, Portugal and Greece) with living standards lower than the average of the other members of the union. In the context of the EU, the most important development in this area was the suggestion made at the Copenhagen Summit in June 1993 by Jacques Delors (President of the Commission of the European Communities). He favoured the introduction of a social progress clause in the policy area of relations between the EU and other countries.

Finally, several international agreements on raw materials have included measures concerning 'fair working conditions'. At national level, only the USA actually introduced social clauses of any importance: between 1985 and 1994 four laws were voted in this area.

References

Adamy, W. (1994), 'International Trade and Social Standards', *Intereconomics*, (November–December): 259–83

Charnovitz , S. (1987), 'L'influence des normes internationales du travail sur le système du commerce mondial: Aperçu historique', *Revue Internationale du Travail*, 126(5): 635–57.

de Maday, A. (1921) *La Charte internationale du Travail*, Paris.

Ducpétiaux, E. (1843), *On the Physical and Social Condition of Young Workers and the Means to Improve It*, Brussels.

Edgren, G. (1979), 'Normes équitables de travail et libéralisation du commerce', *Revue Internationale du Travail*, 18(5, September–October): 557–70.

Follows, J.W. (1951) *Antecedents of the International Organization*, Oxford.

Hansson, G. (1981), *Social Clauses and International Trade: An Economic Analysis of Labour Standards in Trade Policies*, Lund.

Hollande, M. (1913), *La défence ouvrière contre le travail étranger: vers un protectionnisme ouvrier*, Paris.

International Textile Garment and Leather Workers Federation (1980), *The International Division of Labour and International Trade in Textiles, Clothings, Shoe and Leather Products*, Part 3, *The Social Clause*, discussion document (Third World Congress), Vienna, October.

Liemt, G. van (1994), 'The Multilateral Social Clause in 1994', in International Coalition for Development Action (draft discussion paper), Brussels.

Morley, J. (1882), *The Life of Richard Cobden*, London.

Sapir, A. (1996), 'Trade Liberalisation and the Harmonization of Social Policies: Lessons from European Integration', in J. Bhagwati and R. Hudic (eds), *Fair Trade and Harmonization: Prerequisites for Free Trade?* Massachusetts Institute of Technology Press, Cambridge, Massachusetts.

Sengenberger, W. and Campbell, D. (eds.) (1994), *International Labour Standards and Economic Interdependence*, International Institute for Labour Studies, Geneva.

Servais, J.-M. (1989) 'La clause sociale dans les traités de commerce: prétention irréaliste ou instrument de progrès social?', *Revue International du Travail*, 128(4): 463–74.

9. The Impact of Globalization on Employment in Europe

ANDRÉ SAPIR

9.1 Introduction

Since the mid-1970s, the demand for low-skilled workers has fallen considerably in Europe and in the United States. In Europe, this has translated mainly into massive unemployment, affecting primarily workers with low skills. In the USA, it has meant an increase in the wage disparity between skilled and unskilled workers, the latter even suffering a fall in their real wages.

At the same time, globalization has greatly increased. Global integration, which can be defined as the process 'by which markets and production in different countries are becoming increasingly interdependent due to the dynamics of trade in goods and services and the flows of capital and technology' (OECD 1993: 7), has both deepened and widened. Deepening is the process whereby the industrial countries, which had already greatly liberalized their trade through earlier GATT rounds initiated in the late 1940s, have continued to do so through regional and multilateral trade negotiations. Widening is the process whereby hitherto inward-looking developing countries have recently opened up through fundamental changes in their domestic policies. This twin process of liberalization has resulted in extensive imports of manufactured goods from developing countries by industrial countries.

The simultaneous occurrence of falling demand for low-skilled workers in the industrial countries and rising exports of manufactured goods by labour-abundant developing countries has produced a new brand of 'trade pessimism'. Earlier on, developing countries feared that manufactured imports from industrial countries would prevent their own industrialization, force them to specialize in the production of raw materials , and maintain their low income levels. Today, it is instead in the industrial countries that many fear that manufactured imports from developing countries impoverish some of their fellow citizens. As Professor Richard Freeman put it succinctly, the new worry centres on whether the labour conditions 'of low-skilled Americans or French or Germans [are] set in Beijing, Delhi and Djakarta rather than in New York, Paris or Frankfurt' (Freeman 1995: 16).

The debate over whether globalization is responsible for rising unemployment in Europe and falling wages in the United States contains two separate dimensions. The first dimension relates to the respective role of globalization as opposed to other economic factors, such as technological progress, in affecting the demand for low-skilled workers in the industrial countries. The issues here are essentially empirical. One is whether there is empirical evidence on the possible connection between trade and labour conditions in the industrial countries. Another issue is whether future findings may differ from current empirical evidence due to accelerating globalization or increased trade specialization. The second dimension of the problem concerns the origin, rather than the effect, of increased exports of manufactured products by the developing countries. There is some allegation, mainly in developed countries, that these exports are partly linked to the non-compliance of developing countries to internationally-agreed labour standards. This has led to accusations of 'unfair competition' and 'social dumping', and to demands for introducing 'social clauses' in international trade agreements.

This chapter is organized in three parts. The first part examines the extent of globalization, more particularly in Europe. The second part deals with the impact of globalization on the demand for low-skilled workers in Europe and in the USA. The final part studies the link between labour standards and globalization.

9.2. Globalization

Over the past 45 years, the world economy has become increasingly integrated. The main channels of global integration have been international trade and international capital flows. By contrast, international labour mobility has played a rather limited role in the process of globalization.

9.2.1 Trade

During the period 1950–73, the volume of world trade (in goods and services) increased at an annual rate of nearly 8 per cent, while world GDP in volume rose annually by 5 per cent. As a result, the ratio of exports (of goods and services) to GDP doubled for the world as whole, reaching 16 per cent in 1973 (at 1987 prices and exchange rates). As shown in Figure 9.1, this ratio continued to rise steadily during the period 1974–94 (during which world exports and world GDP increased at an annual rate of, respectively, slightly over 4 per cent and slightly below 3 per cent), reaching over 22 per cent in 1994. The main factors behind this phenomenon are well known. Broadly speaking, they fall into two categories: institutional and economic. Institutional factors include regional and multilateral trade liberalization (essentially restricted to the industrial countries until the early 1980s), and unilateral economic liberalization (essentially in developing countries and former socialist countries since the mid or late 1980s). The impact of these institutional factors on trade performance is analysed in Sachs and Warner (1995). Economic factors include mainly technological change, including the reduction in transport costs.

During the period 1963–93, the degree of opening of the European Union (defined as the ratio of extra-EU imports of goods to GDP, both measured in

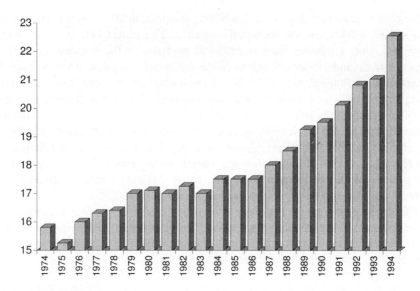

Source: WTO.

Fig. 9.1. Globalization, 1974–94 (%) (world exports of goods and services/world GDP, 1987 prices and exchange rates)

current prices and exchange rates) stayed fairly constant at about 8 per cent, except during the years 1974–85, when it hovered above the 10 per cent mark (partly as a result of high raw material prices). Figure 9.2 shows the degree of opening, together with the unemployment rate. Clearly, there is little relationship between the two.

It may be argued that Figure 9.2, which shows total extra-EU imports (i.e. for all goods and all trade partners), hides the most interesting feature of the recent globalization phenomenon, and potentially the most problematic one in terms of EU employment. This feature is the emergence of developing countries as major suppliers and exporters of manufactured products, which compete directly with EU production. Figure 9.3 confirms that manufactured imports from developing countries have increased faster than total extra-EU imports during the period 1986–93. Thus, whereas the latter stayed fairly constant as a proportion of EU GDP (see Figure 9.2), the former rose steadily faster than EU GDP (see Figure 9.3). Still, in 1994, manufactured imports from developing countries only accounted for 1.5 per cent of EU GDP (1.8 per cent when China is included). The same picture holds for the OECD countries as a whole. During the period 1970–90, the ratio of manufactured imports from 'emerging' countries to OECD GDP increased from 0.24 to 1.61 per cent.

Figure 9.4 shows two important additional features about EU manufactured imports from developing countries. First, these imports have increased somewhat

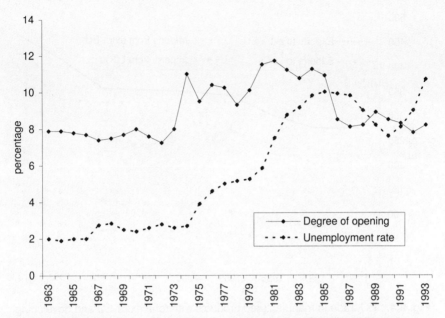

Fig. 9.2. Degree of opening (extra-EU imports/GDP) and unemployment for EU-15, 1963–93 (percentages)

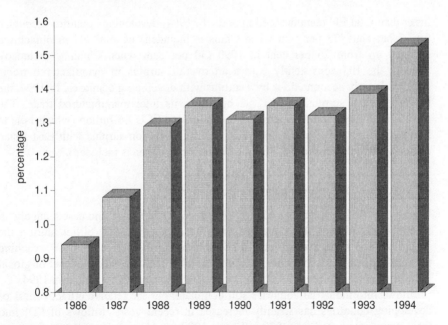

Fig. 9.3. Penetration of manufactured imports from developing countries in EU-12, 1986–94 (manufactured imports from LDCs/EU-12 GDP, percentages)

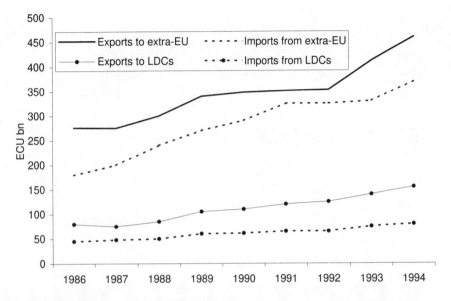

Fig. 9.4. EU trade in manufactured products with total extra-EU and developing countries, 1980–94 (ECU bn)

faster than total EU manufactured imports. In 1994, developing countries accounted for 27 per cent (33 per cent when China is included) of total EU manufactured imports, up from 26 per cent in 1990 (30 per cent when China is included). Second, the EU consistently enjoys an overall surplus in manufactured trade, which is largely accounted for by a surplus with developing countries. In 1994, the EU recorded a surplus of ECU 92 billion in its total manufactured trade. The surplus with developing countries as a whole was ECU 66 billion (which falls to 57 when China is included), including an ECU 4 billion surplus with East Asian countries (which turns into a 5 billion deficit when China is included).

9.2.2 Foreign Direct Investment and Relocation

Worldwide flows of foreign direct investment (FDI) have increased hugely in recent years. Annual flows jumped from an average of $50 billion during the period 1981–5 to an average of $155 billion during the period 1986–90, reaching the $200 billion mark in 1990. According to UNCTAD (1996), the level of global FDI flows reached a record $325 billion in 1995, up from $220 billion in 1994.

Inflows into industrial countries still dominate, but the relative attractiveness of developing countries has steadily increased in recent years. Inflows of FDI into these countries surged from $30 billion in 1990 (or 15 per cent of world flows) to $80 billion in 1993 (that is 40 per cent of world FDI), $86 billion in 1994 (40 per cent of world FDI), and $97 billion in 1995 (or 30 per cent of world flows). Asia attracts most of the inflows into developing countries, with China accounting for the lion's share at $34 billion in 1994 and $38 billion in 1995.

Despite the huge increase in FDI flows, production by multinational corporations (MNCs) in 1990 still accounted for only about 7 per cent of world output (Lipsey, Blomström and Ramstetter 1995). The share was 15 per cent in 'industry', defined as manufacturing, trade, construction, and public utilities.

According to UNCTAD (1994), MNCs employed about 12 million workers in developing countries in the early 1990s, compared with 61 million in developed economies. However, developing countries have accounted for nearly two-thirds of the total increase in employment by MNCs since 1985, thereby fuelling a debate on 'delocalization', that is the relocation of jobs from high-wage to low-wage economies.

9.2.3 Conclusion and Future Trends

During the past few decades, the world economy has become increasingly integrated through international trade and capital flows. Until recently, this phenomenon involved mainly the industrial countries, which acted as the 'engine of world growth'. The developing countries were merely fuelling the engine by supplying raw materials. Today, some of these countries, so far a small band of 'emerging' economies, have become significant producers and exporters of manufactured products.

Over the next quarter century, the new trend is bound to accelerate and to encompass a larger, more populated group of countries. According to the World Bank (1996), the gap in the growth rates of real GDP between developing and developed countries, which reached 3.4 percentage points during the period 1991–4, is expected to remain larger than 2.5 points during the period 1996–2005 (see Figure 9.5). This would imply a gap in the growth rate of real GDP per capita in favour of developing countries of 1.3 percentage points.

Such a prospect is both desirable and inevitable. It is desirable because the current distribution of world income is clearly unsustainable. In 1994, the inhabitants of the industrial countries accounted for 14 per cent of world population and 77 per cent of world income, whereas inhabitants in the developing countries accounted for 77 and 17 per cent of the world's population and income, respectively. In other words, the average GDP per capita (measured in nominal exchange rates) was, in 1994, 25 times larger in the industrial countries than in the developing ones. Despite the growth gap of 1.3 percentage points projected by the World Bank, GDP per capita would still remain, in 2005, 22 times larger in the industrial countries than in the developing world.

The prospect of seeing a larger share of the world's output and trade accounted for by the developing countries is equally inevitable in view of past historical trends. According to Bairoch (1982), in 1830 the Third World (mainly China and India) accounted for over 60 per cent of world manufacturing output, half of it

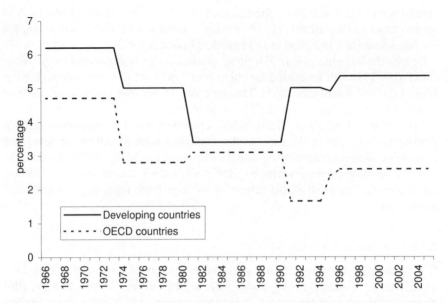

Fig. 9.5. Real GDP growth in OECD and developing countries, 1966–2005 (%)

produced by China, the world's largest economy until 1850. By 1913, the share of developing countries in world manufacturing output had dwindled to a paltry 8 per cent. It is currently about 20 per cent and rising.

9.3 Globalization, Wages and Unemployment

Over the last two decades, wage inequality has risen considerably in the USA. By contrast, in continental Europe, where inequality between skilled and unskilled has remained fairly constant, unemployment among low-skilled workers has reached persistently high levels. There is widespread agreement in the literature that common causes have produced diverging developments in institutionally different labour markets across the Atlantic. As Krugman (1994) and Wood (1994) argue, minimum-wage regulations and other wage rigidities have probably prevented European labour markets from reacting to the factors that caused wider wage differentials in the American labour market. There is less agreement, however, concerning the causes, the two principal candidates generally considered being skill-biased technological progress and competition with unskilled labour-abundant developing countries.

9.3.1 Trade

There have been three approaches to studying the impact of trade on wages and employment, mostly for the United States.

A first set of studies concentrates on the factor content of trade, in order to end up with a total net number of job creations (or destructions) due to exports and imports. Particularly spectacular is the study by Wood (1994), which comes up with a very significant level of net destructions: 5 per cent of total employment in the OECD countries due to trade in manufactured products alone. Key to his estimate, however, is the idea that imports from developing countries are 'non-competing goods' that have practically disappeared in the rich countries. Consequently, Wood argues that the labour–output ratio to use in order to compute employment destructions is that of developing countries, which is much higher than that of industrial countries. This assumption is crucial for Wood's result, and has been much debated in the literature. Another study in this vein is by Sachs and Shatz (1994), who compute the job losses in the USA due to increasing import shares between 1978 and 1990. They argue that rising import penetration has resulted in job losses totaling 7 per cent among US manufacturing production workers, and 2 per cent among non-production workers. However, their computation ignores the other side of rising internationalization, namely US export growth.

A second set of studies econometrically tests the import of imports on employment and wages. A particularly careful study has been performed by Revenga (1992). She finds significant import competition effects. In particular, Revenga concludes that the severe US dollar appreciation between 1980 and 1985 has had a negative impact on wages and employment in trade-impacted industries of 2 per cent and roughly 6 per cent respectively. The relatively small impact on wages reflects a relative ease of relocation for workers in these industries. Moreover, while significant, this impact suggests that trade only contributed modestly to the wage dispersion problem in the USA during the 1980s.

A third set of studies is based on the general equilibrium Heckscher–Ohlin–Samuelson (HOS) model of trade. In a simple 2x2x2 HOS world, with two factors of production (skilled and unskilled labour), two sectors (one skilled-intensive, the other unskilled-intensive) and two countries (skilled-abundant industrial countries, and unskilled-abundant developing ones), increased participation by developing countries in world trade will lead, in the industrial countries, to: (1) a fall in the relative price of unskilled-intensive goods, (2) a rise in the skill premium, and (3) a fall in the skill-intensity of labour in each sector. While (2) has been widely noticed in the USA, the study by Lawrence and Slaughter (1993) fails to find evidence of (1). Instead, Sachs and Shatz (1994) do find some evidence of (1), but of admittedly small magnitude. Finally, (3) has not been observed by any study, since skill-intensity has been rising across all US industries. Both studies conclude that relative prices exerted some pressure on the pay of the less skilled, but not sufficiently to account for a significant widening of wage inequality. Both regard technological change as the chief cause of increasing wage inequality.

Recently, a number of studies have followed these same three approaches to study the impact of trade on wages and employment in Europe.

Cortes, Jean and Pisani-Ferry (1998) estimate the employment content of French manufacturing trade with developing countries. They find that, from 1977 to 1993, trade with non-OECD countries resulted in the loss of about 350,000 jobs, almost entirely among low-skilled workers. This development is ascribed far more to a deterioration in the trade balance than to a change in the factor content of trade.

Neven and Wyplosz (1994) replicate the approach taken by Revenga. Their results are somewhat mixed: they find no significant aggregate effects; at the industry level, however, some evolutions are significant, but not all of them are consistent with a trade-only interpretation. As in a number of other studies, the authors point to the difficulty of disentangling trade and technology, but also to the limited impact of trade on labour market outcomes. Using a different econometric approach, Dewatripont, Sapir and Sekkat (1998) use labour force survey data to estimate the impact of trade on long-term unemployment. They distinguish between several unemployment characteristics: sex, industrial sector (16 two-digit NACE industries), educational level (low, medium and high), and country (Belgium-Luxembourg, France, Germany, and the Netherlands). Their results indicate no significant impact of developing country import penetration on long-term unemployment. On the other hand, workers' individual characteristics appear to play the dominant role: long-term unemployment is largely explained by education and sex.

Krugman (1995) runs a Mickey Mouse computable general equilibrium (CGE) model of Europe. Under the assumption of rigid wages (for both skilled and unskilled workers)—and thus rigid terms of trade—he finds a 1.4 per cent fall in unskilled employment when the economy moves from autarky to observed trade flows. While non-trivial, the effect is obviously small in comparison with the huge rise in unemployment observed in Europe. Cortes and Jean (1996) use a full-blown CGE model featuring three factors of production (capital, skilled labour, and unskilled labour), thirteen sectors, and three regions (the EC, emerging countries, and the rest oft he world). The model postulates imperfect competition in product markets, but assumes that wages are perfectly flexible. A doubling of the size of emerging countries, with an increase of their penetration rate in the European market for manufactured goods from 1.5 to 3 per cent, produces small effects on Europe. The real wage of skilled workers increases by 0.7 per cent, the real wage of unskilled workers falls by 0.1 per cent, and the real return to capital increases by 0.1 per cent. Wage disparity increases (by 0.8 per cent), but so does total welfare (by 0.3 per cent).

9.3.2 Foreign Direct Investment and Relocation

The recent controversy on the relocation of jobs from rich to poor countries dates back to the debate on NAFTA in the early 1990s, during which Ross Perot proclaimed that Mexico would massively 'suck away' jobs from the United States.

In Europe, the debate on relocation has been particularly vivid in France, following the publication of a parliamentary report by Senator Arthuis (1993). The report claimed that 'delocalization' to Asia and eastern Europe threatens over a million jobs in France. The claim was based on the fact that firms in electronics, clothing and footwear have cut their employment in France by half during the past decade.

In reality, the phenomenon of job relocation from rich to poor countries seems to assume a far more modest importance. On one hand, the proportion of French FDI located in Southeast Asia (the prime area for relocation according to the Arthuis report) appears to be in the order of 5 per cent. Similarly, the study of Bernard *et al.* (1995) for the Bureau du Plan in Belgium, indicates that less than 5 per cent of Belgian FDI is located in so-called 'delocalization areas'. On the other hand, only a proportion of FDI in developing countries involves an actual relocation of jobs. According to Bernard *et al.* (1995), the magnitude of the 'delocalization' phenomenon remains, so far, very modest. Moreover, nearly half of the known relocation of jobs from Belgium has taken place in the four neighbouring countries.

9.3.3 Conclusion and Future Trends

The consensus that seems to emerge from the economics literature is that globalization, in the form of increasing trade and investment with developing countries, is not the major determinant of the twin phenomenon of rising wage inequality and rising unemployment observed on the two sides of the Atlantic. Technology appears to be the main culprit. At the same time, there is no denying that globalization may have destroyed jobs in labour-intensive sectors in the industrial countries. As Buigues and Jacquemin (1995) note, imports from non-OECD countries accounted, in 1993, for 5 per cent of EU manufacturing, while exports to these countries represented 7 per cent of EU manufacturing output. However, in labour-intensive sectors, such as clothing, footwear or toys, imports from non-OECD countries accounted for over 15 per cent of EU consumption.

In the future, increased competition from developing countries could represent a mounting challenge for unskilled workers in developed countries such as Europe. There are, however, solid theoretical and empirical indications that the challenge should be manageable. As Richard Freeman reminds us, the fear that '[m]aybe your wages were not set in Beijing yesterday or today, but tomorrow they will be' (Freeman 1995: 30) is based on the HOS model prediction of factor price equalization. This prediction, however, is far from certain, provided low-skilled European and American workers continue to shift from import-competing manufacturing activity to non-traded service sector. A back-of-the-envelope calculation suggests that, already today, no more than 4 per cent of EU workers (that is about 6 million workers) may be in direct competition with low-wage countries. This estimate is based on the assumption that: (1) non-traded activities account for 65 per cent of EU employment, versus 35 per cent in traded activities; (2) among the 35 per cent in traded activities, the unskilled account for one-third; and (3) among the roughly 12 per cent of total employment which is unskilled and in traded activities, those competing directly with low-wage countries account for one-third.

9.4 Labour Standards and Globalization

There are allegations, mainly in developed countries, that the rapid increase in manufactured exports by the developing countries is partly linked to their non-compliance with internationally-agreed labour standards. This has led to accusations of 'unfair competition' and 'social dumping', and to demands for introducing 'social clauses' in international trade agreements. This section first examines whether there is an empirical link between labour standards and trade performance, and then focuses on the issue of 'social clauses'.

9.4.1 Labour Standards and Trade Performance

In 1994, the OECD ministers directed the OECD secretariat to prepare an economic study to establish whether there exists an empirically supported linkage between trade performance and compliance with 'core' labour standards. The OECD's *Trade and Labour Standards* study completed in April 1996 defines the latter as: elimination of child labour exploitation, prohibition of forced labour, freedom of association, the right to organize and bargain collectively and non-discrimination in employment.

The OECD study attempted to analyse possible links between core labour standards on one hand, and trade and investment flows on the other. The main findings of the study can be summarized as follows. First, there seems to be no empirical evidence that low labour standards imply low real wage growth or that raising standards would result in higher real wage growth. In particular, there appears to be no correlation between real wage growth and freedom of association: in a number of countries where there is little freedom of association (including Malaysia, Singapore and Thailand), real wages have grown faster than productivity growth.

Second, there is no evidence that countries with low labour standards have enjoyed a better performance on total trade or manufacturing trade than countries with high standards. It is suggested that economic fundamentals, such as factor endowments and technology, are a much more important explanation of trade performance than the level of labour standards. Indeed, most of the low to medium-income countries reviewed by the OECD secretariat have exhibited rapid export growth, regardless of the level of their core labour standards.

Third, an in-depth analysis of US imports of textile products (which are labour-intensive) indicates that imports from countries with high labour standards account for a large share of the US market. In addition, the price of US imports of textile products does not seem to be associated with the degree of enforcement of child labour standards in exporting countries.

Fourth, there is some evidence that in a few countries (mainly Bangladesh, Jamaica, Pakistan, Panama, Sri Lanka and Turkey) the denial of certain core labour standards has been deliberately used by the authorities in order to attract foreign direct investment to export-processing zones and to improve sectoral trade performance. However, it is difficult to assess whether such policy is or will be successful.

Fifth, although there is some evidence that core labour standards may be factors favouring the choice of non-OECD destinations by OECD investors, aggregate FDI data indicate that they are not major factors in the majority of investment decisions by OECD companies.

Considering these findings, the OECD study concludes that the impact of core labour standards on trade performance is likely to be negligible compared with economic fundamentals such as factor endowments and technology. Hence, concerns expressed by some industrial countries about 'unfair competition' resulting from low labour standards seem unjustified. Equally, the OECD study suggests that concerns voiced by some developing countries that core labour standards would damage their economic performance or their trade position appear to be unfounded.

The OECD findings are partly contradicted by Rodrik (1996), who investigates the impact of child-labour practices on labour costs, sectoral trade performance, and foreign direct investment. Rodrik finds that: (1) labour costs tend to increase as standards become more stringent; (2) the ratio of textile and clothing exports (which is used as a proxy for labour-intensive exports) to other exports is (weakly) positively associated with low labour standards; and (3) the effect of low labour standards on inward foreign direct investment is, if anything, negative.

9.4.2 Labour Standards and Trade Policy

The issue of labour standards and international trade policy has a long cyclical history, whose phases correspond to the globalization process of the world economy. As far back as the early nineteenth century, proposals were made to harmonize national labour legislations in connection with increasing international competition. Demands for international labour standards eventually led to the establishment of the International Labour Organization (ILO) in 1919, at the end of an unprecedented expansionary period of international trade. Recently, the issue has resurfaced in the context of the World Trade Organization (WTO) due to increasing international competition, especially on the part of emerging economies. Concerns of 'unfair competition' and 'social dumping' by labour interests in mature economies of Europe and North America have forced their public authorities to demand that the WTO introduces explicit linkages between trade liberalization and the harmonization of national labour standards.

There are two main facets to the issue of labour standards. One is ethical, the other economic. The ethical aspect relates to the 'universality' of labour standards. The fundamental issue is whether labour standards constitute, like basic human rights standards, a universal principle in the sense that they apply equally to all countries at all times. The alternative view is to consider that labour standards are 'development-dependent' or 'means-related', and therefore that they may vary between countries and across time (see Campbell and Sengenberger 1994). The debate centres, obviously, on comparisons between industrial and developing countries. Essays written in commemoration of the seventy-fifth anniversary of the ILO and edited by Sengenberger and Campbell (1994) present many arguments for and against the universality of standards. Clearly, however, there cannot be any definite answer to such a philosophical question.

If some labour standards, for instance regarding child labour, were considered universal two implications would follow. First, it would mean that all countries should adopt legislation in order to meet such standards, for instance by banning the use of child labour in *all* economic activities. Second, there would be a moral obligation on the part of the community of nations to take actions so as to ensure the application of such legislation.

The question, then, would be whether trade policy, in the form of a 'social clause', is the best instrument to encourage or force nations to adopt and respect labour standards that are viewed as universal. There can be doubts on two accounts. First, a 'social clause' would presumably apply to trade in manufactured products (for instance, to prevent the use of child labour in the production of carpets). Yet most of the child labour in poor countries is employed either in primary activities (including agriculture) or in services (such as shoe shining). Second, it is difficult to understand, on purely ethical grounds, why the scope of a 'social clause' should be limited to working conditions. After all, children in many poor countries are subject to many other evils besides the working conditions, such as prostitution and assassination by death squads, not to mention starvation (Sapir 1995).

The economic facet of labour standards relates to the problem of 'unfair competition' and 'social dumping'. International trade between countries with wide disparities in labour costs is a subject of profound controversy. There are essentially two views. One holds that international differences in wages and other social conditions provide an 'unfair' advantage to countries with lower labour standards and that this threatens social conditions in countries with higher standards. It recommends the international harmonization of labour standards, prior to or concurrently with international trade liberalization, so as to prevent 'social dumping' and 'a race to the bottom'. The proposed instrument of harmonization is the introduction of 'social clauses' in trade agreements. The other view holds that international differences in wages and social conditions reflect differences in productivity and social preferences. It rejects calls for measures of harmonization that would artificially eliminate international cost differences and, hence, reduce international trade opportunities. The message is that trade liberalization will, through convergence in living standards, lead to a convergence in social conditions.

9.4.3 Evidence from European Integration

There is little empirical evidence for choosing between these two views. One exception is Sapir (1996) who analyses the debate on the relationship between trade liberalization and the harmonization of social policies in the context of European integration. The study distinguishes two periods: the early years of integration, and the period since the mid-1970s. It finds that harmonization of social policies was not imposed in the 1960s and 1970s as a precondition for trade liberalization inside the Community. It is argued that two elements were crucial in warding off, at that time, pressures in favour of harmonization: a high degree of homogeneity of economic and social conditions among the six original members of the EEC; and a rapid amelioration of living standards throughout the Community. It also finds, however, that the demand for and the actual measures in favour of harmonizing social policies have increasingly occurred in the Community since the mid-1970s. It is contended that this new regime corresponds to a greater heterogeneity and a slower growth inside the Community. Renewed efforts to liberalize intra-EC trade in the mid-1980s also played a significant part in the shift towards harmonization.

The analysis of the European experience with trade liberalization and social har-monization leads to a certain number of lessons with respect to world trade liberalization. First, although some have insisted on the dangers of trade liberaliz-ation in the presence of differences in social conditions between the member states, the prevailing view inside the Community has been that liberalization will gradually reduce differences in economic conditions and, therefore, lead to the harmonization of social conditions. However, a clear shift in the direction of 'social harmonization' occurred in the mid-1980s. Several factors contributed to the shift: the enlargement of the Community, creating wide differences in labour costs between member states; high unemployment and stagnating real wages; and the 1992 programme, increasing competition inside the common market. The lesson is that trade liberalization among countries with different social standards will inevitably result in accusations of 'social dumping' in the countries with high labour standards during periods of high unemployment and stagnating real wages.

Second, in spite of the Social Charter and the Maastricht Treaty, 'social harmon-ization' remains a distant reality inside the European Union. Differences in labour standards between member states remain substantial. The OECD's *Jobs Study* includes a synthetic index of labour standards measuring the stringency of govern-ment regulations on working time, employment contracts, minimum wages and workers' representation rights. Its scale ranges from 0 to 10. According to this index, regulations are rather light in the United Kingdom (with a score of 0) and Denmark (with a score of 2), but stringent in Greece (with a score of 8), and in Italy and Spain (both with a score of 7).

Finally, it should be stressed that whatever harmonization of social policies has actually taken place in the EC, it would not have been possible in the absence of intra-EC redistributive mechanisms. It is doubtful whether, in the absence of such mechanisms, the harmonization of social policies can be seriously contemplated on a more global scale.

9.4.4 Existing 'Social Clauses'

The issue of a link between trade measures and labour standards has not as yet been raised in the WTO. The proponents of such a link are considering this issue in other fora such as the ILO and the OECD. Some countries (EU, USA) have included labour standards among the criteria used to provide tariff preferences or bilateral aid, while some others (India, Korea) are against any link between trade restrictions and labour standards. International confederations of labour unions are lobbying with governments, as well as with a number of international agencies including the IMF and the World Bank, to persuade them to support the 'social clause' and to incorporate it in their plans. Thus, this issue is being raised at several major meetings of international organizations dealing with socio-economic matters. Meanwhile, at the ILO, a decision was taken to stop examining the issue of 'social clause' and instead to consider ways of improving the mechanisms available within the ILO framework to encourage ratification and compliance of Conventions by member countries.

In the European Community, there was an attempt to include a binding 'social clause' in the Lomé Agreement, but it was not successful. In 1994, the European Parliament adopted a resolution on the need to include the category 'social clause' in the agenda of the WTO and in the EC's Generalized System of Preference (GSP) scheme. From 1 January 1995, the EU altered its GSP scheme by linking trade preferences for developing countries with certain social requirements being met by these countries. The new scheme, announced for the period 1995 to 1998, combines negative and positive incentives. The negative incentives are temporary withdrawal in whole or in part of exported products produced by forced or prison labour; the temporary withdrawal will not be automatic, but will follow the procedural requirements laid down in the regulation. Since 1 January 1998, there has also been a policy to encourage enforcement of certain labour standards. A review was carried out in 1997.

In the USA, social conditionality has been used in providing preferential tariff policies. Certain labour standards were included in the Caribbean Basin Economic Recovery Act of 1983, and a labour clause was introduced in the United States GSP scheme in 1984. From 1984 through 1994, 34 countries have been named in petitions citing labour rights abuses according to GSP law. Ten countries have been denied GSP treatment on either a temporary or a permanent basis for reasons of labour standards. Foreign labour practices and working conditions were included in the Omnibus Trade and Competitiveness Act of 1988, by making systemic denial of workers' rights by a foreign government an 'unreasonable' act that could be retaliated under Section 301 of the 1974 Trade Act, should it prove burdensome or restrictive to the commerce of the United States.

In NAFTA, labour issues have been addressed through a supplementary 'Agreement on Labour Cooperation', which is designed primarily to ensure compliance with the respective national laws of the signatories. The guiding principles for labour standards indicating broad areas of concern, which are specifically noted in the North American Agreement on Labour Cooperation, are freedom of association and protection of the right to organize, the right to bargain collectively, the right to strike, labour protection for children and young persons, minimum employment standards, elimination of employment discrimination, equal pay for men and women, prevention of occupational injuries and illnesses, compensation in cases of occupational injuries and illnesses, and protection of migrant workers. Adherence to national laws is monitored on a trilateral basis, and provisions for consultations are established.

9.5 Conclusion

I draw several conclusions from the discussion presented in this chapter:

First, the emergence of developing countries as major suppliers of manufactured products that compete with traditional producers in the old European industrial countries has only just started. Over the coming decades, the trend is bound to accelerate as new countries join the fray. I have argued that such a prospect is not only inevitable, but also desirable given the current distribution of world income.

Second, globalization is not a zero-sum game. It has raised, and is bound to further raise, incomes and prosperity throughout the world. At the same time, however, globalization implies increased competition among certain factors of production, especially low-skilled labour. So far, there is little evidence that globalization is the main explanatory factor for the current predicament of unskilled workers in Europe, but it could assume a greater role in the future if structural adjustment proves to be too slow.

Third, there is little evidence that the recent export performance of developing countries is linked to low labour standards. Nonetheless, accusations of 'social dumping' and demands for 'social clauses' are bound to continue as long as unemployment remains at the current level.

Fourth, protectionist trade measures, for instance in the guise of 'social clauses', would add to, rather than solve, Europe's problems. The expediency argument, according to which 'social clauses' are needed to preserve the liberal trading system put in place by the old industrial nations after the Second World War, could easily backfire into mounting trade disputes with developing countries.

Finally, there is no substitute to domestic reforms (of labour and other markets) for solving the European unemployment situation. The solution, like the problem, lies not in Beijing or Delhi, but in Paris or Frankfurt.

References

Arthuis, J. (1993), *Rapport d'information sur l'incidence économique et fiscale des délocalisations hors du territoire national des activités industrielles et de service*, Séance du 4 juin, Rapport d'information No. 337, Sénat, Paris.

188 *Sapir*

Bairoch, P. (1982), 'International Industrialization Levels from 1750 to 1980', *Journal of European Economic History*, 11.

Bernard, P., van Sebroeck, H., Spinnewyn, H., Gilot, A. and Vandenhove, P. (1995), *Délocalisation*, Bureau du Plan, Brussels.

Buigues, P. and Jacquemin, A. (1995), 'Les échanges commerciaux entre les pays à bas salaires et l'Union européenne', *Economie Internationale*, 64.

Campbell, D. and Sengenberger, W. (1994), 'International Labour Standards and Economic Interdependence: The Problem of Renovating the Social Pact', in W. Sengenberger and D. Campbell (eds.), *International Labour Standards and Economic Interdependence*, International Institute for Labour Studies, Geneva.

Cortes, O. and Jean, S. (1996) 'Pays émergents, emploi déficient?', document de travail, no. 96–05, CEPII, Paris, March.

Cortes, O., Jean, S. and Pisani-Ferry, J. (1998), 'Trade with Emerging Countries and the Labour Market: The French Case', Chapter 6 in this volume.

Dewatripont, M., Sapir, A. and Sekkat, K. (1998), 'Labour Market Effects of Trade with LDCs in Europe', Chapter 3 in this volume.

Freeman, R. B. (1995), 'Are Your Wages Set in Beijing?', *Journal of Economic Perspectives*, 9.

Krugman, P. (1994), 'Europe Jobless, America Penniless', *Foreign Policy*.

—— (1995), 'Growing World Trade: Causes And Consequences', *Brookings Papers on Economic Activity*, 1: 327–62. Reproduced in this volume.

Lawrence, R. Z. and Slaughter, M. J. (1993), 'Trade and US Wages in the 1980s: Giant Sucking Sound or Small Hiccup?', *Brookings Papers on Economic Activity*, Microeconomics, 2: 161–226.

Lipsey, R. E., Blomström, M. and Ramstetter, E. (1995), 'Internationalized Production in World Output', *National Bureau of Economic Research Working Paper*, 5385, Cambridge, Mass.

Neven, D. and Wyplosz, C. (1994), 'Trade and European Labour Markets', INSEAD and University of Lausanne, mimeo.

OECD (1993), *Intra-Firm Trade*, OECD, Paris.

—— (1996), *Trade and Labour Standards*, OECD, Paris.

Revenga, A. L. (1992), 'Exporting Jobs?: The Impact of Import Competition on Employment and Wages in US Manufacturing', *Quarterly Journal of Economics*, 107(1): 225–84.

Rodrik, D. (1996), 'Globalization and Labour, Or: If globalization is a Bowl of Cherries, Why Are There So Many Glum Faces Around the Table?', paper presented at the CEPR Conference on Regional Integration, La Coruna, Spain, 26–27 April.

Sachs, J. D. and Shatz, H. J. (1994), 'Trade and Jobs in US Manufacturing', *Brookings Papers on Economic Activity*, 1: 1–69.

Sachs, J. and Warner, A. (1995), 'Economic Reform and the Process of Global Integration', *Brookings Papers on Economic Activity*.

Sapir, A. (1995), 'The Interaction Between Labour Standards and International Trade Policy', *The World Economy*, 18.

—— (1996), 'Trade Liberalization and the Harmonization of Social Policies: Lessons from European Integration', in J. Bhagwati and R. Hudec (eds.), *Fair Trade and Harmonization: Prerequisites for Free Trade?*, MIT Press, Cambridge, Mass.

Sengenberger, W. and Campbell, D. (eds.) (1994), *International Labour Standards and Economic Interdependence*, International Institute for Labour Studies, Geneva.

UNCTAD (1994), *World Investment Report*, United Nations Conference on Trade and Development, Geneva.

—— (1996), *World Investment Report*, United Nations Conference on Trade and Development, Geneva.

Wood, A. (1994), *North–South Trade, Employment and Inequality*, Clarendon Press, Oxford.

World Bank (1996), *Global Economic Prospects and the Developing Countries*, World Bank, Washington DC.

Index